LIFE IN FAITH AND FREEDOM

Series II. Modern Scholarly Studies about the Jesuits, in English Translations

Edouard Pousset, S.J.

LIFE IN FAITH AND FREEDOM

An Essay Presenting
Gaston Fessard's Analysis
of the
Dialectic of the Spiritual Exercises
of St. Ignatius

Translated and Edited by
Eugene L. Donahue, S.J.

THE INSTITUTE OF JESUIT SOURCES
St. Louis, 1980

in cooperation with
Gujarat Sahitya Prakash
Anand Press
Anand, India

This book is an authorized translation of
La vie dans la foi et la liberté: Essai sur les Exercices Spirituels de St. Ignace de Loyola,
by Edouard Pousset, S.J., Centre d'Etudes
et de Recherches Philosophiques, 128 rue Blomet,
75015 Paris, France, 1971.

IMPRIMI POTEST: Very Reverend Leo F. Weber, S.J.
Provincial of the Missouri Province
January 25, 1979

IMPRIMATUR: Most Reverend John N. Wurm, S.T.D., Ph.D.
Vicar General of St. Louis
January 30, 1979

This is the
First Edition, for the Americas, Western Europe,
Australia, and New Zealand

Note: There is a *Second Edition*, authorized for
sale ONLY IN ASIA AND AFRICA which
can be ordered from Gujarat Sahitya Prakash,
Anand 388 001, India

Printed in the United States of America
Library of Congress Catalog Card Number 79-84200
ISBN 0-912422-39-4 paperback
ISBN 0-912422-40-8 Smyth sewn paperback
ISBN 0-912422-41-6 cloth bound

Edited by George E. Ganss, S.J., and Philip C. Fischer, S.J.
The Institute of Jesuit Sources, St. Louis, Missouri
Published by Xavier Diaz del Rio, S.J., Gujarat
Sahitya Prakash, Anand 388 001, India
Printed by S. Abril, S.J., Anand Press, Anand
388 001, India

TABLE OF CONTENTS

EDITOR'S FOREWORD

In this book Father Edouard Pousset presents the substance of Father Gaston Fessard's interpretation of St. Ignatius' *Spiritual Exercises*—in far fewer pages than Fessard's two volumes which are still in French. Pousset makes Fessard's important analysis more readily intelligible to a general reader who might otherwise be deterred by the density and Hegelian terminology of the original French commentary. Fessard praises both the fidelity of this book to his own thought and the creative originality of Pousset's book.

Among modern commentators who have published studies in depth on the *Spiritual Exercises* we find such names as Erich Przywara, Gaston Fessard, Karl Rahner, Hugo Rahner, Gilles Cusson, Daniel Gil, and Leo Bakker. The Institute of Jesuit Sources has made the substance of Karl Rahner's interpretation of the *Spiritual Exercises* available to English-speaking readers in Harvey D. Egan's *The Spiritual Exercises and the Ignatian Mystical Horizon*, with a Foreword by Karl Rahner (1976). This Institute is now happy also to present the substance of Gaston Fessard's interpretation.

It is well known that Fessard drew the inspiration for his interpretation of the *Exercises* chiefly from Hegel. Some of the prospective readers of this present book will perhaps ask: What is to be gained by interpreting Ignatius' *Spiritual Exercises* according to the principles and terminology of Hegelian philosophy? These did not yet exist in Ignatius' lifetime. What then was Fessard aiming to do when he wrote his book?

A compressed sketch here of the history and circumstances of its composition will give at least an initial answer to these questions; and this information will expand below, little by little, as the pages of the book are read.

From about 1920 onward many French Catholic thinkers observed that Marxism and Communism were spreading in France and elsewhere, and also the Hegelian philosophy from which they sprang. Some thought, in fact, that it would be advantageous, in this new cultural atmosphere so prevalent in many dechristianized areas, to present Christianity itself to nonbelievers through

Hegelianism. "Many Catholic professors in France," a colleague recently returned from doctoral studies there told the present writer in the 1950's, "are now studying Hegel more than St. Thomas." With other Catholic thinkers there, however, including ecclesiastical censors, Hegelianism was something not deeply or sympathetically understood and was in much disfavor.

In this environment, Fessard's book arose gradually and un-expectedly from some notes which he wrote in 1931, for his private use, to clarify some insights of his own on Ignatius' *Spiritual Exercises* (as he explains more fully in his Letter below on page **xx**). These insights sprang from his study of Blondel and his first acquaintance with Hegel. He tried to expound, through Hegelian methodology, the intellectual and affective conversion which takes place in an idealized retreatant who earnestly, capably, and profitably makes a thirty-day retreat according to the content and directives found in the *Spiritual Exercies*. This interior process is *La dialectique des Exercises* which Ignatius' book sets in motion and which Fessard tried to expound in his notes.

The existence of Fessard's notes gradually became known among his friends. Hence more and more of them, especially among his Jesuit brethren, asked to read them and became enthusiastic about them. In the early 1950's some young Jesuit theologians urged him to let these notes be published as part of the forth-coming celebration, in 1956, of the four-hundredth anniversary of St. Ignatius' death. He acquiesced, made relatively minor revisions, and saw the book appear on time with the title *La dialectique des Exercices Spirituels de Saint Ignace de Loyola* (Paris: Aubier, 1956). But the hastened circumstances of publication made it more difficult to understand than it should have been. In his Letter below he tells (pages **xx-xxviii**) how Pousset's present book largely remedies these shortcomings.

Fessard's aim was to analyze and explain the process stimulated in an exercitant who through thirty days faithfully followed the content and directives of Ignatius in the *Spiritual Exercises*. Fessard found that process to be one of liberation or freeing. It is a process from a state of relative non-being before the act of freeing decision into a better state of being. He also applied his analysis to Igna-tius' Rules for the Discernment of Spirits.

His book produced considerable excitement in philosophical and theological circles. Scholarly reviews of it appeared, for example, by G. Martelet, *Nouvelle revue théologique*, 78 (1956), 1043-1066; F. Roustang, *Christus*, no. 12 (1956), 561-573; H. M.

de Achával, *Gregorianum*, 38 (1957), 317-327; M. A. Fiorito, *Ciencia y fe*, 13 (1957), 333-352; J. Granero, *Manresa*, 29 (1957), 311-320; L. Roy, *Sciences ecclésiastiques*, 9 (1957), 303-311.

Within a few years the need to reprint the book became apparent and the publisher suggested the possibility or even desirability of some revisions and expansions. Fessard decided instead (1) to reprint the original volume unchanged except for the addition on the title page of "*Liberté—Temps—Grace*," three words designating the main topics which the original book had stressed, and (2) to compose another volume in which he applied his same methodology to "*Fondement—Péché—Orthodoxie.*" Thus he composed a commentary on three additional areas of Ignatius' book: the Foundation, the Meditations on Sin, and the section commonly though incompletely termed the Rules for Thinking with the Church. The result was the appearance in 1966 of the two-volume set: *La dialectique des Exercices spirituels de saint Ignace de Loyola. I. Liberté—Temps—Grace* (367 pages). *II. Fondement—Péché—Orthodoxie* (283 pages). Fessard left it to his readers to insert the new themes treated in Volume II into the framework of the *Exercises* which he had already presented in Volume I. Pousset has rearranged Fessard's key thoughts on the four Weeks and the Rules for Discernment of Spirits.

Fessard's volume of 1956 is, as the late Ignacio Iparraguirre states (in *Orientaciones bibliográficas sobre san Ignacio de Loyola* [Rome, 1965], page 122), a valuable and profound work. To view the Exercises from a new frame of reference which was not yet existent in Ignatius' lifetime brought many new insights into their meaning and functioning.

A retreat director who understands Fessard's thought as presented in Pousset's present book could use this book as a means to refresh his memory, step by step, about the fruits which he hopes to stimulate in an apt retreatant whose Exercises he is guiding. To such a retreatant he could also suggest the book as a means which might help him—but only *after* the retreat—to analyze the process which went on in his mind and will and heart.

Pousset himself points out (see below on page xvi) that his book mitigates the philosophical jargon which is necessary in Fessard's work but is nevertheless unfamiliar to many readers. Pousset's book makes the theological and spiritual content of Fessard's analyses more explicit. It is addressed to those who have made the Exercises for at least eight days, and to those who give them. It is also addressed even to those unacquainted with the Christian faith. However, it is not a Directory intended to give practical directives. An analysis of a thought process is something different from a practical directive.

The Institute of Jesuit Sources is happy to make Father Fessard's thought available in English through this faithful medium of Father Pousset's present book.

George E. Ganss, S.J.
Director and General Editor
The Institute of Jesuit Sources
February 2, 1979

TRANSLATOR'S INTRODUCTION

A key insight of Ignatius of Loyola, in the process of his conversion, was that human existence is basically a vocation.[1] The full dimensions of his own personal calling took many years to unfold, and hence he liked to refer to himself as the "pilgrim."[2] The *method* of discerning the will of God for himself, however, was something that Ignatius learned relatively early in his conversion, and he began to share his method with others who were also interested in finding their most profound identity in terms of their relationship to God. The "exercises" which Ignatius himself undertook, and which he later suggested to others, eventually took the form of a small book, the *Spiritual Exercises* of St. Ignatius.

The fact that many other people, in all walks of life, have found St. Ignatius' "exercises" helpful in charting their own spiritual journey testifies to Ignatius' respect for each individual's freedom. For the originality of St. Ignatius is found in the form of the Spiritual Exercises rather than in their content.[3] The latter is drawn from standard Christian sources, the Bible and the Church's spiritual tradition. But rather than giving the exercitant ready-made answers, the book of the *Spiritual Exercises* offers the person a method for discovering just how God is calling him or her to live in deeper faith and greater freedom.

Pousset begins with a modern existential and phenomenological analysis of human freedom (chap. 1), and he then briefly outlines the internal dynamic of creation itself (chap. 2). He next describes the inner structure of the Spiritual Exercises as the unfolding of four key aspects or "moments" which are involved in the historical becoming of any free person (chap. 3). This general structure

---

1 Leonardo R. Silos, S.J., "Cardoner in the Life of Saint Ignatius of Loyola," *Archivum Historicum Societatis Iesu*, 33 (1964), 40-41; the whole article is on pp. 3-43.
2 See André Ravier, S.J., *Ignace de Loyola fonde la Compagnie de Jésus* (Paris: Desclée de Brouwer, 1974), pp. 96-99, on the importance of the notion of "pilgrimage" for Ignatius and his companions.
3 Dominique Bertrand, S.J., *Un corps pour l'Esprit: Essai sur l'expérience communautaire selon les Constitutions de la Compagnie de Jésus* (Paris: Desclée de Brouwer, 1974), p. 8.

is then explicated and deepened in the following chapters, which enter into the particular dynamics of each portion of the Spiritual Exercises. Taken together, these dynamics provide a theological foundation for the process of making free decisions within our personal life histories.

The idea of translating Pousset's work came to me after I had been asked to teach a graduate course in the theology of the Spiritual Exercises for the summer program in Christian spirituality at Creighton University. The positive reception which the course has received, plus my own discovery of the value of the principles highlighted by Pousset, convinced me that there is a need for this work to be available in English. The treatment of St. Ignatius' rules for the discernment of spirits (chap. 10) is very valuable for spiritual direction in general, even outside the context of a retreat, and I believe the same is true for many of his analyses concerning the growth and development of spiritual freedom.

Although Pousset draws heavily on Gaston Fessard's *La Dialectique des Exercices Spirituels de Saint Ignace de Loyola* for much of his inspiration,[4] he has creatively worked out a *theological anthropology* that underlies his treatment of various forms of prayer in the Exercises (chaps. 1, 4-6). As a result, he is able to explain how praying in faith, with the help of grace, can effect a fuller integration of the entire person (sensation, imagination, reason, and affectivity) by bringing the person into deeper contact with the mystery present in Scripture.

Pousset's quotations from Fessard have all been verified, and since Pousset has frequently made slight emendations in Fessard's language for greater clarity and simplicity, I have usually followed Pousset's terminology and expressions. I have also occasionally supplied the exact Scripture reference or bibliographical data when it was lacking in Pousset's text, but other additions of the translator have been indicated by brackets.

I would like to thank the author, Edouard Pousset, for his personal help and encouragement. I would also like to thank Philip C. Fischer, Brian W. Van Hove, and Leonard A. Waters, all of the Society of Jesus, for their generous assistance in reading the entire manuscript and for their many valuable suggestions and

---

4 See Pousset's own Introduction and Fessard's letter that follows it. For a study of Fessard's entire thought, see Nguyen-Hong Giao, *Le Verbe dans l'histoire: la philosophie de l'historicité du P. Gaston Fessard* (Paris: Beauchesne, 1974).

corrections. In addition, I would like to thank Dean Richard V. Andrews of the graduate school of Creighton University for a grant to help defray expenses in preparing the typescript.

Eugene L. Donahue, S.J.
Department of Theology
Creighton University
Omaha, Nebraska
Epiphany, 1979

AUTHOR'S INTRODUCTION

The *Spiritual Exercises* of St. Ignatius present a reasoned procedure for one's conversion and decision leading to action in conformity with God's will. Their goal is a choice in harmony with God or, in philosophical terms, the actualization in one's life of a unity of theory and practice, a unity of the universal (God's will) and the particular (my action inserted into history). In *La dialectique des Exercices Spirituels de Saint Ignace de Loyola*, Gaston Fessard, S.J., has highlighted this doctrine of freedom which develops in and by the decisions which weave the thread of its history. There we see freedom unfolding as it joins the objective historical movement of the Son of God becoming man for us. The movement of the incarnation-redemption-resurrection and the movement of freedom constituting itself are one and the same: Freedom itself and my freedom. Christ himself neither is nor does anything that is not entirely for us and in us. According to this principle, the most objective dogmas, even those concerning the being of the Word of God *in himself*, such as the union of the divine and human natures in the single person of the Word, are decisive and significant *for us*. Fessard's reading of the *Spiritual Exercises* thus helps us come to a better understanding that the life of faith is a life of freedom, our freedom and God's Freedom, completely united. His interpretation also enables us to perceive that in at least some dogmas—and indeed the most important ones of creation, original sin, the incarnation, death, and resurrection of Christ, the Eucharist, and the divinization of man—the stakes are absolutely decisive for us today.

It is this reading of the *Exercises* that we are offering in this work. It follows closely Fessard's book, which was first published by Aubier in 1956, and which was reissued unchanged in 1966 as the first volume of a trilogy whose final volume is yet to appear. Our treatment of Fessard's work mitigates the technical philosophical jargon unfamiliar to many, and it makes the theological and spiritual content of the analyses more explicit.

The present book is addressed to all those who have made the Exercises of St. Ignatius (for at least eight days) and to those who give them. But it is also meant for a much larger audience. It is even directed toward persons unacquainted with the Christian faith but who recognize that Christianity is part of their cultural heritage and therefore has a claim on their attention.

Those who have made or who give the Exercises should take care not to consider our book a Directory.[1] It has none of the practical orientation of the directories, and it even points out in a few passages the danger there would be in transposing some of its analyses into spiritual directives for a retreatant. On a broader scale, one should avoid confusing this philosophical and theological or spiritual reflection with the simple exercise of faith which is an adherence to God in prayer, with a minimum of reflection. That is why this book is not for reading just *before* a person enters into a retreat. For one's retreat it is advisable to forget this type of speculation and to stick to the summary hints given by St. Ignatius in his booklet. On the other hand, reading this book can be helpful *afterwards*. It can help the reader find in the Exercises a way of converting not only his disordered behavior and affections, but his understanding as well. And the theologian of freedom can find a method here for grappling with the human problems of our time.

Is there anyone today who does not need to be a theologian of freedom? We are thinking of priests, of course, but also of Sisters, especially those who make Ignatian retreats, and of all Christians who are trying to understand their existence and to guide their lives by faith. We are thinking in particular of those who readily make use of the Ignatian method for spiritual discernment and decision making. We hope that our work can bridge the gap between lived spiritual experience, expressed with the help of images and representations characteristic of the tradition of faith, and everyday existence, forced to situate itself within the context of contemporary currents of thought and to espouse a problematic of freedom.

It would be a mistake to think that our analyses bring to light a new *meaning* (more adequate for our times) which has remained hidden or implicit in the traditional *representations*. The meaning is found in these representations themselves, and it becomes crystal-clear when we grasp the movement immanent in them. The task of grasping this movement, however, falls to each succeeding generation, and it is always fulfilled amidst believers dialoguing

---

1 In the tradition of the Society of Jesus, a commentary which helps in making or giving the Spiritual Exercises in greater conformity with the spirit of St. Ignatius is called a Directory.

with their age. This was already the case from the outset of Christianity, when the first Christian thinkers made use of Stoic and Platonic concepts in order to express the content of their faith to one another and to others.

The problematic of freedom, which is at the center of our reading of the *Exercises*, is what may enable this work to hold the attention of readers unacquainted with Ignatian spirituality or even with Christian faith.

Christian Faith and Freedom.   Those who do not share the Church's faith, but who at least value freedom as much as we do, may find a doctrine of freedom elaborated in function of faith, within a modern problematic, important and significant. They have the right, moreover, to ask us to direct them towards the interior of the world of faith, which should, without being their world, nevertheless become familiar enough to them so that the present dialectic of freedom, in all its implications, may become evident to them. This world should become familiar enough to them so that they are able to form and accept a notion of what we insist on calling the coherence of faith. If at the outset faith seems senseless or arbitrary to them, reading a work like this does not even appear possible. But we must present to their critical reflection a path of faith that organizes the reflective experiences which are the believer's very reasons for believing and which may be reasons for others' granting a rational value to faith.

Without this progression towards the interior of faith, without this statement of reasons whereby a believer accounts for the hope which is in him, our presentation of the dialectic of St. Ignatius' Exercises would appear to nonbelievers as a construct which may be intelligent but which is wholly gratuitous (in the least acceptable meaning of the word).

We have suggested this progression in an earlier work which presents the philosophical problem of God, *Un chemin de la Foi et de la Liberté.*[2] Human existence points toward absolute otherness or, to use a more traditional term, *transcendence:* God as totally other and, for that very reason, present at the heart of the world, the principle, foundation, and meaning of all that is. Experiencing our human condition as based on an irreducible and mysterious

---

2 Edouard Pousset, S.J., *Un chemin de la Foi et de la Liberté—Première partie: Existence humaine et question de Dieu.* Printed for private circulation, 1972. A few copies are still available by writing the author at 128 rue Blomet, 75015 Paris, France. No English version is available.

presence which bestows this condition on us is a prelude to the Exercises. The latter are prefaced by a Principle and Foundation which invites us to renew, at least in principle, our basic adherence to God as man's creator and end. But the Exercises presuppose more than faith in God; if they introduce us to the logic of Christian faith, and if they offer us a way of appropriating it unreservedly, they presuppose that we recognize at once the value of this logic, at least in theory.

It was necessary, therefore, to map out a prior path of faith and freedom within the realm of religion, particularly the Christian religion. Of what value is Christianity from the viewpoint of reason which has acknowledged God's presence at the heart of the world? Is Christianity the spot where there occurs an authentic mediation between man and God who makes himself present? Is Jesus of Nazareth the sole foundation of human existence for one who seeks to live in truth? We have asked ourselves these questions in a second part of *Un chemin de la Foi et de la Liberté*.[3] The answer which we think we have found in that study of Israel's history and the Christ-event leads directly into the world of the Spiritual Exercises, and it enables us to accept their help for living henceforth in faith and freedom.[4]

Edouard Pousset, S.J.
Centre d'Etudes et
de Recherches Philosophiques
128, rue Blomet
75015 Paris, France
February, 1971

---

3 Available on tape (Association Didakè, 310, rue de Vaugirard, 75015 Paris) and partially mimeographed (Faculté de Théologie-Publications, 4, montée de Fourvière, 69006 Lyon, France).

4 Volume I of G. Fessard, *Dialectique des Exercices*, will be cited as *Dialectique*, I, followed by the page number(s). Likewise, Volume II will be *Dialectique*, II, followed by the page(s). The booklet of the *Exercises* will be referred to simply by citing the paragraph number (e.g., [116]). It would be difficult to follow our analyses without being able to refer easily to the text of the *Exercises*.

[Translator's Note. We will use the English translation of *The Spiritual Exercises of St. Ignatius*, by Louis J. Puhl, S.J., originally published by the Newman Press in 1951, currently available from Loyola University Press, Chicago, IL 60657.]

A LETTER FROM GASTON FESSARD, S.J.

Dear Father Pousset,

Do the readers for whom your work is intended really need my endorsement of it? I don't believe they do, for two reasons. First, they will hardly be drawn except from among persons capable of making their own judgment about the quality of the spiritual fare they want to live on. Secondly, the very nature and purpose of what you are offering them is likely to attract their attention and to be chosen as indispensable even before they have been able to appreciate the clarity, accuracy, and depth of your exposition.

It is true that you refer frequently to my two volumes, *La dialectique des Exercices Spirituels*, where I have tried to state how I understand Ignatius' work, at the same time bringing to light the reasons for its extraordinary efficacy. Not content with repeatedly quoting one or the other volume, you sometimes refer to my work purely and simply as if your readers could find nothing better. So that, in relationship to my work, your book can appear to have no other ambition than to make my work accessible to a wider audience which then seems justified in expecting me to guarantee the fidelity of your essay. Such an appearance is not entirely false—provided, however, we notice that this appearance stems more from my own work's liabilities than it denigrates the worth of one that is concerned with bringing an indispensable corrective to them.

But the meaning of a reservation like that runs the risk of remaining enigmatic for a number of your readers. I must therefore explain it, especially for your younger readers who scarcely knew or experienced the Church's atmosphere during the half-century preceding Vatican II. To recall briefly how and in what circumstances I began to reflect on the *Exercises* will, I think, be the best way of helping them understand to what extent your interpretation, while following mine, reveals itself as more original than faithful because, like all true fidelity, yours is creative.

At the very start of my first volume I said that the essential core had been composed as far back as 1931, and that its first six chapters, dealing with the four Weeks and their division, were being published almost as I had drawn them up twenty-five years earlier.[1]

1 Only chapter four on the Choice, whose original text came to two pages of brief

When I undertook this work in the final months of my tertianship, and still more when it was finished, never for an instant did the idea occur to me that it could ever be printed and made public. My sole intention was to clarify for myself some insights about Ignatius' booklet by consigning them to writing. Although my reflections, initiated much earlier, had been developed till then principally under the influence of Maurice Blondel's early works which I studied about 1922, they were at the time if not dominated, at least certainly influenced, by my first contact with Hegel, especially his *Phenomenology of Spirit.* Since 1926 I had tried to penetrate the mysteries of that book by translating some fragments of it for my personal use: the preface and introduction, the beginning of the section on consciousness, manifest religion, and absolute knowing. At that period in France very few people were interested in this philosopher, and his basic work, almost universally ignored, remained a book as "sealed" as that in the Apocalypse.[2] For my part, the more Hegel fascinated me because of the place he awarded Christianity in the genesis of absolute knowing, and also because

notations, includes some developments which date from 1948 or are contemporary with the book's publication (see *Dialectique*, I, 18).

[Translator's Note. Following the example of Puhl in his translation of the *Spiritual Exercises* and the arguments he gives on pp. 183-184, along with the example of other recent works on the Exercises, such as John English, *Spiritual Freedom* (Guelph: Loyola Retreat House, 1975), we have translated the French *élection* (Spanish: *elección*) as *choice* rather than use the older term, *election*. When *élection* is used to refer to the retreatant's major decision in the Second Week of the Exercises, as is the case here, we have frequently capitalized *Choice*. In all cases the meaning should be clear from the context.]

2 Remember that Jean Wahl's *Le Malheur de la conscience dans la philosophie de Hegel*, the first French work devoted to the *Phenomenology*—and which studies just one aspect of it, appeared in the course of 1929.

In connection with this, perhaps it is not irrelevant to recount a little anecdote which is fairly significant. During my study of theology at Fourvière, from time to time I went to visit Auguste Valensin, then professor of philosophy on the Catholic faculty at Lyons, in order to consult him or to borrow some books from him. In the course of one of our conversations, as I was telling him how excited I was about Hegel because the basic plan of his *Phenomenology* seemed analogous to Blondel's *L'Action*, he cried out, "My poor friend, they have nothing in common! Hegel is all being, non-being, becoming, and so on, which are mere logical abstractions! Blondel, on the other hand, is concrete, real life!" Like a modest disciple, I protested somewhat, but of course without making a dent in the master's convictions. Well, shortly after the publication of Wahl's book, when I happened to return to see him, he welcomed me with uplifted hands and numerous exclamations, "You are a wonderful, astonishing, extraordinary fellow! Jean Wahl says the same thing about Hegel as you do!" And he immediately quoted the beginning of Wahl's preface: "Hegel's philosophy of his reflection on historicity which I noticed underlying everything, the more I was aware of being a long ways from penetrating the maze of questions which he raised by this twofold claim. How could I therefore have dreamt of publishing an interpretation of the *Exercises* which drew its inspiration from a philosopher so forgotten and so very poorly understood by those who had some acquaintance with him?

What's more, supposing that such an idea had entered my head, the mentality prevailing at that time in ecclesiastical circles excluded any hope of my being listened to. Wasn't Hegel the philosopher of Protestantism who, by exacerbating Kant's negations, had paved the way for Marx's atheism, and the errors of evolutionism and historicism, giving birth to modernism? To want to clarify Ignatius' procedure by one who, in the phrase of Father de Régnon, "had wielded the standard of non-being" could only have been a foolish conceit at a time when the whole horizon of clerical studies was the development of a neo-scholasticism whose most intelligent representatives were struggling to appropriate the foundations of modern philosophy. Let us not forget that an open Thomism like that of Pierre Rousselot was very poorly thought of by Church authorities, and that Joseph Maréchal's cahiers on *Le point de départ de la métaphysique* ran into so much resistance from religious censors that the fifth cahier on Thomism and Kant's critical philosophy appeared only after "sixteen months of retouching and modifying."[3] Finally, let it be enough to recall, as René d'Ouince has recently done with all the accuracy one could hope for, that the "initial difficulties between Teilhard de Chardin and

cannot be reduced to a few logical formulas. Or rather, these formulas cover up something which is not of purely logical origin....At the beginning of this doctrine ...there is a kind of mystical intuition and affective warmth....Before being a philosopher, he was a theologian." Because of his enthusiasm Valensin soon put me in touch with Jean Wahl, who at that time was a professor at the University of Lyons. But need I say that my whole merit in this affair was limited to having tried to decipher a book which, until then, my patron had not even bothered to open?

3 André Hayen, in a biographical account of Joseph Maréchal (1878-1944). He adds, "Maréchal will say with a smile later on that everyone then wanted to add their two cents' worth," *Mélanges J. Maréchal* (Paris: Desclée de Brouwer, 1950), p. 52.

[Translator's Note. For an introduction to several major traditions within recent Thomistic metaphysics, including Maréchal, see Helen James John, S.N.D., *The Thomist Spectrum* (New York: Fordham University Press, 1966). Translations of major parts of Maréchal's cahiers are available in *A Maréchal Reader*, edited and translated by Joseph Donceel, S.J. (New York: Herder and Herder, 1970).]

his order's administration date back to the years 1925-1926."[4] Today everyone knows that these difficulties were to disappear only with the changes in mentality which took place in the course of Vatican II.[5]

Since I was fairly conversant with the obstacles put in the way of any intellectual innovation at that time, when I carried on this work I was thinking only of drawing up a text which would serve as an aid to my memory. At the very most, I envisaged sharing it with a few long-standing friends who were familiar with my train of thought and who would be able to take my hint, as it were, and help me follow up my reflections by their questions or objections. This is why, when I hastily dashed off a literally rough draft, I merely typed it out in triplicate, intending it actually for Henri de Lubac and René d'Ouince who, thanks to our seminary years together studying philosophy and theology, met these conditions.

Besides, the reader of my first volume can still verify today that I was not at all concerned about giving any detailed information on the source of my inspiration. The preface written in 1947 filled up this lacuna. But in the introduction of 1931 it is more a question of Descartes, as the father of modern philosophy, than of Hegel, who is just mentioned at the end in connection with the word *dialectic* which I had picked up from Henri Brémond. Likewise, in the first chapter on "The Division of the Exercises," I am careful to refer as much to the tradition of the first directories as to a recent commentator, Jaime Nonell, in order to ground the objectivity of my starting point: "How can I get the four Weeks and the three Ways to coincide?" The solution which I then propose in the form of a purely *a priori* "deduction" contains no clear allusion to Hegel. For the initiates, there is perhaps an implied reference to Hegel in the bringing together of the two definitions of freedom ("positing of self by self" and "passing from non-being to being") and their being related to temporality. I contented myself with brief notations in the commentary of the next chapter on the First Week, so convinced was I that it was merely a matter of preserving the memory of some perspectives for myself. In this way I could find their outline again later on, if they were worth

---

4 *Un prophète en procès: Teilhard de Chardin dans l' Eglise de son temps* (Paris: Aubier, 1970), I, 51.

5 In connection with this, see the final sections of Volume I cited in the previous note: "L'oeuvre au feu de la polémique" and "Vers la révision d'un procès," pp. 188 ff.

the trouble of being worked out. As a matter of fact, the fruit-fulness of my interpretation revealed itself to me the more I continued it. It became more and more illuminating for me so that my commentary on the other Weeks expanded much more than I had anticipated, even becoming disproportionate in relation to that on the First Week.

When all is said and done, the entire work filled some eighty pages which I kept in my possession, without bothering to make it known or, on the other hand, refusing to share it with anyone who had heard of it and asked to read it. After tertianship was over, as my superiors did not grant me any leisure for deepening my knowledge of Hegel or for following up these reflections on Ignatius, but rather assigned me to high schools for three consecutive years, a job involving nothing intellectual, I let this Ignatian study lie dormant in my notes. Its destiny developed all by itself, without my even being concerned about it.

Actually, apart from an attempt at publishing it in 1947 (which fizzled out very quickly, but which spurred me to write a preface and the start of various complementary studies), the text which was lent out left and right was reproduced by one or another person, so that copies began to spread around, especially among Jesuit seminarians studying philosophy and theology during the postwar years.[6] Meanwhile, Hegelian studies had not stopped developing. Jean Hyppolite published his translation of Hegel's *Phenomenology of Spirit* from 1939 to 1941, and in 1946, his thesis-commentary, *Genèse et structure de la Phénoménologie de l'Esprit de Hegel*, followed shortly by the publication of the course lectures which Alexandre Kojève had delivered at the Sorbonne from 1933 to 1939.[7] Finally, in the same period Jean-Paul Sartre and

6 For example, in a letter dated Easter, 1949, Valensin wrote me from Nice: "Young F—— (son of the former minister) handed me your typed essay on 'The Dialectic of the Exercises,' and I am delighted with the little bit I have read. I would like to be able to read it at my leisure. Have you another copy you can give me? You are obviously a good example of the benefit which comes from keeping company with a great thinker. Hegel has taken you out of the crowd—or rather, you were already emerging from the crowd on your own." To my great regret I was unable to satisfy this request, since I had only my own personal copy left. Besides, I was not at all interested in a "clandestine" distribution of my work in the manner of Teilhard, who had himself, for that matter, long been firm in not resorting to such a method.

7 [Translator's Note. Hyppolite's commentary has recently been translated into English by Samuel Cherniak and John Heckman (Evanston: Northwestern University Press, 1974). Heckman's Introduction (pp. xv-xli) surveys the development of interest

Maurice Merleau-Ponty ensured the success of "existentialism" and of Husserlian phenomenology, while Marxism was intruding on everyone's attention thanks to the propaganda of the Communist party, which ascribed the merits of the party and of the U.S.S.R in the struggle against Nazism to the infallibility of the "dialectic."

One tiny and unforeseeable result of this evolution was that the text which had been almost incomprehensible in 1931 ended up being fairly intelligible. So that in 1955, when there was talk about celebrating the fourth centenary of Ignatius' death and I was no longer thinking about my old manuscript, some young theologians insisted that I should have it published for this occasion. Since they had become acquainted with it, they assured me, its perspectives had constantly nourished their intellectual and spiritual life better than anything else.

If I yielded to their pleas and published the text then without modifying it, the reason for it is, first, that this kind of invitation seemed to me to demonstrate that the text had already found its audience and that its form, however faulty, should not prevent it from pursuing its career. Above all, having no more than a few months at my disposal before publication, which had to be in the course of 1956, I preferred to clarify the initial version by completing it through the commentary on the Ways of Making a Good and Correct Choice, and especially on the Rules for the Discernment of Spirits, rather than to embark on a modification whose outcome I didn't know. This decision was quite prudent, as it turned out, since the revision ended in the publication of a second volume, not to mention the projected third volume!

This rapid historical account will suffice, I think, for your readers to grasp the advantage and value of your work: Without needless effort, it enables them to benefit from a study which was made more difficult than it should have been by the circumstances of its composition and publication. While following the interpretation of the *Exercises* which it initiated, but without enslaving yourself to the letter, you have brought out its essential argument and freed it from an overly technical form and a forbiddingly laconic style which threatened to hide its spirit. In order to succeed, you had first to explicate the underlying philosophy which my

in Hegel in France after World War II and its connections with Marxism. Kojève's lectures are also available in English, *Introduction to the Reading of Hegel*, translated by James H. Nicholas, edited and with an introduction by Allan Bloom (New York: Basic Books, 1969).]

remarks presupposed rather than stated. This is the special merit of your opening chapter on freedom. It unfolds a problematic which is indispensable for an understanding of the *Exercises* as I present them, but which your readers will not find any trace of in my work—unless they have the gift of reading "between the lines," as you do.

Furthermore, at other times, you have experienced the normal reward of intelligent commentators. By trying to clarify this or that expression of mine through comparisons drawn either from my book or from your own resources, you have succeeded in giving it a more satisfying explanation and especially in making the depth of some Ignatian insights stand out better than I did. Thus, while reading your Notes added to chapters four, five, and six on the representation, the application of the senses, and the immediate relationship between God and the creature respectively, I remembered Kant's remark and reconfirmed its accuracy: "It is by no means unusual, upon comparing the thoughts which an author has expressed in regard to his subject, whether in ordinary conversation or in writing, to find that we understand him better than he has understood himself. As he has not sufficiently determined his concept, he has sometimes spoken, or even thought, in opposition to his own intention."[8] Hence, thanks to the particulars which your work contributes in these Notes and on other points too, your fidelity has enlarged and deepened the field which I began to do the spadework on; in the same measure, your fidelity reveals itself as therefore already creative.

But it is also creative in a more profound sense, one from which I derive a good deal of deep-seated joy, believe me. In your own personal output, this commentary on the *Exercises* follows a first volume, *Un chemin de la Foi et de la Liberté*, which presents the problem of God first from a simply philosophical viewpoint and then from the viewpoint of history. In point of fact, man cannot pose for himself the problem of his own destiny without a minimum of rational reflection. And in order to grasp the novelty of Christ's revelation, if we want to comprehend the Christ-event and the meaning of the solution which Christ's message offers us, we must plunge this revelation back into the reality of the Jewish and Greek world of that period which, for the believer, suddenly becomes the center of universal history. This is, moreover, the very approach

8 *Critique of Pure Reason*, A 314; B 370; trans. N. K. Smith (London: Macmillan and Co., 1963), p. 310.

of Ignatius who, before having us meditate on the mystery of the Incarnation and on Jesus' life, first proposes for our reflection the Principle and Foundation as the "path of freedom" and then the truths of the First Week as the man "of faith" who lives them out gets ready to hear the call to a momentous destiny.

Consequently, that work was a kind of propaedeutic to this commentary on the *Exercises* which you rightly entitle *Life in Faith and Freedom*. Moreover, even now you let us look forward beyond this second volume to a third which will elucidate, from a properly theological angle, the meaning of the dogmas implied in the unfolding of the *Exercises'* four Weeks. Your previously published articles on the Resurrection, the Eucharist, and religious life[9] give some idea of the way in which you conceive its realization. Beginning from the cares of our everyday life, taken as the existential and historical basis of questions which the declaration of faith puts to the unbeliever, as well as to the believer's own understanding, you show how reflection resolves the theoretical problems each time—insofar as human freedom agrees to transcend the apparent antinomies of reason in order to enter a life directed by hope and charity. Thus fulfilling a properly speculative task, you remain faithful to the direction mapped out by the *Exercises*. Am I mistaken in thinking that you are thereby beginning to fulfill the wish I expressed in my preface of 1947: "to transcend the classical distinction between asceticism and dogma" by taking as our guide "the pedagogy of the saints"?[10]

It is undoubtedly necessary for the theologian to constantly transform dogmatic expressions in order to translate their content into a language intelligible to his contemporaries. Consequently, he must be conversant with discoveries in the natural or social sciences and he must stay sensitive to sound trends in contemporary philosophy. After fulfilling this condition, however, it will always fall to the theologian to show, in the face of the most modern problematic, that his own competence is to seek and find a solution by

---

9 [Translator's Note. Pousset's articles in English translation are: "The Eucharist: Real Presence and Transubstantiation," trans. John Ashton, S.J., in two parts, *Chicago Studies*, 9 (1970), 307-320; and 10 (1971), 91-110; "Human Existence and the Three Vows," trans. Wm. Russell, S.J., *Review For Religious*, 29 (1970), 211-237; Pousset's contribution to the article, "Homme," in the *Dictionnaire de spiritualité* appears as chapter three, "Christian Man in Dialectic," in *A Christian Anthropology*, trans. Sr. Mary Innocentia Richards, S.N.J.M. (St. Meinrad: Abbey Press, 1974), pp. 31-50.]

10 See *Dialectique*, I, 11, and the note there concerning an article by Hans Urs von Balthasar, "Théologie et sainteté," *Dieu Vivant*, no. 12 (1948), pp. 15-32.

situating himself within the movement of *conversion* by which the believer strives to reproduce the life of the dead and risen Christ in his thought as well as in his existence in order to become one with Him. Even if the theologian is merely raising questions about problems not yet decided on by the magisterium, and searching for a "way of speaking according to the true sense of the Church," his understanding cannot find a better guide for its own conversion than attending to the all-inclusive model of the process which the *Exercises* have so subtly analyzed. For even in his choice of the words and propositions which he must then find and enunciate, it is always a question of the decision of a sinful freedom which must here and now, in the thick of a continually fresh juncture enlightened only by salvation history, aim at uniting itself to the divine Freedom, revealed by the incarnate Word once and for all. Isn't this what Ignatius teaches when, in the most subtle of his Rules for Thinking with the Church, he recommends no other criterion for the language of his disciples, apostles as well as theologians, than the bond of symbolic relationships in which the Spirit establishes a conjugal link between Christ and the Church, making the Church our mother?

Insofar as your works continue to aim at an ideal which culminates in advice like that, I am sure they will play an efficacious role in making available to people today the truth of revelation in the form of that "historical and concrete theology" which Paul VI hoped for in his allocution of October 17, 1963. As for myself, I will see fulfilled the wish I made when, after having explained in detail this thirteenth Rule for Thinking with the Church, I expressed the concluding hope that such an interpretation of the *Exercises* would be able "to usher in their future fruitfulness as well as explain their past effectiveness."[11]

Therefore, accept my deep gratitude as your first reader who ardently hopes that many others, as many as possible, will benefit from your work and share the same feeling.

Gaston Fessard, S.J.
Maison Saint-Louis
Chantilly, France
May 6, 1971

11 *Dialectique*, II, 251.

LIFE IN FAITH AND FREEDOM

Chapter 1

FREEDOM

Invincible Freedom

I am my body in the world. All my perceptions, thoughts, reflections, certitudes, decisions, and actions are based on this body which is rooted in the world and by which I am present in the world and the world is there for me. But I am not merely my body in the world. At the heart of my consciousness which sees, thinks, reflects, believes, doubts, and decides, I experience myself beyond this body. For the time being I will not worry about whether this "beyond" is an escape and an incoherent dream, an illusion of "pure consciousness," or whether, on the contrary, it is an indication of a reality which is at least as real as my body in the world. *It is* in the sense that it is experienced and lived, and this is enough for now. I am my body in the world, but within this body, I am also a consciousness. The two are connected, but one is not simply the other.

This consciousness expresses itself through the body. I speak, I gesticulate, I connect motions together to form one deed; but I am not merely a word or this particular gesture; nor am I even a huge sum of gestures or deeds. By means of this body others enter into relationship with me. They see me, hear me, sometimes listen to me, and they form an idea of me. They approve my works and recognize me as this or that: I am a teacher, carpenter, nurse, and so on. They consider me intelligent or slow. All these qualifications belong to this animated body which I am, but I do not experience myself as coinciding purely and simply with these objectifications. I am somehow not merely beyond what others think of me, but even beyond what I think of myself. At one and the same time, I acquiesce and even voluntarily accept being this body. Or rather, I am this body, and deep down I am confortable there. I can

3

deride my looks, and yet I would not want to change my face for another.[1]

The consciousness by which I am beyond whatever I am here and now, for myself and for others, is an insuperable universality which cannot be confined by any limitation. Consciousness can be an immeasurable power of escape and illusion, or on the other hand, it can be a subject capable of reflecting and making a firm decison which involves the subject in reality in a permanent, definitive way. Perhaps these alternatives, moreover, are not mutually exclusive. In any case, I am this insuperable consciousness, beyond whatever I am for myself and others. It seems nothing can determine consciousness from outside. Here it is impossible to distinguish my freedom from the feeling of being free.

Someone can coerce my body and even "make me talk," but it seems quite evident to me that no one could definitively abolish my feeling of a clear or muffled disclaimer. No one can make me adhere interiorly, if I do not want to. Some famous trials have given us staged confessions which suddenly proved not to be confessions.

We can appeal to some more common situations. We know that in many of our deliberations it is not our motives which bring about the decision. Instead, it is a secret prior decision which confers value on this or that motive rather than on some other ones, and which sees to it that the former and not the latter motives weigh upon our reflection which leads to the decision. As for those who invoke their temperament as the origin of their choices and actions, they forget that their temperament exists only for the second-order knowledge that they gain about themselves when they see themselves as others see them,[2] and insofar as they acquiesce and secretly choose to allow their temperament to follow its bent.

I am a freedom more profound than all my deliberate deeds. Some have pushed their affirmations very far in this direction. They have forcefully and courageously maintained that there is "ultimately nothing that can set limits to freedom, except those limits that freedom itself has set in the form of its various initiatives,

---

1 See M. Merleau-Ponty, *The Phenomenology of Perception*, trans. Colin Smith (New York: Humanities, 1962), p. 434. We are drawing our inspiration here from some of Merleau-Ponty's analysis in his final chapter, "Freedom."
2 Ibid., p. 435.

so that the subject has simply the external world that he gives himself."[3]

Understanding freedom in this way, however, makes freedom impossible. Let us see why.

Within Duration and under Conditions

If my freedom exists absolutely; if it is more profound than all my voluntary or forced deeds; if it is a universal and necessary *a priori* factor dictating how I am affected by the world in my body; if it is uniformly free in my every course of action—then it also exists nowhere. It is the fundamental *given*, an acquisition which is present from the beginning, and not a freedom which is acquired within time, and which bestows itself on itself by developing gradually. In such a conception, freedom is condemned to itself, whatever it may do and whatever may happen. "The very idea of choice vanishes, for to choose is to choose *something* in which freedom sees, at least for a moment, a symbol of itself. There is free choice only if freedom comes into play in its decision, and posits the situation chosen as a situation of freedom. A freedom which has no need to be exercised because it is already acquired could not commit itself in this way: it knows that the following instant will find it, come what may, just as free and just as indeterminate."[4]

It seems quite essential to freedom that it will itself—in other words, that it choose and become by doing something. Freedom is not a necessary fact or a pure act which could not be other than it is. Freedom is a temporal movement which unfolds through choices.

The very notion of freedom demands that our decision should plunge into the future, that something should have been *done* by it, that the subsequent instant should benefit from its predecessor and, though not necessitated, should be at least required by it. If freedom is doing, it is necessary that what it does should not be immediately undone by a new freedom. Each instant, therefore, must not be a closed world; one instant must be able to commit its successors and, a decision once taken and action once begun, I must have something acquired at my disposal, I must benefit from my impetus, I must be inclined to carry on, and there must be a bent or propensity of the mind.[5]

3 Ibid., p. 436, though Merleau-Ponty does not agree with this view.
4 Ibid., p. 437.
5 Ibid.

This implies, at the very least, that I am a body in the world, and a body which endures. And that is why I value being a body as much as being conscious. This body is not simply identical with me (for my consciousness goes beyond it), and it requires that I submit to something other than myself. But this body is simultaneously the power and the means of my gradual becoming, and of my becoming free by doing something. In and through my body temporal instants are connected and built into a continuum; in my body acquisitions are stored, resources are developed, and that propensity of the mind which favors (or opposes) my action takes shape.

Thanks to my body, I experience duration and continuity, but I thereby also acquire some constraints and determinisms. My consciousness, which is not a spray of instants, can at any moment affirm itself as an instant which breaks the duration in two. This instant would not exist, however, if the two "pieces" of the fracture did not come together again for me into a before and an after. Only within my bodily duration can I experience and situate myself in relationship to a before and an after.

In this way a *field*[6] is constituted for me, without which no instantaneous freedom could irrupt, because it neither would nor could *do* anything. The *before* lays constraints on me, but it also affords me resources. The *after* separates me from my goals, but it also raises my hopes. The distance which separates the possible from the real, even if this distance is protracted by encumbering weights from the past and the uncertainty of far-off hopes, is the very milieu in which freedom develops; it is the necessary condition for freedom.

In summary, we have extricated two central ideas. The first is that of an invincible freedom, which may be just as empty as the feeling of being free, but it is basically just as undeniable. This freedom emerges as consciousness, surpassing all those qualifications and determinations which define me, and which even make me what I am here and now. Do I employ consciousness for reflection and decision, or for dreaming and escape? The second idea is that of a field where, from before to after, connections are joined and distances are stretched: my body in the world, and a body which endures. Without this field my freedom would be nothing because it could neither choose, nor act, nor consequently come to be.

Now we must search for, and think in terms of, the unity of

6 We are borrowing this word from Merleau-Ponty, ibid., p. 438.

these two contrary aspects: the *unity* of a person who lives, decides, and acts, while the decision and action are articulated within a spatio-temporal *manifold*. The goal of this search is to know whether or not there exist some free acts which are more important, more decisive, than others. Such acts would constitute a cleavage within a human existence for a long time, if not forever. Such acts, decisive as an instant and replete as duration, would make the person cross over the abyss from what is not to what is.

Are There Decisive Acts and Definitive Commitments?

So many situations in daily life are bound up with one another, and so many of them are controlled for me by an impersonal "system," that my freedom appears quite relative, limited, and unfit—or at any rate unable—to create itself by producing something original. Some choices do present themselves, to be sure, but within a very limited range. Free decision, lost in the tide of occasions, scarcely intervenes, even for important issues. A profession in which one is engaged for a long time, if not for life, is often "chosen" in conformity with a concatenation of circumstances which are linked in the same way as those which make me take the 6:30 rather than the 7 o'clock train. I did well in high school; I was "good in math"; I graduated when I was 17; I passed the entrance examination at Central, flunking it at another school, which was otherwise easier academically—and there I was, an engineering student at Central University for Arts and Manufacturing. I chose and I did not choose. In any case, I did not have the feeling of having invested my all in this series of events which, nevertheless, involves my entire social and professional existence until the age of retirement.

What about the man or woman whom one marries? Was he or she really chosen? Yes, of course. And yet it is so obvious that a host of frequently very fortuitous circumstances were operative there, too, and they undoubtedly conditioned the choice. Moreover, this is why a number of people, in their heart of hearts, secretly nurse the idea that they have been "trapped" or at least that they did not reflect enough, that they were not free enough, that the result—a definitive commitment institutionally ratified by the state or church—is too weighty with respect to the imponderability of the decision.

Today the very idea of a definitive commitment is disputed and challenged. Some will go so far as to say that such an idea

7

contradicts the true reality of a human choice. Those who are disposed to think along these lines are obviously more attentive to the temporal dimension of freedom in which a later moment can call the former decision into question. They find the field brought about by space and time filled with an unending dialectic in which decisions and circumstances continually modify one another. And our life is, in fact, woven by this kind of dialectic.[7] But is that *all* our life is?

We should at least look at the other side of the coin, the fact that people, and a lot of them, make commitments which they consider definitive, and which they maintain. They build their lives on these commitments without ever admitting the possibility of calling them into question. "I married Frances, and we will stay together until the end." "I made my religious profession, and if I should ever ask for a dispensation from my vows, I declare today that this would be, *in my case*, a breach of faith." Is this to have said too much, and to have passed oneself off for "the hero [who] lives out to the end his relation to men and the world"? If I say that there are some decisions which commit my entire life and which, in any case, constitute a cleavage for a long time, I am thereby saying that I have already somehow gone "to the end." At least this is what should follow from my resolve, and it must be explained.

Such decisions are facts. But are they justified and, if so, in what framework? The entirety of this book will be needed to answer such a question. This chapter merely aims at warning the reader regarding decisions of this nature. For anyone who considers such decisions impossible, or who cannot perceive anything corresponding to them in his own experience, would be very hard put to

---

7 Merleau-Ponty has not only frequently described this dialectic with great eloquence, but he has developed it into a theory, running throughout his works. He has, however, sometimes touched on points where the inadequacy of such a conception makes itself felt. But he has proceeded no further in the matter. Whether his silence is due to inability, modesty, or a decision, is hard to say. He ends *The Phenomenology of Perception* on this reflection: "Whether it is a question of things or of historical situations, philosophy has no function other than to teach us once more to see them clearly, and it is true to say that it comes into being by destroying itself as separate philosophy. But what is here required is silence, for only the hero lives out to the end his relation to men and the world, and it is not fitting that another speak in his name" (p. 456). [Smith's translation, slightly emended.]

   The truth of this conclusion is that philosophical language is not completed by words, but by action. There is no word which can definitively clear up words; in the last resort, it is the deed which sheds light. A word which is also deed is Truth.

understand what the Spiritual Exercises of St. Ignatius are about. Such a person would also be unable to grasp what we are talking about when we define freedom as the power of "becoming oneself by oneself" by passing from non-being to being. It will therefore help us if we can conceptualize, as nearly as possible, the nature of such decisions, which are at least known to some people.

The Absolute and the Relative

Today we encounter a quite futile but striking manifestation of that absolute power which freedom has of suddenly irrupting and severing the dialectic of particular circumstances and decisions. There are masses of men and women who go along with the daily routine of going to work and providing for the necessities of life day after day, and even hour after hour. This whole series of motions in which freedom stays buried—others would say it was suffocated or destroyed even before being born—is described on Paris walls as: Subway-Sweatshop-Sack Out [*Métro-Boulot-Dodo*]. But those people who scrawl these graffiti on subway walls are protesting. They are saying No, and they say it absolutely, or almost so. In their No we recognize an irruption of that invincible freedom— empty perhaps, but undeniable.

This irruption of freedom is so violent that it breaks duration or time in two, the breach preventing the before from passing into the after, and there ensues an action that is somewhat coherent, a beginning of history. At least we have here an Instant. But how can this absolute Instant become inscribed in duration? How can it become history, which develops patiently, day after day? This whole book is concerned with answering the question: How does a decisive Instant, the instant of a Yes rather than a No—and that obviously changes everything—become history? The Instant is categorical, even absolute, and yet it is capable of becoming embodied in a duration where, in a sense, there is nothing except what is relative; but without the relative, the Instant itself would be nothing.

The anonymous crowd which leaves for work each day also provides some (less striking) manifestations of the absolute power of freedom, namely, the definitive decisions which people make without full awareness of what they are doing, but they make them. These decisions extend from the most solemn variety to the most surreptitious. Because the latter are hidden, we cannot speak of them, but everyone talks about the former. Someone gets married in a church or before a justice of the peace, and it is "till death do us part." And, in fact, it often is "till death." After all, a signature on the state's register merits as much attention as graffiti in the subway.

People know and do not know what they do. The reflection which presumably accompanies the act which a person is going to posit and be accountable for frequently is very brief. The reasons why Peter marries Margaret are often not the same reasons why he lives with her until the end. But ultimately, the decision is made; and from one day to the next, their marriage vows never lose their meaning and value. On the contrary, they discover the meaning of their life together. They continue to carry out their decision through routine, of course, but appearances can be deceptive. They continue *through fidelity*, too, even if that word never occurs to them. The decision, and there was one, continues to be made. Motives change because the reality changes.

Without the couple thinking about it, such a life combines the two aspects differentiated by our analysis: the absolute quality of the Instant, and the duration in which things develop little by little. How well an entire life matches the absolute of an Instant, and unfolds it to the end point, when "the hero has gone to the end," is a secret which each person carries to the grave. The necessary condition for my going to the end is not to want to know "clearly" what I did and said in the Instant of my decision, and conversely, it is never to separate what I say and do each succeeding day from that decisive and fundamental Instant.

In Search of Unity

The intellectual (there has to be one every so often) is often enough trapped by his own scalpel. He scrapes the instant, and then he dissects the viscera of duration: its series of unthinking gestures, words, and all its constraints. He contrasts the instant with duration, but he no longer knows how to think in terms of their unity, nor even whether this unity exists. In the meantime, millions of people live and die who one day vowed fidelity to each other, and who never got divorced.

The authors of graffiti caution us against getting bogged down in things as they are. The men who go to work every morning and bring back a paycheck to their wives and children remind us that decisions made once and for all are inscribed in reality slowly, day after day, year after year. The daily labor of urban jobs is necessary in order to provide the conditions which allow personal decisions to become embodied in a human community.

But not just any instant of decision can develop into a history, nor can just any duration embody an absolute. Whoever suddenly demands the absolute of freedom and love is sentencing himself to rave in his own mouthings, in speech without any history, and to the throes of being refused. Conversely, whoever gets caught in the chain of movements which procure the paycheck needed for what is important lacks an essential element. For he is no longer the author of a history in which a decision is being accomplished. He is not leading a *decisive* life.

A decision made once is actualized in history not only by fidelity, which tirelessly repeats necessary motions, but equally by the intervention and creation of a new act from time to time, at an opportune moment, one which takes a risk and assumes even unforeseeable consequences in advance. The first decision becomes diluted in a series of quasi-automatic motions if their sequence is not broken once in a while by an act which renews, corrects, and deepens what was once decided. Changing one's profession or residence, building a house, welcoming a new baby are ways of continuing to create one's life, and of creating it together. Such ongoing creation includes parties and funerals; quarrels and the reconciliation which discovers the joy of even deeper understanding; the gift of flowers, as on the day of the engagement, but offered on a drab, ordinary Sunday; forgiveness without reserve, which renews and perfects the gift of self. All of this means creating one's life through the renewed and ever fruitful irruption of freedom, the instant which innovates not by arbitrary impulses, but through acts of lavish generosity.

The rebel who records his anger in graffiti is haunted by the dream of creating his own life. But is this not just a dream in him? He is unacquainted with, or incapable of, limiting himself by a particular decision that does not will everything at once. He is unacquainted with, or incapable of, plunging into the constraints and determinisms which would be the death of his dream, but perhaps the birth of a history. He does not have the power to live because he does not have the power to die a bit. For deciding on something, and plunging into things in order to bring it about, means dying to many dreams and passions.

But conversely, those who die to all their dreams by dint of things, rather than by their own energy, end by dying to the power to dream, to form a plan, and to decide.[8] They no longer make

---

8 We must believe in the reality of our desires and not take our desires for realities!

their own history, but are content to witness the history which others make, or perhaps only talk about: "sweatshop, subway, *TV*, sack out."

To make one's own history, one needs to "dream," that is, to communicate in symbols. The symbol is an act which unites a universal thought and some particular material into a simple, powerful image capable of spurring one into action, of sustaining the action, and bringing it to completion. The union of man and woman is thus a symbol: the founding act of a community, a language, and a history. Every life that is lived originates in a symbol and is nourished by one. When a person is no longer able to be in communion with reality through symbols, he falls into imaginary illusions.[9] If the imaginary (in the pejorative sense) proliferates, it is because the individual who feeds on it has retired into his shell, alone with himself and a fate which he submits to. He then experiences his interior emptiness to the point of aberration, and he seeks to fill it by an unending production of unreal fantasies. Television supplies only too many of these. But used with discretion, television could strengthen our sense of the symbolic, which enables us to be in communion with all of reality and gives rise to action.

Slave of necessity that I am, who compensate for my condition by fantasizing, may heaven help me some day to hear the message of two young men who, with their music under their noses, played the flute and violin in the aisle of the subway train for the harried passengers who no longer had the time to dream a little or to make a decision. The vicious circle will be broken the moment the graffiti writers and the commuters dispel their incomprehension. A decision has been taken by someone, and it is beginning to be inscribed in an intelligible history: I am playing Mozart for men, my brothers.

A Choice Uniting the Absolute and the Relative

We are inquiring whether there exist any instants of freedom in which we die to our dreams and passions so clearly, so deliberately, and so decisively that we are at once reborn to an incipient history. The history emerging from such instants never loses its power of novelty and creation in the time remaining to us. Facts prove that we make decisions without thinking or knowing what

9 See the Note on the Application of the Senses at the end of chapter 5.

we were doing at the time, though we stick to them afterwards. But we are wondering whether there also exist decisions in which we commit ourselves, not with an impossible and useless "clarity," but with a conscious and reflective resolve which evaluates the import of the act, the precariousness of our resources, and which calmly relies on hope.

In short, we are looking for instants of *responsible* freedom, or rather, for the source of a responsible attitude. *Responsibility* designates, in a global fashion, what we are seeking, for it unites the intensity of an instant of reflective decision with the sluggishness of something that develops slowly within duration, no matter what happens on the way. It holds together the two sides of our dialectic of freedom, the absolute *instant* and *duration* in which everything happens in and through the precarious and the relative.

Basically, responsibility takes account of our spirit-flesh condition: quick as spirit, but halting as flesh, Spirit decides and posits itself in a flash of lightning; but this lightning is still nothing, because I do not know what it contains. It is, in the present, fraught with the secrets of the future. But what secrets? What I decided in that moment includes things which I neither intended nor wanted, and yet which are part and parcel of my decision, as the future will bring home to me. A man and woman, for example, one instant wanted to love each other, and now they discover that their act of love has been inscribed in their bodies as an inchoate presence that they did not want; a baby is going to be born from an instant of love. Their being responsible means, first of all, admitting that this child was part of their decision as a possibility, indicating the infinite dimension of their finite act. Whoever does not want to accept his or her deed beyond what is intended and foreseen is not positing an act which is responsible or free. Any act posited in an instant of decision naturally goes beyond itself during its temporal development. Our body does not thereby "trap" us; it reveals and actualizes the very thing we did. Thus freedom exists in the determinisms of the body and of the universe no less than in the non-temporal and non-corporeal instant of decision.

This book records the history of this kind of freedom, the freedom which "passes from non-being to being by becoming itself." Do such instants of responsible freedom exist? We believe they exist in some lives, at least, and that these instants can exist for anyone who is not yet acquainted with them, but who lets a dormant element in himself be awakened and enjoined to attend to them.

In an earlier book[10] we brought up the God-question in human existence, and faith in God is undoubtedly necessary for an intimate understanding of St. Ignatius' Spiritual Exercises. But faith in man and the experience of freedom as we have just defined it are no less indispensable for understanding the Exercises. That first book, moreover, was both an investigation of our own reasons for believing and a study of Israel's freedom journeying towards a threshold of decision. Examining religion as a historical narrative in which men develop in and through their relationship to God consists simply in spotting *instants of freedom*[11] where men die to themselves and are born into an intelligible history. This history even reveals itself as absolutely intelligible insofar as its earlier hopes are wholly matched by subsequent events; we thus believe that the Christ-event is the fulfilment of Israel's hope since the call of Abraham. Within the framework of a history which involves an entire community's destiny, such instants of freedom would be more precisely designated as founding events.

Now, however, it is no longer a question of reflecting critically on human existence as a path to faith and freedom, nor of examining a historical religion as a progression on this same road. Once the threshold of faith in Jesus Christ has been crossed, it is a question of living in faith and freedom, according to a logic whose value is presupposed from now on.

The Spiritual Exercises implement this logic, according to an arrangement in which Ignatius' own genius plays a role. At the center of the Exercises there is a decision to make, the Choice. Prior to this are two "Weeks" which prepare for it, and afterwards, two Weeks where the consequences (foreseen and unforeseen) of this decision unfold. I ready myself for the Choice by being converted and following Christ (first two Weeks); when I have made my decision, I then die in Christ and rise with him (last two Weeks). I move from my furthest past, where I lived without really existing (sin is less than nothing), to the ultimate of life which has conquered death and which *is*. From one extreme to the other, the freedom which becomes itself passes from its own nothingness and becomes embodied in what is. Without minimizing the difficulty of the analyses which unfold this movement of self-creation, we can say that

10 Mentioned in the Author's Introduction, p. xviii above.
11 For example, the convenant with Abraham, the Israelites with Moses at Sinai, the establishment of the Davidic kingship, the destruction of Jerusalem. Part II of our earlier book *Un chemin de la Foi et de la Liberté* deals with the religion of Israel and the Christ-event from this perspective.

14

the principal difficulty is the risk involved: Will a connection be established between my own lived experience of freedom and the content of these analyses, or not?

The freedom in question here is not a matter of verbal outbursts or of daily motions bound in routine. The latter are bogged down in a duration where the dialectic of circumstances and "decisions" is indeed too feeble, But the former irrupt in an instant which is absolute only in its language. The freedom "which becomes itself by itself" and hence "'passes from non-being" both concentrates itself in the intense instants of creative decisions and unfolds itself calmly, powerfully, and patiently in the consequences and even constraints of duration. This freedom creates something novel in knowing that its deeds will go beyond what it has foreseen. But it takes responsibility for those deeds—that is, it disposes itself for courage, and it awaits, in faith and hope, the increase of the gift already bestowed on it. This freedom believes in the God of Jesus Christ who is present in history at the root of our decisions, at the heart of our actions, and at the end point of our accomplishments.

Therefore, in becoming itself, freedom is received from Another, and in gradually passing from the less good to the better, it crosses over the abyss from non-being to being. "I was as though non-existent, and now, by the grace of our encounter and decision, I exist and we are. I exist through You, for You give me being through myself."

There are acts which liberate definitively, even if the liberation they confer must yet be won, day after day. There are acts which re-create the person who posits them, even if he still has to develop patiently, day after day. What grace enables us to do for better, violence enables us to do for worse. The history of our freedom, according to the logic of faith, goes from worse to better, through the grace of Him who became the victorious victim of our violence.

15

Chapter 2

THE PRINCIPLE AND FOUNDATION

Man is created to praise, reverence, and serve God our Lord, and by this means to save his soul. The other things on the face of the earth are created for man to help him in attaining the end for which he is created. Hence, man is to make use of them in as far as they help him in the attainment of this end, and he must rid himself of them in as far as they prove a hindrance to him. Therefore, we must make ourselves indifferent to all created things, as far as we are allowed free choice and are not under any prohibition. Consequently, as far as we are concerned, we should not prefer health to sickness, riches to poverty, honor to dishonor, a long life to a short life. The same holds for all other things. Our one desire and choice should be what is more conducive to the end for which we are created (*Spiritual Exercises*, [23]).

The booklet of the *Exercises* proposes this rather dry text for our *preliminary* reflection. Everything begins with the First Week, but nothing could begin if God our Creator had not inscribed this vital logic in the depth of our hearts. It is the vestige, the first fruits, we could even call it the totality in hope, of the gift which he wants to give us and already did give us at the very beginning: before we entered upon the Exercises, before we committed our first sin, before the fall of Adam.

History begins with man's sin; but there could be no history without the gift of God our Creator and Lord. The difficulty here is to form a correct notion of this primordial gift, since it is not effective *before* we exist as subjects who make history by our own deeds. We are created, that is, entrusted to ourselves, and this gift is included in the sending[1] of Christ our Lord "even as he

---

1 The sending here is not a question of Jesus' birth, but of God's "purpose which he **set**

16

chose us in him before the foundation of the world" (Eph. 1:4). But the act which creates us and orders us to Christ is the foundation of our freedom's history, which begins with our existence; it is not a preexisting reality before we ourselves exist. Thus sin, the first deed belonging to this history, did not come after we had enjoyed God's gift for a while—we have known his gift only in our act of grabbing it and brushing aside the giver (this could be the radical definition of sin).

The Exercises begin by reflecting on sin, the original deed of our history. But they presuppose what makes sin possible, namely, the creation of the world and our establishment in Christ as the source of the divine life which we are called to share. It is fitting to celebrate this creation and establishment beforehand, as the Principle and Foundation of a life which we are then going to try to set in order by these same Exercises.[2]

The idea of creation took shape within the heart of the Israelite people. The Israelites' primary and fundamental experience was their election by God as the Chosen People, their covenant with God, and their liberation. God lavishly gives his people life and the conditions which make men free and masters of their destiny. "A wandering Aramean was my father; and he went down into Egypt. ...And the Egyptians treated us harshly, and afflicted us, and laid upon us hard bondage. Then we cried to the Lord the God of our fathers, and the Lord heard our voice, and saw our affliction ...and the Lord brought us out of Egypt with a mighty hand and an outstretched arm...and he brought us into this place and gave us this land, a land flowing with milk and honey" (Deut. 26:5-9).

The idea of creation emerged only secondarily, thanks to Israel's reflection on its history. Creation was conceived as the primordial spring whence gushed out God's gift of living water, which made the valleys green and the deserts blossom. For Israel, that men are created means that they are assured of God's generosity, from which they came, and that the fidelity of yesterday guarantees that of tomorrow. Man's relationship to the Creator does not entail a dependence which would alienate man from himself, as so many moderns imagine it. On the contrary, this relationship generates life and freedom for every person who abides in life and freedom.

forth in Christ as a plan for the fulness of time, to unite all things in him" (Eph. 1:9-10).

2 See J. Labarrière, *l'Existence réconciliée*, Collection Christus (Paris: Desclée de Brouwer, 1967), chap. 1, "Le dessein de Dieu."

If this is the case, I am happy with God, and I can acknowledge the charter of my existence and freedom in the dry formula: "Man is created to praise, reverence, and serve God our Lord, and by this means to save his soul." The dynamic here is obvious, and I fall on my knees because love is comfortable on its knees, welcoming the outpouring of Love.

To praise. In order to praise, a person must be like God, completely forgetful of self and truly free, with an expansive heart, ready to be awed by the unforseeable blossoming of a rose, an infant's smile, the tenderness of God.

To reverence. "In the measure that man is man, he is reverence. Reverence for the presence of meaning which is scarcely perceptible to our gaze. And precisely because we are dealing here with a basic attitude, beyond which there is nothing else, we can by no means prove it. We can only suggest or indicate it by a clue which immediately fades away. This attitude is man's heart, his integrity, and the slightest violation of it ushers in the dehumanizing process. For there is only one *human* possibility for man: the desire for and attention to (re-spect) meaning for its own sake....The person who seeks God for God."[3]

To serve. Through service I return what I have received to the one whom I reverence. "Whoever would be great among you must be your servant, and whoever would be first among you must be slave of all. For the Son of man also came not to be served but to serve, and to give his life as a ransom for many" (Mark 10:43-45).

The rest of Ignatius' text is equally obvious: "The other things on the face of the earth are created for man...." They are the first fruits in this world of the gift which God made of himself. "Hence, man is to make use of them in as far as they help him in the attainment of his end.... Therefore, we must...." This is the response of love to Love.

If this response is not obvious to someone, he is a "stiff-necked" slave heading for death, who imagines God as a tyrannical and threatening master. The Israelites learned from God, for all of us, that they and we were this slave. The Principle and Foundation then comes down like a judgment, and we must employ the full force of the reasoning which remains at the heart of our unreasoning to convince ourselves of the undeniable accuracy of these "mathematical" propositions.

---

3 G. Morel, *Problèmes actuels de religion* (Paris: Aubier, 1968), p. 180.

We must make ourselves indifferent: We must attain the condition of a preferential desire and longing for whatever leads us to love more. Indifference is lived out amidst continual choices, that is, at the heart of freedom, of life with others in the world.

He must rid himself of them insofar as they are a hindrance: "And if your hand causes you to sin, cut it off; it is better for you to enter life maimed than with two hands to go to hell, to the unquenchable fire. And if your foot causes you to sin, cut it off. . ." (Mark 9:43-45).

More: This is the unbounded measure of love. To love is to love more: "Take heed what you hear; the measure you give will be the measure you get, and still more will be given you. For to him who has will more be given; and from him who has not, even what he has will be taken away" (Mark 4:24-25).

The Lord is my chosen portion and my cup;
thou holdest my lot.
The lines have fallen for me in pleasant places;
yea, I have a goodly heritage.
Thou dost show me the path of life;
in thy presence there is fulness of joy,
in thy right hand are pleasures for evermore. (Psalm 16)

This was only a preliminary reflection. We have not yet begun, and all is said. Yes, all is said. From now on, long is the road which is MORE conducive to praise, reverence, and service.

Chapter 3

THE FOUR WEEKS

The Spiritual Exercises last about a month, and they are divided into four "Weeks" of six to ten days each, according to the needs of the retreatant. The First Week proposes exercises on sin and aims at an initial conversion, passing from sin to acceptance of grace. The Second Week is introduced by a contemplation of Christ the Lord who calls each person to follow him, according to his own vocation. Then we follow Jesus from his birth to the end of his public life, preparing ourselves for a decision in response to Christ's call, the Choice, which is the center of the Exercises. With the Choice, we enter into the Third Week, allowing ourselves to be united to Christ in his passion and even in his death. Dead with Christ, we rise with him in the Fourth Week. The fruit of the entire Exercises is harvested in a final contemplation, the Contemplation to Attain the Love of God, which enables us to see everything in God and God in everything.

We will first reflect on how the four Weeks relate to each other, in function of our freedom which has to make a decision. God did not create the world once and for all in the beginning; he creates it today, as yesterday, and again tomorrow. The creative act grounds our history in its origin and development, but each and every person's history begins only with acts of freedom. In the First Week of the Spiritual Exercises, St. Ignatius is not directly interested in the relationship to the Creator which constitutes the creature. He is concerned with the *act* by which a freedom has begun to exist and to make history. The relationship to the Creator, which is presupposed at the beginning of the First Week and re-called briefly in the Principle and Foundation, could be thus defined: Of itself the creature is nothing, but God entrusts the creature to itself by enabling it to become and to be by itself. As for the act constituting a human freedom, it can only be the "yes"

20

or the "no" by which this freedom becomes itself in the world and ultimately posits itself in relation to the Creator, whether or not its affiliation with God is recognized.

According to revelation, the original "yes" is the Virgin Mary and Christ, and we all hope to be included in them. The original "no" is Adam and Eve, and our sinful past, or "old man," incorporates all of us in them.[1] The Virgin Mary said *"Fiat"*: in this word can be heard the acknowledgement of the creature recognizing itself as a creature, "I am not." This acknowledgement ratifies the concrete difference between the created "I," who by right is nothing, and God who IS. But since God made us exist in ourselves, that is, in an essential difference from him, solely with an eye to uniting us to himself, such an acknowledgement immediately inserts the creature in a movement which proceeds from God, goes beyond (without abolishing) the difference, and ends in union. This is the history of the Virgin Mary; the handmaid of the Lord is made spouse, mother, and queen.

This kind of acknowledgement is impossible without the help of him who IS. In fact, an intelligent creature masks its own fundamental nothingness from itself. It is before God that it discovers its nothingness; as conversely, only to the degree that it discovers its own nothingness does it arrive at the presence of God. This double movement constitutes a unique relationship, whose foundation and origin is God and God alone. "I am not" is hence enveloped by a more basic affirmation, "God is."

Freedom's original act of saying "yes" unfolds in a history which is structured in four moments.[2] The *first* is the Virgin's "I am not"; Mary understands and conducts herself as the handmaiden who is nothing by herself, and who owes everything to him who IS. This attitude is highlighted for us in the account of the Annunciation, but it is fundamental in Mary, constituting her entire life.

The *second* moment is the negation of this self-abasement. From her who is not, God makes the mother of his Son, but by paths

---

1 The meaning of *original* here is primarily logical, not chronological; thus, whatever is foremost is "original." Foremost in salvation history is the Virgin's "yes," made possible by Christ's "yes." Adam's "no" precedes this "yes" in time, but the "yes" abolishes the "no."

2 *Moment* does not have primarily a chronological meaning. It is one phase in a dialectical movement which always contains three, four, or more moments. Each moment forms a whole, and each even contains everything which unfolds in the entire dialectic, but each moment contains it according to one particular aspect different from, and even opposed to, those which characterize the preceding or following moments.

in history where self-effacement and sometimes suffering predomi-
nate. Hence this negation goes even to the limit where the creature dies wholly to itself (*third* moment: Mary at the foot of the
cross), but thereby finds itself overcome by him who is (*fourth*
moment: the mother participates in the resurrection of her Son
and will be taken up into the heavens in the Assumption). The
logic of this freedom likewise applies to Christ, or rather, he is its
author and principal cause. In Christ, finally, it applies to everyone; we will see what the difference is.

The logical moments which structure a historical becoming
subsist together, but in individual situations one is more dominant
than the others. This compenetration of moments is remarkably
verified in the life of the Virgin Mary. For example, at the instant
when she says her *fiat*, the "I am not" of the first moment, the
Holy Spirit overshadows her, as in the fourth moment. And when
she is taken up into the heavens, she remains the humble handmaid of the Lord. But all is contained within the sign of the first
moment at the Annunciation, of the second during the years at
Nazareth, of the third at the foot of the cross, and of the fourth
starting with Jesus' resurrection.

Entirely contrary to the creature who says yes to God, the
sinner's freedom is an affirmation of himself as the principle and
end of all his acts, "I am." Through this sort of self-affirmation,
the creature grabs the something which it indeed is (but as gift)
and subjugates the world of creatures to itself as far as possible. But
in thus affirming itself, the "I" severs itself from its source of being
and clutches only its own insignificance and nothingness. This is
a contradiction which separates the sinner from himself, from
others, from the world, and from God. The sinner experiences
this contradiction before he understands it; he understands it when
he begins to be delivered from it. Of course, for a while the particular pleasures which he relishes in things and the satisfaction of
affirming himself hide from him the growing emptiness within.
But the void does deepen; it is the immanent judgment within
sin pronounced by him who is.

In the sinner, the "I am" is in fact the creature's own nothingness
withdrawing, becoming attached to itself, and doubling back on
its own self. The sinner draws the power of thus doubling back on
his own self from God's gift, himself and all the things around him.
But he grabs this gift and thus refuses to acknowledge it as gift,
an obstinacy which is more and more contradictory and destructive. One who of himself *is not* can become so hardened in his own

22

wretchedness that he wills it, even to the terrifying identification of himself with a hence subsisting contradiction, hell.

But this immanent judgment which the sinner feels can be the starting point of an "awakening" in which the sinner begins to reflect and uncover the truth of his deeds. The pseudo-affirmation of his own self is really obstinacy in his own insignificance, emptiness rather than fullness, non-being rather than being. He then needs to admit: "I wanted to make myself; I wanted to be and to be able to say 'I am,' but in fact *I have freely posited myself as non-being.*" "Sin is nothing but the negation of self which freedom began to posit, or rather, posited at the outset. An irrational negation, without motive...."[3]

The First Week of the Spiritual Exercises is a reflection whereby the "I" discovers the irrationality of its behavior. Under the pretext of affirming itself, it has posited the *negation of its own self* by its sins. This is the first moment.

But the immanent judgment which the sinner feels in his deeds, and which brings about this inward reflection, carries him still further. This divine judgment within the sinner becomes the principle of a *negation of this negation of his own self.* The thoughts and feelings of Jesus Christ—he who is and who reunites himself with the sinner in his sin—take the place of his sinful thoughts and disordered feelings. This is the second moment, the Second Week.

The negating of sin extends even to its radical exclusion. In Jesus Christ who dies on the cross, the sinner dies to his sinful I, the free and contradictory "positing of his own self as non-being" (Third Week). Dead, he is reborn to the life of the risen Lord, that is, he allows himself to be overcome by him who is (Fourth Week), the positing of being.

The Spiritual Exercises thus unfold a unique act of freedom, which is all man's and all God's. All is done by me, and all is from God, who is more myself than I am.

We recognize here the same four moments as in the history of the Virgin Mary: without sin in her, with sin in us. Each moment corresponds to a quite determinate stage. The I passes from one stage to another by crossing a threshold, the threshold of a conversion: the colloquy of mercy throughout the First Week, the Choice at the end of the Second, and compassion in the course of the Third. To the degree that the conversion deepens, the four moments

3 *Dialectique*, I, 46.

in the I become what they are logically, internal to one another.

The freedom which posits itself by going through these moments is entirely internal to itself; it posits itself by itself. At one and the same time, it executes and submits to a negating of its own self which makes it pass from the nothingness which uselessly doubles back on its own self (non-being) to the life of God who is all in all (being). We can thus give a twofold definition of *freedom:* (1) the act of positing its own self, and (2) passing from non-being to being.[4] As the positing of its own self by itself, freedom is its own principle. As passing from non-being to being, freedom must, in order to exist, cross over the abyss which separates what is nothing, and less than nothing (the sinful creature), from him who IS. Freedom cannot cross over this abyss by itself since, of itself, it is nothing; it can only do so by the mediation of the Being which gives it being, God the creator, and this creator precisely as mediator. In one and the same movement, freedom thus posits its own self by itself and through Another, within the simplicity of an undivided act and a historical development which takes time.

If we now reread our brief presentation of the Exercises, we will there see the two definitions of freedom outlined and combined. The four Weeks constitute a becoming which rises from non-being to being. The first two Weeks consider the negative side of this becoming, that of non-being; the final two Weeks consider its positive side, that of being. The Choice takes place at the juncture of these two sides. This central act of freedom cannot be represented in itself, and yet it is represented in the form of its *antecedents* (the preliminary situation and conditions which make it possible, the first two Weeks) and its *consequences* (the death which it brings to the converted sinner's heart, and the life which springs from death itself, the Third and Fourth Weeks).

The first two Weeks describe the development of freedom *before* the decision; the latter two Weeks describe it *after* the decision. The Choice which separates, or rather joins, Before and After is this *positing* of self by self, an act wholly internal to itself and incapable of being represented, which both concentrates itself in this point and permeates each of the four moments. The first moment is the reflection on sin by which the I *posited itself* as non-being; the second is the life of following Jesus, in which *is posited* the negation of the first positing; the third moment is the passion and death in which *is posited* the exclusion of all non-being; and the

4 We justify the use of these categories (being and non-being) in a Note at the end of this chapter.

fourth is the resurrection in which *being will posit itself.*[5]

In summary:

A. Before the act of freedom
    I.   Positing of non-being   First Week
    II. Negation of this positing   Second Week

B. After the act of freedom
    III. Exclusion of non-being   Third Week
    IV. Positing of being   Fourth Week

This schema *represents* the act of freedom which is intrinsically incapable of being represented; accordingly, only its four moments appear here, spread out in the time of the representation, which is the time of reflection.[6]

Note on "Being" and "Non-Being"

These two categories do not designate distinct and successive states, but rather two aspects of the same reality, in dialectical relationship (that is, involving both cooperation and opposition). Moreover, a formula like "passing from non-being to being," one of our definitions of freedom, should not fool us. We cannot pass from pure non-being to being without any admixture of non-being. For one reason, pure non-being is that whence we were drawn (if we can use that expression) by the creative act; but the creative act is not a *passage.* For another reason, being without admixture of non-being is God.

---

5 We have intentionally used and italicized the verb *to posit* four times here, despite some awkwardness. This emphasis draws attention to the fact that the act of freedom (positing of self) is spread over the four Weeks, vivifying them from within, without ceasing to be internal to itself. Moreover, this is why the truth of our representation of the four moments is their mutual inwardness, even if the representation spreads out the four moments into successive Weeks which are external to one another.

6 We have not been able to avoid having recourse to some technical terms such as *being, non-being, becoming* or *development, positing of self by self.* As soon as they are understood, they allow us to define the four Weeks by means of a homogeneous language, and to shed light on relations which would scarcely appear otherwise. Translated into this language, the ensemble of four Weeks appears as a single, well-knit system of remarkable correlations and oppositions. The movement running through these relations belongs to the act of freedom which is not represented anywhere in this schema because it is everywhere. Concentrated in itself, the act of freedom is *the Instant* which connects Before and After; spread out in the Before and After which it permeates, the act of freedom is, on one hand, its own anticipation and, on the other, its consequences.

As concrete existents, we are always becoming: some fluid combination of non-being and being (being which refers to Being). In the Exercises, therefore, the dialectic of freedom goes through the phases of a becoming. The first phase, however, is not pure non-being, but rather an already concrete situation of becoming, and thus a mixture of being and non-being. This initial situation is marked by the predominance of non-being over being, a tendency towards non-being, and not exactly towards the non-being we were created from, but towards the less than nothing which is sin (non-being doubled back on itself, an unthinkable contradiction). As for the last phase in the development of freedom, we say it is being; but this being is not purely and simply God. It is the being of a creature, hence still connoting non-being. This creature, however, has become a participant in divine Being, in the strong and precise sense of our divinization in Jesus Christ.

But it is true that each phase in the development of freedom is not unrelated to radical non-being and absolute Being, even though it is and remains a relative situation in historical becoming. That is the difficult and important point: We are always in a relative situation; what we do is relative to this situation, and yet our deeds carry with them a properly ontological content. It is ultimately a question of being and non-being. "To be, or not to be!" We will look at this more closely.

The difficulty can be expressed by using an example borrowed from our analyses. We said that by her *fiat*—"I am the handmaid of the Lord"—the Virgin Mary expressed the creature's acknowledgement of its own createdness, "I am not." We said this was the first moment of a freedom's concrete development, *non-being*. But, by the power of God, the handmaid of the Lord was made mother and queen, maternity...assumption: *being*.

As for the creature which cancels itself, as it were, by its sin, and descends below the nothingness proper to the creature, we said that, by wanting to be, the creature has in fact freely posited itself as *non-being*. Forgiven and re-created, it becomes a son in and by the dead and risen Son: *being*.

Now it seems clear there should be a difference between "handmaid of the Lord" and the *non-being* proper to every creature—their equivalence is not obvious. "Handmaid of the Lord" designates a relative historical condition, intermediate between pure and simple non-being and the Being proper to God, while *non-being* is the negation of any ontological reality, however meager it may be. Likewise, the sinner's confession lowers him in relation to his earlier pretension, but not to the point of annihilating him below the nothingness proper to the creature. We can make the same comment, in opposite fashion, for the term *being* in relation to "mother of God," "queen," or "son in and by the Son."

In short, beyond the obscurity of terms not used in everyday language, what causes difficulty is the radical ontological meaning which they superimpose, like a double exposure, onto the relative situations of repentant sinners or the improving faithful. Each person lives out his or her freedom's development in a personal history which is always situated between "absolute zero" and infinite Being, without ever coinciding with one or the other. Is it then legitimate to use these terms, with their strong ontological meaning? Is it really necessary?

We would like to make the legitimacy and necessity of these terms felt by having recourse to a rather eloquent example. It is even more than a question of an example; it is a question of the peculiar history of our freedoms as the Bible speaks of it. In its own way, the Bible also uses language with strong ontological meaning.

The history of Israel unfolds between a beginning situated within temporal becoming (the call of Abraham, the exodus from Egypt) and an end point which is also situated within time, the messianic event. Everything Israel says about itself is measured by events which occur between this beginning and the end point to which its account refers. God's choosing Israel, its sins, the new covenant ...designate a historical reality (or its contrary), not an immediately ontological reality in the sense of non-being or being. And yet these historical realities are ultimately about the first and final ontological Reality. They are about the people's relationship to God, who drew the people from nothing, and who calls the people to partake in his own Being. The people is this relationship. And, by virtue of this relationship, at the end point the people's being will be God's Being as shared by the people.

The people's participation in the Being of God is ultimately going to be actualized in the messianic age which extends to the end of time: a recapitulation of time in the absolute. If this relationship were broken, the people would fall back into non-being, an absence of being experienced (in a relative way) at the time of the destruction of Jerusalem and the exile.

So true is it, therefore, that Israel's history has an ontological density, and that the stakes are all or nothing (being or non-being), that Israel's historical consciousness developed a *Before* all the way back to the origin of the world (the first eleven chapters of Genesis) and an *After* all the way up to the absolute fulfillment (St. John's Apocalypse). The Before is about God the Creator's victory over non-being and the creature's fall into a redoubled non-being (sin); the After is about our life with God, our participation in the very Being of God.

By virtue of this initial rooting in the creative act and this ultimate fulfillment, the biblical expressions which designate historical events and typical or particular situations have an absolute content, not merely a relative one. God's favor towards Abraham or David speaks simultaneously of God's favor towards every creature called to be (creation) and re-created (the messianic age...until the end). And David's particular sin speaks simultaneously of the typical sin in chapter three of Genesis, and it gives an inkling of the sin which calls forth the Apocalypse.

In the same way, the use of *being* and *non-being* in our text helps us perceive a definite ontological reality in each particular and relative moment: the all-or-nothing stakes Israel expressed by tracing its history back to the very beginning, while Jesus' disciples extended it until the final end.

_____

Chapter 4

THE FIRST WEEK

The First Week aims at acquiring sorrow for sins at the feet of Christ on the cross or, in other words, at making the retreatant experience the absence of God, and God's presence in this absence. This latter formulation will be justified by the rest of our commentary.

The God who thus reveals himself through the very paths of sin is the Father who sends his Son, Christ, whom the Father made "to be sin who knew no sin, so that in him we might become the righteousness of God" (2 Cor. 5:21). The spiritual experience of the Exercises can be lived on several levels. A beginner will often remain on the surface of his sins, and he will then encounter Christ principally by externals, by a representation of the Crucified, rather than in the full mystery of "Christ made sin." But whoever receives the grace of going to the root of sin will feel his prayer becoming extremely simplified. All representations will disappear in a soul-piercing emotion which conveys this fundamental and overwhelming truth: "For our sake he made him to be sin who knew no sin, so that in him we might become the righteousness of God." Then, by dint of the five exercises suggested by St. Ignatius, the retreatant's contact with his sins becomes for him contact with Jesus Christ: at first shame and confusion at himself, then deep and intense sorrow, and tears.

In a commentary on the Exercises two viewpoints necessarily interweave with each other: that of the *consciousness* which advances step by step with good will but limited vision, and that of the *principle* or *logical viewpoint* which surveys beginning and end in a single glance. Only at the end point does consciousness, emerging from its limited and sometimes deceptive awarenesses, catch up with the logical viewpoint. The latter, in short, transcends every viewpoint that is still particular (the situation of consciousness in each Week) and it grasps, in global and simple fashion, the whole mystery that has taken place.[1]

We can explore the First Week's content from the logical viewpoint by starting with a proposition we formulated earlier: "I wanted to be and to be able to say, 'I am,' but in fact I have freely posited myself as non-being."

Let us compare the beginning and end of this proposition. "I am" and "non-being" are two contradictory terms. They define sin in itself. In the person who commits it, sin stems from a will to be and not from a will not to be; the sinner does what he does in an effort to realize himself. But what precisely impels him is a resolve to become himself by and for himself. The sinner ignores or scorns the necessary mediation of him who IS, or he suspects his intentions, as appears very clearly in the account of the fall of Adam and Eve: "You will not die. For God knows that when you eat of it your eyes will be opened, and you will be like God, knowing good and evil" (Gen. 3:4-5). God is suspected of jealously wanting to retain something for himself, which he would deny to man. The sinner's freedom, failing to will itself for God and in God, whom it distrusts, establishes the contrary of what it aimed at: non-being, error, vain and empty self-affirmation, the contradiction of "I am" and "non-being."

Now let us look at the middle section of our initial proposition, "...I have freely posited myself...." This sin, which in its pure state is a subsisting contradiction, has a history, and a history which can hide the true nature of sin for a long time. The sinner first pursues a good, his own self-realization, and to attain it he uses the things of the world—all good in themselves—and he uses other people, but by relating them to himself and his egotistic ends. His act first presents itself to him as entirely positive, and he thoroughly commits himself to it, freely. In actual fact, this commitment is marked by a lie and whoever refuses to face up to the truth ceases to be free.

Falsehood and contradiction are at the root of our history. Sin is not one particular act among others. Sin is the act which is at the origin of the I, a global positing which develops of itself and tends to include an entire facet of existence—my entire "past" up to the present moment when I reflect and begin to be converted. Moral conscience left to itself cannot experience the totalitarian

---

1 St. Ignatius himself distinguishes these two viewpoints as that of the director and that of the retreatant who is told not to be curious about what lies ahead.

hold of sin. What makes it known as original sin, in mysterious connection with the sin of the fallen angel, is revelation.[2] Whatever my personal sins may be, my present concern as I reflect is first to recognize my own history in the history that develops from the original sin: I am capable of all sins.

To reflect is to suspend time. By simply entering into the reflection of the First Week, I suspend the course of my sins; and in relation to this reflection, my entire life is in the past. But sin is not sporadic in my past—it penetrates my life completely and entirely. This is what must be seen. The retreatant in the First Week should be able to hear Yahweh saying to Jerusalem: "This city has aroused my anger and wrath, *from the day it was built to this day*" (Jer. 32:31). This experience is absolutely essential for the spiritual life, and without it a person remains a "juvenile." According to revelation, this is the meaning of sin—including my sin.

From what we have just said we can deduce (that is, perceive the logical connection of) the five exercises proposed by St. Ignatius. "From what we have just said," meaning that we start from a given which is revealed. There is no question of a deduction that would, by virtue of a principle taken elsewhere than from revelation, point out any necessity linking these exercises. Rather, it is the reflection of faith itself which here exhibits its own internal coherence, within the Exercises, in representing to itself the growth of sin down to the non-sense of hell.

First Exercise

The subject matter for this exercise is "the triple sin": the sin of the angel, original sin, and the sin of an ordinary man. Revelation alludes to a perplexing sin at the edge of our history, a sin which exceeds and precedes human freedom, and which has, through temptation, exerted a primordial influence on human freedom: *the sin of the angel.* Evil entered the world by the door which the

---

2 Sin, as understood by Christian faith, cannot be known by the mere reflection of moral conscience on its intentions and acts. Of ourselves, we can agree on certain faults against others or against ourselves, but not on that for which God reproaches us in Scripture, the adultery of the beloved, the idolatry which consecrates to those other than God the gift received from him. Such a revelation is not totally discontinuous with our moral experience, but it does unveil, beneath our conscious intentions and concrete situation, a sense or rather a non-sense which would never have entered our minds. It is, therefore, true that sin obfuscates the sinner's conscience and keeps the import and intrinsic malice of his deeds hidden from his eyes.

31

freedom of man's consciousness opened to it, but man is not the first inventor of evil. Man has made himself a liar and a murderer, but there is a "father of lies" and a "murderer from the beginning" (John 8:44). Such is the teaching of revelation, which clarifies our everyday experience: As sinners, we are both guilty and victims, liars and deceived.

This connivance of man with the inventor of sin is not merely an accident which happens every hour of each day of our poor lives. It is a global "principle" enveloping our freedom; we are born into this connivance, and the acts which renew it are already owing to it: original sin. We will explain this a little.

The existence of Satan is often challenged or even denied today. Nevertheless, Jesus' words and actions throughout the four Gospels do not permit us to eliminate from the mystery of Jesus the aspect of spiritual warfare against one whom he calls the enemy in the parable of the wheat and the tares. This name is fully justified. Satan, by his twofold title as the "father of lies" and "murderer from the beginning," is the enemy of the Word (Truth) and of the Son (Life), and the enemy of men. The undeniable reality of this spiritual warfare compels the Christian to believe Christ when he speaks of this enemy and of defending oneself against him.

Whoever has seriously experienced the spiritual life knows of what or rather of whom the Lord speaks. "Of whom"—is it then a person? Yes, but a person who, by reason of his sin, does not stop depersonalizing himself, and who ceaselessly depersonalizes others: Satan divided against himself.

The Scriptures give us clear and sober indications about this enemy. First and foremost is the saying of Jesus: "I saw Satan fall like lightning from heaven" (Luke 10:18). This saying takes up the words of Isaiah, in a satire on the king of Babylon: "How you are fallen from heaven, O Day Star, son of Dawn!...You said in your heart, 'I will ascend to heaven; above the stars of God I will set my throne on high'" (Isa. 14:12-13).

Ezekiel's twenty-eighth chapter, in a satire against the king of Tyre, has enlarged upon Isaiah's text. The saying of Jesus entitles us to see outlined in these personalities the complete tyrant, the one of whom it was first said: "...your heart is proud, and you have said, 'I am a god, I sit in the seat of the gods'" (Ezek. 28:2). Only the austerity of Scripture can correctly express this absolute act of freedom, this perplexing creation of evil and iniquity out of nothing: "You were the signet of perfection, full of wisdom and perfect in beauty. You were in Eden, the garden of God...you were on the holy mountain of God. . . . You were blameless in your ways from the day you were created, till iniquity was found in you" (vv. 12-15).

There is no process, no sequence of causes and effects, that makes him shift gradually from good to evil. By an arbitrary act that apes the gratuity of creation, the best becomes the worst. We thereby learn that it is not our faults, our imperfections, and our limitations which produce the greatest evil in us, but our good qualities and perfections when a spirit of pride and a will to power take possession of them. "I cast you as a profane thing from the mountain of God. . . . Your heart was proud because of your beauty; you corrupted your wisdom for the sake of your splendor. I cast you to the ground. . . . I brought forth fire from the midst of you; it consumed you. . . . you have come to a dreadful end and shall be no more for ever" (vv. 16-19).

Original sin also presents a problem for the understanding of believers today. Some preliminary indications will help dispel any reservations about entering into the meditation proposed by St. Ignatius.[3] The New Testament teaches us two things about man's sinful condition: (1) all men are sinners and need to be freed from their sin by Jesus Christ; (2) this sinful condition is linked to the sin of the first man, Adam.

The first of these two affirmations is found on every page of the New Testament. The second is only formulated two times, both in the letters of St. Paul: 1 Cor. 15:20-22 and Rom. 5:12-19. What is directly affirmed in these two texts is the redemption by Christ; the role attributed to Adam is indicated in a subordinate way: "Then *as* one man's trespass led to condemnation for all men, so one man's act of righteousness leads to acquittal and life for all men" (Rom. 5:18). From the way Paul speaks, we see that Adam's role was supposedly better known by his Jewish and Judaeo-Christian readers than was Christ's role. And in fact the Jews at the time of Jesus and Paul did admit that the torrent of sins in the world originated with Adam. If God was able to allow such a source of sin and evil to spring up, he could create its analogue for good. For people who had put their hope in justification by the Law, it was this affirmation of Christ as the

---

3 We will return to this question of Original Sin in another volume dealing with the principal dogmas put to use in the Exercises. See Charles Baumgartner, *Le péché originel*, in the series "Le mystère chrétien" (Paris: Desclée de Brouwer, 1969).

unique source of all righteousness which posed a problem.[4]

Three centuries later, St. Augustine argues in the reverse direction. Beginning from Christ's universal role as savior, widely admitted and believed at that time, Augustine reasoned there must be an original sin which envelops all of us, since Christ came as savior for all men without exception, including those who die before having committed any personal sin. There is one salvation given to all by Christ and by Christ alone; hence there is a sin common to all. If all persons are united in the salvation given by Christ, it is because they were locked up in the same sin. We cannot be partners in the salvation of Jesus Christ but every man for himself in the sin. Thus faith arrived at a more complete formulation of its content: The concept of salvation (*one* salvation, *for all*, in Christ who justifies us down to the roots of our being) is equally fitting for sin. There is one sin which confines *all* men by striking them at the root, at the root of their historical freedom— a sin which is not merely produced by men's deeds, but is the principle of their actions.

The dogma of Original Sin was then fully formulated and its meaning is as follows. What is first in the history of our relations with God is not sin, but the Father's will to unite us all in his Son. In one and the same act he creates us and directs us to this unity in Christ. He sees all of us in each of us, gathered in his Son; in the first man he already sees Christ and all of us in Him. This is why he sees in man's first sin a sin of every man, but even more he sees his Christ who saves and gathers us.

The underside of the Mystical Body of Christ is Adam the sinner and our sin in him: God gathers us; man sins. The very act which unites us for love thus begins by confining us in sin. God's loving act of gathering us for our "yes" of love is changed by sin to confinement in disobedience. But we would not be enclosed in sin if Christ were not already present in our sin itself, working to unite us in his body. So that ultimately, to recognize Original Sin is already to proclaim, but on a level with our wretchedness, Jesus Christ as savior of men.

After these suggestions about Original Sin, our relationship to Adam still needs to be clarified, for it likewise poses a problem today. Traditionally the relationship has been thought of in terms

---

4 We are drawing our inspiration from a study of Stanislas Lyonnet, which he later developed in his book *Les étapes du mystère du salut selon l'épitre aux Romains* (Paris: Le Cerf, 1969).

of generation: Original sin is propagated in each and every person through generation. In the Church's thinking, this concept of generation excludes the notion of imitation: some have imagined original sin as a prototype which each and every person would copy by his personal sins. This conception is erroneous because it fails to take account of the radical reality actually involved in generation. All men are one, communicating among themselves at the roots of their existence and freedom, and not merely because they may imitate some prototypes.

But it is well to avoid a misconception about generation which we of the twentieth century are in danger of falling into. We spontaneously think of generation as a completely biological process of nature, pertaining to the history of our physical life. Ancient peoples, and especially the Semites and people of the Bible, did not look at generation that way at all. For them *generation* designated the most fundamental relationship by which a man, in the totality of his being, was linked to a human origin. Through generation, the member of a community was connected to his ancestor, to the father of the community (human history), who was at the same time the first witness of the religious events which founded this community (supernatural history, that is, history of men in their relation to the divine). It is in this sense that the Jews said they were all sons of Abraham, their father.

We ought to appropriate this full significance of generation, so that the term designates not so much a physical relation to a primogenitor, but a human relationship to an origin where there occurs not merely a human history (the origin of humanity) but a supernatural history (a founding event for a human-divine community). We should also understand the role of him whom the Bible designates with the name of Adam ("man") according to this fullness of meaning. Our relation to Adam is essentially a human relationship in a history with a supernatural dimension.

But a human relationship is analyzed in terms of language and political relations. Original sin is not communicated on the level of flesh and blood, but on the level of a jointly human and supernatural history. The basis of human unity cannot be shown on the biological level, but rather on the historical plane. In the same way, the bond between brothers and sisters is not primarily blood (animals issuing from the same parents have consanguinity and no fraternity), but rather history. A man and woman become father and mother of numerous brothers and sisters not merely because

35

they engender bodies, but persons—freedoms in a history. Reflecting along these lines could dissipate the problem many have concerning our relation to Adam. We can now return to Ignatius' text on "the triple sin."

Sin of the Angel

"I saw Satan fall like lightning from heaven." Lightning flashes for an instant without duration, with the end coinciding with the beginning. It makes us think of an act which would take place outside of time: simple, but more decisive than resolutions ripened in a prolonged becoming. Such is the first sin. If the end coincides with the beginning, the act locks onto itself; it is completed, definitive; everything has happened once and for all. There is no "one time, then another time..." because this instantaneous act, which we represent succinctly as lightning, has in fact a (nontemporal) scope at least equal to the entire history of the world.

In our acts, on the other hand, which stretch out in duration, the beginning only connects with the end through a history in which it brings about its effect little by little. Even if the beginning is an intention which of itself leads to a sin which damns, the condemnation is not immediate because in fact the meaning, content, and end of the intention are not yet actualized. And there is room for an eventual retraction. But in the case of a freedom that does not have to be attained by struggling throughout a history and that posits itself in the Instant, what is willed is done and what is done immediately locks what is willed within itself. Such is the first sin: the sin of the angel.

Original Sin

First is a term with a twofold meaning: It can denote the first *above* the entire series (the sin of the angel), and it can mean the first which *orders* the series and is itself part of the series (original sin). Satan's sin is above the series of human sins, but it encompasses this series, in the sense that he is its supreme instigator. Satan is the tempter, and every human sin goes back to him in one way or another. The sin which orders the series and belongs to it if original sin. Fundamentally, original sin is distrust of God, who is suspected of jealously wanting to retain something for himself which he would deny to man. At least this appears to be the meaning of the text in chapter three of Genesis. And it is the serpent who inspires this distrust in man by flattering him.

Our present reflection is not a passage from the angel's sin to original sin by way of a necessary deduction, as if the first sin above the series necessitated a first sin that would order the series and belong to it. Man was not created under Satan's yoke: "It was he [the Lord] who created man in the beginning, and he left him in the power of his own inclination" (Eccli. 15:14).[5] However, all is related in creation (and the angel belongs to creation), for God creates in his own image and God is one.

Thus revelation hands down to us, from the depths of a mystery as disturbing as it is baffling, some words of warning: Man's sin is not unrelated to the sin of the angel who bestowed on himself the essence of liar, tempter, and murderer. At once guilty and victim, man freely placed himself under Satan's yoke by succumbing to temptation. Once he had fallen, his downfall appeared in his own eyes as fated, if not necessitated. Hell becomes a dim and disturbing reflection of our original capacity for freedom.

Our reflection, then, is not inventing the *necessity* that connects all sins to one another, *once they have been committed*. Reflection, as its name indicates, *comes afterwards*; it recovers and utters what is revealed: Our sin is not unrelated to the angel's sin, and it appears as fated. As for the necessity that seems to follow from this mystery, it does not impose itself on creatures before they create it for themselves. Whoever sins places himself under the yoke of necessity. Such is original sin: the second sin.

The Sin of Any Man Whatever

Whatever has been posited at the foundation of history also exists at any point in history. Original sin is, by definition, sin at the beginning and as such it is not repeated. But the same sad history begins again in every sin: A man suspects the intentions of the Creator, more readily believes Satan than God, and acts accordingly. The *third sin* occurs at any point in the series.

What this reasoning gives us to understand is that all sins are related because every sinner is in collusion with another sinner. Since it is outside time, the first sin is truly at the beginning, influencing the destinies of others. It cannot but strive to introduce its own lie and contradiction into all of creation through its own brand of logic which is merely the perversion of the one and only

---

5 The entire passage of Eccli. 15:11-20 is worth rereading. It insists on man's freedom in relation to every compelling necessity which would lead him into evil.

logic, that of the works of God. According to this argument concerning the "triple sin," a community of destiny encloses all sinners, and individual freedom expands to embrace all of history: My sin is as vast as original sin, and it aims at nothing less than becoming coequal with Satan's sin beyond history.

This reasoning, however, casts a different light on the first exercise than does the book of St. Ignatius. We have been concerned with an objective portrayal of the history of sin, with an eye to its interiorization by consciousness. Ignatius' text is concerned with rousing the torpor of the retreatant by making him compare his numerous sins to "that of one who went to hell because of one mortal sin" or at least "for fewer sins than I have committed" [52]. Ignatius places himself on the level of the retreatant's *consciousness* and addresses himself to it as it is—rather removed from feeling sin as it is. We have placed ourselves at the *logical* point of view which, encompassing the beginning and end in a single glance, says straightaway what it sees: The objective history of sin (portrayed here for me) presents the ultimate extent and fatal result of the personal sins of anyone, outside of redemption. It is my history as it has developed thus far, and it can be the entirety of my history. This logical viewpoint provides the basis for the following comparison proposed by St. Ignatius.

The Comparison Proposed by St. Ignatius

"This will consist in using the memory to recall the first sin... to be the more filled with shame and confusion when I compare the one sin of the angels with the many sins I have committed. I will consider that they went to hell for one sin, and the number of times I have deserved to be condemned forever because of my numerous sins.... Consider also countless others who have been lost for fewer sins than I have committed" [50, 52.] This comparison at first surprises and even shocks the reader. What mutual proportion can there be between my sins, however numerous, and the sin of the angels? And isn't there something arbitrary about divine justice if "countless others...have been lost for fewer sins than I have committed"?

Whoever raises questions of this nature simply shows that he has not yet understood who God is nor what kind of person he himself is.

The sin of the angel teaches me the fallibility and infallibility of created freedom. By the example of the angel I see that, however perfect its nature, however lucid its understanding may be, the free creature, before taking possession of itself, must still earn its being and win its own freedom.... This implies the greatest risk; one instant is sufficient to lose oneself and to lose oneself irrevocably. Of course, my own instants are stretched out in the temporality of my Befores and Afters.... Nevertheless, though my freedom is distended by time, it also decides in an instant, and the sum of the decisions taken in each *present moment* differs in no way from that which constitutes the good or bad angel....

Any one of my instants can be the one which attains that totality.[6] Once we have taken into account all the environments or external influences which can have a bearing on freedom, we must ultimately get to the root of freedom, under pain of destroying all responsibility.

Freedom exists in every person. We are not affirming this *a priori*, but because of the duty imposing itself on everybody when he intends to reverence his fellow man and to recognize in him a real possibility of his making or remaking himself. A clear case will help us understand this. An alcoholic is a being who has fallen into misfortune, and it is advisable to treat him at first as a victim and sick person rather than as a guilty one. His illness is physical, and then mental (subject to compulsions, locked in complexes, and so on). But no alcoholic will be cured if he is merely treated as ill. Aided at first by the care of a physician and put on his feet again, then restored to a minimum of equilibrium and psychic strength, he will not take the road of a true cure until the day when he is able to face his former and present situation as a responsible human being. Only then, arriving at freedom of behavior, will he be in condition to repair, through his restored freedom, what he acknowledges his freedom had destroyed. Of course, this supposes that he takes his entire past (including his half-conscious alcoholic binges and the violent outbursts of an irresponsible brute) upon himself in *terms of responsibility*. But thus recognizing himself as responsible for everything is no longer *then* morbid guilt or social disapproval, but the fruitful step of a man who is freely rebuilding the life his freedom had destroyed.

If this man cannot acknowledge the freedom at the root of his past life, he has no possibility of restoring himself as a man; he will be the prey of complexes, the victim of compulsions and pyscho-somatic automatisms. To acquit a man of his responsibility is not

6 *Dialectique*, II, 78.

to liberate him, but to alienate him, as all those who work with alcoholics know. This one fact is worth all the metaphysical proofs: At the core of a human being we cannot do otherwise than ultimately *presuppose* his freedom.

In the course of a human life, confused and partially determined from outside, there are therefore *cleavage points*, instants when the man secretly but freely decides. By reason of these instants which are the man himself, no matter how his consciousness may portray them, his freedom can be compared to that of an angel. At the root of his being, anterior to any reflection on himself, and prior to all the outside influences that are channeled into him by way of his character, pyschology, or atavism, each person ultimately is what he makes of himself. This freedom cannot be proven by starting from something else, for what is basic—as our freedom surely is—cannot be proven by an argument, but it reveals itself.

Everyone is here referred to the intimate testimony of his own personal existence: On the whole I am free, even if I am not always free at each particular instant. But those moments when external influences or subjective forces are the strongest do not eclipse my freedom. In one way or another, my freedom ultimately gives its own direction and meaning to my entire life. There are thus, in a man's whole life, cleavage points where something definitive can be inserted. And whoever, in such an instant,[7] would throw himself into the absolute contradiction of sin known as such, without a backward glance, would lose himself as irrevocably as the angel—even if his condemnation would not bring about its full effect immediately. We write these words hesitantly, knowing that judgment is reserved to God. It is God's formidable secret. But the secret of my own existence, at the moment when I begin to meditate on sin, is no less formidable: half-unconscious and in any case incapable of discerning what is going on and has gone on in me, I do not know where I am going with my freedom before God. I do not know whether or not I have frequented these instants when the possibility and proximity of the irrevocable have existed together. Whoever suddenly becomes aware of his thoughtlessness feels shame and confusion. If I am still here, and here in order to reflect, it is because God has undoubtedly saved me from falling in such an instant. But what does this mercy mean? Not that God is less God with me than with the fallen angel, nor that I am less

---

7 *Instant* does not necessarily mean a "time sudden as lightning," but it does designate an indivisible whole in duration.

free to lose myself. "So, too, the understanding is to be used to think over the matter more in detail, and then the will to rouse more deeply the emotions" [50].

Comparing the *bulk* of my sins with the sin of the angel is an effort to make me realize the *intensity* of a decisive instant which, however temporal it may be, cannot be measured by time or number because it brings into being the essence of a destiny. Comparing my numerous sins with the fate of "one who went to hell because of one mortal sin" [52] leads to the same result, if I take it as St. Ignatius proposes it. First, he presents the pure affirmation of faith: one mortal sin leads to hell; then he offers the means for deriving profit from this: "Consider also countless others who have been lost for fewer sins than I have committed." Both of these propositions make us uncomfortable, especially the second one, but even the first one does, if we take it in St. Ignatius' concrete sense: to consider "the third sin, namely, that of one who went to hell because of one mortal sin."

Let us try to dispel our discomfort and get in touch with the weighty mystery of our freedom. We say "mortal sin," and we try to think what it could well be. We imagine some external deed which would give us a feeling of righteous condemnation for anyone guilty of it. But it is misleading to thus try to imagine an act that we could classify as mortal sin. Even the methodical extermination of a million Jews in a Nazi gas chamber does not furnish the idea of the mortal sin *which would have led a man to hell*. A mortal sin, as it is in itself, does not crop up in a concrete situation, and it should never be confused with the latter. In the proposition, "one who went to hell because of one mortal sin," Ignatius is taking *mortal sin* in its dogmatic and canonical meaning, which we always confuse with the spiritual and personal meaning (likewise present in the text). We will clarify these two meanings. The dogmatic and canonical meaning is situated on the objective plane where the Church as a society proposes definitions and laws. This objectification of the Church is an abstraction derived from particular situations and human subjects, each having his secret which no societal procedure can scrutinize.

Thus the Church objectively defines the conditions for mortal sin: full knowledge, full consent, and grave matter; and it states that every culpable deed which fulfills these three conditions is a mortal sin. But it is left to each person to judge, with the help of a confessor if necessary, to what degree his act does or does not fulfill these three conditions. The Church thus differentiates the objective and societal dimension from the dimension of spiritual and personal existence. On the level of personal existence, the massacre perpetrated by a criminal may not fulfill the canonical definition of mortal sin; as conversely, an unperceived decision that takes place in the secrecy of a person's consciousness and is only expressed by a word or the winking of an eye can be an unpardonable sin.

What would correspond, in a man's existence, to the sin of "one who went to hell because of one mortal sin"? It would be a decisive instant, a steadfast cleavage point, completely fulfilling the canonical definition of mortal sin. It would be a deed which perhaps goes almost unnoticed, but in which a resolute human freedom would have verged on the freedom of the angel who said No. There is no need for one to cast about trying to represent such an instant which is the act of an I and not the flux of states of consciousness. "Whatever the subject matter and occasion may be, mortal sin actualizes in the individual the attitude of Adam, and at the fine point of his spirit, it repeats the revolt of Satan. Without a doubt, passions of the heart, impulses of the senses, and errors of the understanding count for much in the straying sinner. But, once having taken account of all the causes and individual or social conditions which psychology and sociology can discover, in order to explain culpable behavior it is ultimately necessary to come to its root."[8]

A human being is never deprived of the power of deciding the direction of his life, whether he be a monk in the desert or the lowest alcoholic left to the chances of the street. This is said not in order to judge (for it is impossible for one person to know where, when, or how another person makes decisive choices), but out of reverence for man and his Creator.

Every one of the saints shows a frightening realism in this area because they believe in God and consequently in man. For them the sin which damns can spring forth like lightning in anyone's life, and hell exists. What is a mortal sin? It is an *act*...along with the whole preceding road which leads up to it by more or less direct ways. We must not allow the thousand and one detours in the road, which psychologists and sociologists analyze, to make us lose sight of the freedom traveling that way. Mortal sin generally has a history: culpable negligences, various compromises, lies and equivocal behavior patterns.... Whoever sins mortally began by flirting with evil before the exact instant when he

8 *Dialectique*, II, 101.

suddenly and deliberately falls; or he followed a deliberate decision taken beforehand, but a decision that occurred at a fork in the road, leading him to the fatal instant. He falls "deliberately," that is, in a supreme equivocation—for the clarity proper to sin is ambiguity, and it has no other because sin is a lie, and a lie is the opposite of clarity.

Before being concentrated in a specific act, the malice of mortal sin originated in a more or less diluted form by spreading over a stream of prior actions or omissions. But this stream, which we know only too well, very often hides from us the malice of the decisive act, which only the dogmatic and moral definition of mortal sin retains. It is precisely this malice—the seriousness and perversity of sin against the Creator and Lord—which the Ignatian comparison, starting from the turbulent stream of our numerous sins, undertakes to make us realize. Here again, as in the comparison with the angel's sin, the passage from the *bulk* of my sins to the *intensity* of a decisive instant does not lend itself to any temporal or numerical measure because it brings into being the essence of a destiny. Anyone who, in such an instant, coincided with the creature's proud revolt against its Creator and Lord could perhaps have gone to hell "for fewer sins than I have committed."

If the gravity and perversity of the sin which damns consists, in the final analysis, in contempt for the divine Goodness, in refusing to respond to the Love which calls me, Ignatius has the right to ask me, however innocent I may be, to compare myself to those "countless others who have been lost for fewer sins than I have committed." For the guilt of another, even that of the worst criminals, is unknown to me, whereas mine has revealed itself, and it has not stopped discovering more about itself in the spectacle of the angel's sin and then of Adam's sin. Deepening this awareness even more by thinking of sinners whose sentence has already been pronounced should succeed in destroying the rigidity and pride in which I station myself so much more easily as long as I believe I have nothing serious to reproach myself with. Success is assured, for nothing can so increase my shame and confusion as the secure feeling of a good conscience, if it comes to grasp the comparison called for by Ignatius.[9]

9 Ibid., 103. [Translator's Note. Fessard's text goes on to explain that if sin essentially consists in refusing God's free offer of love, then the essence of sin might better be found in a "pure" soul which is freer and closer to God than in a great criminal who is further away from God's freedom.]

Here there is no question of quibbling about the arbitrary or non-arbitrary nature of divine justice. It is a matter of surrendering to the questioning which tears me from my thoughtlessness: What divine mercy has so far kept the bulk of my sins from bringing about the *intensity* of a decisive and steadfast instant? I feel "shame and confusion," for I literally do not know where I am with my freedom before God. What does this mercy mean? Is it the postponement of wrath or a day of grace? If I am here to reflect, it can only be a time for sorrow, a moment of grace, which Christ crucified established for all men.

At this point in my reflection, I find myself at the feet of Christ on the cross, and the question rises from my heart: "What have I done for Christ? What am I doing for Christ? What ought I to do for Christ?" (Colloquy, [53]).

Suggestions for Presenting This Exercise

The preceding commentary in no way constitutes suggestions for prayer in a retreat presentation. At the very most it can inspire some explanations to offer, with an eye to preventing difficulties. As for material for prayer itself, one could find it in scripture texts, such as the following.

For the sin of the angel one could use Luke 10:18, which recalls Isaiah 14:10-15: "How you are fallen from heaven, O Day Star, son of Dawn!" And this passage of Isaiah is taken up and expanded by Ezekiel 28:1-19. In Ezekiel's so powerfully symbolic text, notice verse 15, among others, which expresses what we have called "the Instant" with impressive succinctness: "You were blameless in your ways from the day you were created, *till iniquity was found in you.*"

For original sin one could use Romans 5:12-20 and Genesis 3, stressing the symbolism of man divided against himself, against his fellowman, against God, and against nature, drawing attention to this sin as distrust of God and, instead, trust of the lying serpent.

One can approach the sin of an ordinary man with the Gospels. There are lists of "flagrant" sins in the Gospels, but what Christ warns us to be on guard against are those things which we would call sins of omission (Matt. 25:31-46); sins stemming from lack of vigilance and scandalous frivolity (Matt. 24:37-44), either in the order of service or the duties of one's state (Matt. 24:45-51), or in the order of love, with the symbolism of the virgins and their lighted or snuffed out lamps (Matt. 25:1-13). See also a dictionary of biblical theology. Another approach is with the sin of David; what at first had been weakness of the flesh can contain criminal and shrewd malice.

Second Exercise

The first exercise proposed the objective content of sin to consciousness as the horizon of its own history. This objective content is, in a sense, external to the reflecting consciousness, but it has been presented to consciousness as measuring the extent of its own sin. This relationship of the objective history of sin to the retreatant's own personal history is what must now be worked out in the second exercise. Here freedom relates the history and objective content of sin to its own history by way of its personal sins.

Consciousness is on the same level with its immediate awarenesses, and hence it is still rather external to this objective history, even at the end of the first exercise, and even after the comparison established there has borne some fruit. But the five points of the second exercise will contribute towards educating this consciousness' spiritual judgment about itself. Thanks to these five points, consciousness will open itself to a truth that is not acquired by reasoning and still less by autosuggestion, but which it must dispose itself, through prayer and reflection, to receive as a light from God. Consciousness, in accordance with its grace, thus comes to recognize that it is joined to original sin and that it rests only with itself not to repeat "at the fine point of spirit the revolt of Satan."

This acknowledgement is made in the present. Freedom grasps that what it has done leads to hell. The gap between this fatal end point and my sins which have not yet actualized this end point becomes for me the time for repenting and for thanksgiving towards God our Lord "that up to this very moment He has granted me life" [61].

From the logical viewpoint, the second exercise is one of relating to oneself: Consciousness relates to itself the content of the first exercise, and there is nothing else to say about it. But St. Ignatius constructed the second exercise in function of the subjective needs of the retreatant's consciousness. The latter is unable either to directly interiorize the vision of the past presented in the first exercise or to comprehend its own sins in light of it. Five points will help it.

"*First Point.* This is the record of my sins. I will call to mind all the sins of my life, reviewing year by year, and period by period" [56]. "This is an exercise of the memory where the overall view is more important than exact detail because it does not directly aim, even remotely, at getting ready for a general confession; instead, it should simply furnish the understanding with material for the work outlined in the following four points."[10]

"*Second Point.* I will weigh the gravity of my sins, and see the loathsomeness and malice which every mortal sin I have committed has in itself, even though it were not forbidden" [57]. To weigh is to measure, and what St. Ignatius wants to measure is the loathsomeness and malice which such a sin contains in itself, "even though it were not forbidden." But how can we "weigh" or measure anything whatever without using some unit of weight or measure? In the moral realm one such unit of measure is furnished by the laws and rules which fix the limit between what is permitted and what is forbidden. But such a reference is here expressly excluded by Ignatius: "even though it were not forbidden."[11]

St. Ignatius excludes any such reference because what is at issue here is something quite different from extrinsically applying an *already constituted* standard to an empirical case, a procedure which would remain within a legalistic framework. Rather, it is a matter of entering into the movement by which a very interior and very objective evaluation of events *may be constituted*. In this movement consciousness at first grasps sin within the wholly qualitative determinations of a subjective deed; consciousness then relates sin to objective moral norms which allow sin to be measured somewhat, in quantitative terms. Thus quantified, sin is then gradually related, passing beyond every confine, to the respective attributes of the sinner and of God our Creator and Lord, who is the measure beyond measure of this sin. Consciousness' evaluation thus passes from viewing sin as an infraction of the moral law to viewing sin as a mortal outrage carried out against an interpersonal relationship, something which would be judged unspeakable even though it were a question of an act or deed "which were not forbidden" by law.

Let us illustrate this analysis by some scriptural passages. Sin is at first grasped "within the wholly qualitative determinations of a subjective deed." The sin of David (2 Sam. 11) is at first lived and presented according to all sorts of contingencies with various qualities: David, towards evening...nonchalant on the

10 Ibid., 111.
11 Ibid., 112.

palace roof, alone...and Bathsheba likewise alone, bathing....
Their encounter...Bathsheba annoyingly pregnant.... David's
astuteness in calling Uriah back from the war.... But his astuteness
is frustrated by this soldier's nobility. Astuteness then becomes
criminal calculation in order to try and get out of the quandary....
There is material here for a rich and colorful short story, but not
yet a moral judgment on a transgression.

"Consciousness then relates sin to objective moral norms which
allow sin to be measured." This would be the moral judgment
ranking David's deed in the categories of adultery and murder,
an evaluation which is still "quantitative" and wholly "legalistic."
As a matter of fact, Nathan's parable of the ewe lamb (2 Sam. 12)
does much more; it brands a deed as unspeakable, even supposing
there were no moral law forbidding adultery and murder. The
sin is viewed here within the framework of personal relationships:
the rich and the poor; David, whom God has provided abundantly,
and Uriah the Hittite; God who provides, and David who covets
and robs the poor.

Sin is thus related "to the respective attributes of the sinner and
of God our Creator and Lord, who is the measure beyond measure
of sin." This movement is recognized still better in Yahweh's
peremptory questioning of the people of Israel (Hos. 2) or in the
symbolic history of Israel (Ezek. 16). Passing straightaway beyond
all moral evaluation and "quantitative" measuring of the people's
sins, Yahweh declares the people purely and simply adulterous
and given to prostitution, like a worthless woman who has been
well provided for by her husband, but who is cynically unfaithful.
"You also took your fair jewels of my gold and silver, which I had
given you, and made for yourself images of men, and with
them played the harlot.... Also my bread which I gave you—I fed
you with fine flour and oil and honey—you set before them for a
pleasing odor, says the Lord God" (Ezek. 16:17-19).

Over against Israel's infidelity is described the Lord's wholly
gratuitous bounty: "I passed by you, and saw you.... I spread
my skirt over you, and covered your nakedness; yea, I plighted
my troth to you and entered into a covenant with you...and you
became mine.... And I decked you with ornaments, and put
bracelets on your arms....and a beautiful crown upon your head"
(vv. 6-14).

Between the sinner and his Lord there is no reciprocal measure;
the Lord is truly the measure beyond measure of the former's sin.
Ignatius wants to make us feel this incommensurable standard.

or else gradually comprehend it, "passing beyond every confine" in the third and fourth points of the exercise. The latter consist in two progressions to infinity (the infinity of my nothingness and the infinity of God) which "oppose one another and pass into one another, until 'loathsomeness and malice' appear incommensurable in the fifth point, thereby unveiling for me, as nearly as possible, the essence of sin in itself."[12]

"*Third Point.* I will consider who I am, and by means of examples humble myself" [58]. "Ignatius could not say more clearly that it is a question of making my own idea of myself proceed towards the infinitely small, towards non-being. To this end, he points out five comparisons which it is important to distinguish. The first two are purely quantitative, though the second does contain a qualitative ingredient."[13] (1) "What am I compared with all men?" (2) "What are all men compared with the angels and saints of paradise?" The third is situated on the ontological plane: (3) "Consider what all creation is in comparison with God. Then I alone, what can I be?" The last two are solely qualitative and even aesthetic: (4) "I will consider all the corruption and loathsomeness of my body." (5) "I will consider myself as a source of corruption and contagion [literally, a sore and ulcer] from which has issued countless sins and evils and the most offensive poison."

"*Fourth Point.* I will consider who God is against whom I have sinned, going through His attributes and comparing them with their contraries in me: His wisdom with my ignorance, His power with my weakness, His justice with my iniquity, His goodness with my wickedness" [59].

After the process which reduced me more and more, down to nothingness and to a nothingness which is a source of an annihilating infection, these new comparisons, on the contrary, will make God rise (in my eyes) towards an equally incommensurable positive infinity....

And what will be the result of these two series of comparisons where a process towards infinity, on one side, carries the I towards nothingness, the source of non-being, and on the other side, magnifies God as Being in possession of every perfection? Carried to the extreme, this redoubled opposition, which ought to make me weigh the loathsomeness and malice of sin in itself, can only have one effect: to lead to the incommensurable and

---

12 Ibid.
13 Ibid. For Fessard's analysis of this third point, see his pp. 112-114.

bring about an explosive tearing asunder which will effect a dialectical turnabout of the situation. This is exactly what Ignatius heralds in his own language.[14]

"Fifth Point. This is a cry of wonder accompanied by surging emotion..." [60]. "Without any doubt, mystical experience is at the origin of this 'cry of wonder.'...Ignatius here lets us think of religion as a 'cry' or at least as beginning with a cry. But for Ignatius this cry is far from being what a contemporary philosopher called the nostalgic expression of a 'metaphysical and moral consciousness [which] dies upon contact with the absolute.'[15] Quite the contrary, Ignatius' cry is like the infant's cry as he emerges from his mother's womb, an awakening and irruption from mortal darkness and torpor, if it is true that astonishment or 'wonder' is the point of departure for philosophical reflection."[16]

This cry of wonder is accompanied by a profound love which rises to balance the two incommensurable infinities of God and the nothingness of the creature who has sinned. It disposes the understanding to turn back and go through the entire series of creatures again (but in the opposite direction as compared with the third point), in a humbling motion in which "the vibrating of the explosion produced by the two progressions to infinity reverberates in successive waves of emotional questioning."[17] These questions will not appear exaggerated except for those who are still on the threshold of knowledge about God and themselves. But these "exaggerations" express very precisely the truth which the saints know well; as St. Gertrude, for example, said: "the greatest miracle for me, Lord, is that the earth continues to support a sinner like me."

In the colloquy, the consciousness which converses with God our Lord gives him thanks that he has granted it life up to this very moment. Thanksgiving goes much further than repenting. The latter confesses its sins and repudiates them; the former sees only God, even in the sins themselves.[18]

Third and Fourth Exercises

These are repetitions of the first and second exercises. The third exercise is more subjective, and it invites us to "dwell upon those

14 Ibid., 114, 115.
15 M. Merleau-Ponty, *Sense and Non-Sense*, trans. H. L. Dreyfus and P. A. Dreyfus (Evanston: Northwestern University Press, 1964), p. 95.
16 *Dialectique*, II, 115-116.
17 Ibid., 116.
18 This thanksgiving should be compared with the final Contemplation to Attain the Love of God. See *Dialectique*, II, 119-121.

points in which we have experienced greater consolation or desolation or greater spiritual appreciation" [62]. The fourth is more objective, and it proposes that "the intellect, without any digression, diligently thinks over and recalls the matter contemplated in the previous exercises" [64].

Deepening our experiences, being more and more faithful to the spiritual motions produced in us by the Holy Spirit, and at the same time readjusting our thoughts and feelings to the objectivity of revelation (biblical images, dogmas) are just what is needed.

Fifth Exercise

This is a meditation on hell. The movement of reflection that relates the past (first exercise) to the present (second exercise: my personal sins) is to be completed by a determination of the future—that is, what my destiny would be if my sins actually catch up with their sense or rather their non-sense, hell.

The future is my encounter with the Absolute: God who justifies or God who condemns. In this encounter all the particular deeds of my historical freedom, all my usual behaviors in temporal existence, are gathered, totaled, and transcended. The result is either that I am united with God who maintains everything in unity (the kingdom of God) or, conversely, that my deeds are locked in a subsisting contradiction which never stops disintegrating (the empire of Satan, hell).

What is revealed in this encounter is the infinite power by which the Creator constituted each human being. An act of my freedom is both mine and God's all in one. For better or worse, "Man infinitely transcends man."[19] In the encounter with God which consummates our union, it is the God "more myself than I" who manifests himself. He is simple and immediate presence, magnifying to the utmost the self's own positing of itself worked out in its course of temporal existence. The servant's humbling through the *fiat* of an entire life (we are thinking of the Virgin Mary) becomes elevation into glory. The particular "yeses" strung out day after day then appear as they really are already: the unfolding of a freedom whose breadth God alone can measure. "Give, and it will be given to you; good measure, pressed down, shaken together, running over, will be put into your lap" (Luke 6:38).

19 Pascal, *Pensées*, trans. A. J. Krailsheimer (Baltimore: Penguin, 1966), Brunschvicg no. 434, p. 65.

Hell is likewise the self's own positing of itself "magnified to the utmost": empty self-affirmation indefinitely crossing the boundary of particular deeds, forever running after itself. Hell is vain self-pursuit, perpetuated in the non-sense where nothingness lasts.

For the retreatant it is a question of *realizing* this situation which for him is still in the emptiness of the future. But how can he "magnify to the utmost" the futile affirmation-negation of self which perpetuates itself in the contradiction of hell? Where can the I find some kind of content which will allow it to portray definitive non-being to itself? How can the I set hell before itself?

But is it exactly a question of setting hell *before* oneself? No. Rather, it is a question of allowing reality (here, the underside of reality, the subsisting non-sense which hell is) to come *into* the innermost part of our flesh-and-spirit being. It is the *imagination*, reproducing in us the symbols employed by revelation—fire, tears and grinding of teeth, the worm of conscience—which will make this non-sense present to us. But it must be a purified imagination, simplified by faith and founded on faith. At the point where we are, the non-sense of hell is spread out in the triple sin of the first exercise and in our own sins of the second exercise.

At present it is a question of realizing the unity of the first exercise (which furnished me with an intelligible content to ponder) and the second exercise (where this content was loaded with my sins as concrete material). To the degree that freedom notices it is very near to being enclosed within such a unity, freedom can portray its own non-being to itself, as hell would fix it forever. The imagination, reproducing the symbols of revelation, will present freedom with its own non-being.

"But this unity is realized for me in 'remorse': an absolute, eternal remorse, invading the entire field of my being, penetrating my consciousness through all its 'doors and windows,' and thus identifying itself with consciousness by way of my senses. That is how the I can complete the growth of sin, magnifying the non-being of its freedom to the absolute degree: *by applying the senses to hell*."[20] "To taste the bitterness of tears, sadness, and remorse [worm] of conscience" [69].

I hit upon the definitive non-sense of sin in the revealed representations and dogmatic affirmations of the first exercise—but as external to me. Now I want to get in touch with existential non-sense, the non-sense in me and for me, and not merely the non-sense

20 *Dialectique*, I, 48.

of sin as represented outside myself. The only way for me to do this is to recognize by faith that the non-sense of sin (as salvation history portrays it in the fallen angel and the first man) belongs implicitly to my own sins. I must recognize this by faith, but by a faith that is embodied and sensuous—in my body, my sensuousness (*sensibilité*). My freedom will thus experience what its end point, outcome, or definitive non-sense would be, if it should go along with what it has done. Of course, this exercise, which takes place on the level of my spiritual sensuousness, remains a *representation*, but one which is internal to me and no longer external, as the first exercise was. Hell is not realized in the depths of my being (this would be the actual hell from which the Redeemer precisely saves us), but in the senses of the imagination and there only.

The impact of the entire First Week on one's sensuousness can go quite far. The application of the senses is a difficult exercise for beginners. People miss the point, and the exercise is disappointing as long as some progress in union with God has not yet simplified the forms of their prayer very much. No untimely effort of the imagination should seek to replace this grace of simplification, for the basis of the exercise is not the imagination—even though the latter is brought into play here—but faith. It is a faith which abides by this revealed truth: sin is non-sense; and it is a faith which has properly digested the content of the first exercise: "Recall the first sin, which was that of the angels.... In the same way...the sin of Adam and Eve. Recall to memory how on account of this sin they did penance for so long a time, and the great corruption which came upon the human race that caused so many to be lost in hell" [50, 51].

The application of the senses[21] consists in the I opening its eyes, ears, and all its senses to this truth in such a way that the non-sense of hell sinks into it: the non-sense lived by the damned in the bitterness of an eternal *remorse*. St. Ignatius' text permits the use of this word: "to taste the bitterness of tears, sadness, and remorse [Spanish, worm] of conscience" [69]. Remorse is an impotent and futile disavowal of sin; a contradiction which does not succeed in suppressing itself; a self-destruction which perpetuates itself; the worm which gnaws conscience.

Remorse is not repentance. The principle of repentance is Christ made sin, who was buried in the depths of our sinful existence, in

---

21 See the Note on the Application of the Senses at the end of chapter 5.

the depths of non-being, and who dies in us to sin in order that we may live in him for righteousness. Repentance is the contradiction as overcome and suppressed. The principle of remorse, on the other hand, is the sinful consciousness which deep down does and does not will itself in its sin. It is the sinner left to himself who repudiates and does not want his contradiction, and yet who always begets it again because he is attached to himself. Remorse is unendurable, and it makes life impossible, driving one to despair, like Judas.

We cannot label this infernal circle an ordinary "pathology" as if its principle were necessarily psychic guilt. Remorse is the terrible awareness of a fallen freedom—at least in the strong and precise sense in which we understand it here. We are distinguishing remorse from repentance and from all the confused ways in which a conscious experience of moral guilt wavers between one feeling and another. Can one live with remorse? If it does not lead to suicide, will it not destroy the understanding by drawing it into pathological behaviors which will be like a kind of compromise with it? As for routine guilt, it also presents a vicious circle of thoughts and feelings, but it should not be confused with remorse (in the strong sense we just mentioned). We should try to heal it and to keep the afflicted person from living as though it were remorse.

Does St. Ignatius want to bring about remorse in the retreatant's consciousness? Absolutely not. He wants repentance and thanksgiving (see the colloquy). If he speaks of the worm of conscience, it is not for the purpose of my abandoning myself to its gnawings; no more than he conjures up the "vast fires" for me to give myself to them, nor the "howling, cries, and blasphemies" for me to utter them. On the contrary, it is in order that, grazed by them in my senses, I may conceive a horror which would set up an insurmountable barrier between my weakness and sin: "that if because of my faults I forget the love of the eternal Lord, at least the fear of these punishments will keep me from falling into sin" [65]. The fruit of the exercise is gathered in the colloquy which invites me to give thanks to Christ our Lord...that up to the present moment he has always had so much tenderness and mercy for me.

Remorse, rearing its head for a time within the field of sensuous consciousness, can present some danger in this exercise, unless the I has a stable psyche. But remorse, objectively speaking, is a lofty truth. The paths of conversion—and even of progress in the spiritual life—can move through deserts of God's complete absence, an absence that is not at the same time felt as a sort of hollow presence. God so abandons some men to their past sins that, from a certain angle (the only one they are actually aware of), there is nothing else in them. Christ is undoubtedly there, but so clothed in sinful flesh that he only manifests himself in and through this sinful feeling.

For one who finds himself in such a situation, there is very often only a hair between despair (or remorse) and repentance. He no longer knows where he is: repentant or remorseful? Peter or Judas? He wavers between the two; and if he is reinforced in repenting, it is because another, Christ made sin, frees him.

End of the First Week

"When consciousness of sin has grown in me to the point of realizing the *sense of hell*, sin negates itself in a *contrition* which dissipates its false existence, and correlatively there appears *faith* in an Incarnation of Being in the 'sinful body.' "[22] This passage briefly indicates for us the logic and end of the First Week. For the retreatant the First Week means "growth" of sin. It is not a quantitative growth—sin does not abound on the edge of my reflection as it did in the period when I was not reflecting—but a growth in intensity: intensity of experienced feeling and progressive interiorization.

"The *triple sin* is sin in the *past*, as my *memory* is capable of representing it. The *unfolding of personal sins* is sin *present* to my soul, as my *understanding* ought to know it. Finally, the *application of the senses to hell* is sin which begins to make me feel its *future* and absolute reality and thereby come into contact with my *affections*. Sin outside of me or in itself—sin for me—sin in itself and for me."[23]

The principle of this growth—growth of an increasingly keen sense of sin—is not the reflection of consciousness; it is Christ. In each exercise he is present to the I who is reflecting, but in the form of a representation: Christ on the cross, and consequently more or less external to the consciousness that gazes on him and addresses itself to him. And it is likely that for a rather long time the retreatant of the First Week will not perceive Christ otherwise. But, in fact, it is not merely in the form of such a representation that Christ is there. He is sinful flesh, hence present within my sins; and it is there that he is really crucified.

And it is precisely because the sinner who repents passes, by the action of grace, from the *representation* of Christ on the cross to the

22 *Dialectique*, I, 50; see Rom. 6:6; 8:3.
23 *Dialectique*, I, 49.

intimate feeling of his presence as Christ made sin, that he sometimes goes through these distressing phases where remorse contends
with repentance for his soul. The vanishing of Christ on the cross
from the eyes of his imagination is actually admittance to a more
intimate knowledge of the mystery of redemption. It is on this
level of experience that it is helpful to read the passage we are
commenting on: "sin negates itself in a *contrition* which dissipates
its false existence, and correlatively there appears *faith* in an
Incarnation of Being in the 'sinful body.'"

Beyond the uncertainties of the distressed soul that no longer
succeeds in *representing* Christ on the cross, beyond the remorse
that threatens to invade and crush it, rises contrition which proceeds
directly from the Redeemer's presence recognized in the thick of
one's sins. In this kind of contrition sin negates itself. Not that sin
is capable of disavowing and suppressing itself; the sin which
negates sin is Christ made sin, the Christ who is more myself than
I, and hence I in him.

For one who arrives at this meaning of sin, at this recognition of
Christ made sin in him, it is not so much the *representation* of Christ
on the cross that puts him in touch with his Creator and Lord.
Rather, it is his sin itself—his meager reality, reality for him here—
that is from now on Christ crucified for him. Sin is the path of the
revelation of Christ; sin is revelation of Christ. On this level of
truth, the retreatant no longer *passes* from his sins to representations
(especially the representation of Christ on the cross) which tell him
their meaning. He *is* within the correlation sin/Christ-made-sin;
his soul is enlivened by this very correlation. Then he comprehends
God's purpose: If God permitted sin, allowing us "freedom" to
take liberties, it is because he intended the manifestation of true
Freedom, the manifestation of his holiness and mercy in his
incarnate Son. Given the existence of sin, the fact is that from
God's viewpoint the paths of sin are, in Jesus Christ, the path
of Love.

The Love of God (Being) is so absolutely necessary (as sovereignly
gratuitous Freedom, beyond all necessity) and sin, by reason of
God's purpose, is so much the path of the manifestation of Love
that sin itself appears necessary in this logic. In fact, sin is not at
all necessary. The logic which first makes it necessary as the manifestation of God to sinful man is based wholly and entirely on divine
generosity, the liberality of Being, the gift of Love.

"Non-being, therefore, can be posited at the beginning of freedom
only in order to be negated. And non-being is in fact magnified by

freedom to the absolute degree only in order to make the very nature of this freedom appear. Thus, as soon as non-being magnifies its existence to the absolute degree by itself, so to speak, it erases itself from existence in order to give place to the existence of this freedom. But in doing this, non-being achieves its *truth*, which is to be the *necessary condition* of the manifestation of Freedom in itself, that is, of *Love*."[24]

Such is the First Week of the Exercises in its ultimate truth: a very deep experience of God's absence—to the point where his absence is recognized as the presence of Jesus Christ made sin. Christ seems less present in language expressing this level of experience of the First Week than he does in the more representational language of the booklet of the *Exercises*. But he is truly there, simply and absolutely, in his own unportrayable mystery: "For our sake he made him to be sin who knew no sin, so that in him we might become the righteousness of God" (2 Cor. 5:21).

When the retreatant arrives at the end of the First Week, contrition for sin [4], and finds himself in the presence of Christ, he is by that very fact in the Second Week, the life of our Lord Jesus Christ.

Practical Note

Not every retreat leads all the way to this ultimate truth of the First Week. It is necessary to take time into account and to allow people to travel according to their own rhythm and grace. Nevertheless, unless they pass some day or other through a more radical purification which makes them feel God's absence and perceive Christ at the heart of their sins, as the one who has been made sin, they risk staying within the representation. Christ on the cross is the "sinful body." He represents what is in fact *in* us: sin and himself crucified by our sins: he is so identified with sin that he dies from it and by his death saves us. To represent Christ on the cross to oneself is fine, but it is necessary to go to the final truth of this representation: Christ made sin, buried in the depths of my being.

Besides this, some people are struggling so much against difficulties with their own sins and complexes, their repentance and guilt, that it is hardly possible and not very helpful to tell them to "look at Christ on the cross." Instead, it is necessary to help them recognize Christ in their very condition: Christ clothed in sin, working in them, suffering and enduring his unique passion, during the entire history of the world—all out of love. Whoever sees Christ

24 Ibid., 50.

on the cross as merely external to himself ("Imagine Christ our Lord present before you upon the cross" [53]) risks getting no further than a representation.

But it goes without saying that the retreatant can have attained the end of the First Week in a relative fashion, even if he does not experience the mystery in its full reality. It is advisable to reverence the progressive motion of God's gift in each person. To insist on making the retreatant pass from the representation of Christ on the cross to the mystery of Christ made sin would be to force the Freedom of God, who is master of his gifts, and the freedom of the retreatant. (This is all the more so because the revealed representations are already bearers of the meaning of the mystery.) Whoever gives the Exercises should never take such an initiative, which would moreover be quite useless. It is the Lord himself who introduces whom he wants, when he wants, as he wants into the heart of his mystery.

Consequently, one should not take our logical presentation of the First Week and its end as a practical rule for conducting retreats. We have already said that two perspectives are interwoven in our account: that which is on a level with the awarenesses of the retreatant's consciousness, and the logical perspective which includes everything in a single glance and which goes straight to the depths of the reality. These two perspectives are present in the *Exercises*, especially in Ignatius' introductory observations about what is for the director and what is for the retreatant [1-20]. Each retreatant is called to arrive at the most profound level, but according to his own rhythm and with reverence for the way God gauges his gift of time.

Note on the Term "Representation"

Various forms of the word representation (for example, to represent, to represent to oneself, representation, getting no further than a representation) will continue to recur, and they have a very precise meaning, which we will now explain.

The Spiritual Exercises aim at making consciousness pass from the representation of the mysteries to their reality, but by way of the representations themselves. Without going outside each representation, the Exercises make the internal negation of the representation come alive. They help us unite ourselves as closely as possible to him who is for us God's Image, the Word of God made man, the Representation who is identically the Reality.

In short, as creatures we are representations, beings who are not our own origin. But in him who has been made Image (representation) of the invisible God, we are what he is. Our vocation in Jesus Christ is to go beyond the representation as disconnected from its source, the initial motion which made it to be. Transcending the representation does not mean arriving at some conceptual truth or other, deemed to be absolute truth—although conceptual accounts are very important. It means uniting ourselves to the Image by allowing the Image to be in us what it is, the Image who is the Son, hence who is his own truth.

Some instances of representations in us are our own sensations, feelings, and ideas. They make the content of reality present to us, but they insert their own thickness between us and this content. They remain more or less external to our mind which begets them, and at the same time they keep distant from us the very thing which they are meant to make present to us. They are means whereby we can attain the real, but they can become like things which substitute themselves for the real and cause us to slip into illusion. This happens when a man in prayer, for example, becomes attached to the ideas which come to him and to the feelings he experiences, rather than to God alone who can be neither thought nor felt.

The representation must be distinguished from the *act* which produces it, examines it, negates it, surpasses it, and thus makes us come into contact with the real by way of it. What begets comprehending and communion with the real is not the heap of representations in our mind, but this act—which is a *thinking* and a *living*.

Exist as they may in our mind, representations remain external to us. We can have as many of them as there are words in a dictionary and phenomena in nature. But neither their number nor their wealth increases our comprehension and renders us true and discerning in our being, clear-sighted and free in our deeds. The representation by itself remains external to the act of understanding and still more to the act of freedom. The representation embodies these acts, and the latter are internal to it, but the representation should not be confused with them. Whoever dallies in the "materiality" of his representations, rather than living out—in his way of being and acting—the acts of comprehending and deciding which connect, examine, negate, and complete them, deservedly "gets no further than representations," in a pejorative sense.

The representation belongs not merely to the inner realm of a subject's mental and affective life, but to the external world of history and societal life as well. Everything in the world and in history (things, events, human beings) is a representation, in the sense that everything there is a manifestation of "something" else, of an originating source. And between what is manifested and its manifestation there creeps in a certain gap or inadequacy: the antinomy of being and appearing. People, things, and events *are* not what they first appear to be. It is necessary to inquire after the being of their appearance, examining and negating the representations by the operation of the mind which comprehends, decides, and acts. This kind of examining and negating attains, or at least aims at attaining, true reality.

We have said that Christ, as a man in history, is a representation for us. As such he is and he is not immediately what he reveals to us. Of course, he is in himself what he reveals; he is God. But he is God for himself and *for us* only by the negating movement which fashions him from the crib to the cross, and which will make him the absolute revelation of God in and by the act of his death, resurrection, and disappearance (ascension).

We have differentiated between the representation and the examining-negating activity, but the latter activity (comprehending and deciding) is the very inner movement of the representation. The movement advances by negating the representation, and hence it compels the representation to go through a death, ending in a resurrection which is proportional to this death. We see the Christian mystery dawning here, but it is just as much a question of the life of understanding and freedom in every person.

Every representation is meant to be comprehended (that is, entered into and then transcended in the direction of its meaning) by coming into contact with the act which posits and *negates* it. For in order *to be* a representation which makes what it represents present, it must be negated, once it has been posited. Otherwise, it subsists in its obscure "materiality," inserting itself between our mind and what it represents, hiding the latter and concealing it from us. (This happens in all forms of illusion.) Such negating is constitutive of every sign; a sign is a sign only to the degree that it contains and manifests its own negation—like the word which dies away the instant it is pronounced and comprehended, in order to give way to another word and finally to a meaningful silence. Without this kind of negating, the signified does not appear in and by the sign.

Let us place matters within the framework of the mystery of Christ and salvation history. Why is Christ the image of the invisible

God? We can answer: Because he is in himself the Word of God. This response is true but insufficient. For whoever says "image" speaks not only of the relationship of the image to its origin, but also to itself and to us for whom the image exists. Consequently, we must answer the question not only within the framework of what Christ is in himself, but also in terms of what he is for himself and for us.

Why is Christ the image of the invisible God for himself and for us? Because from the first instant of his life in the world, even from his conception, he is fashioned by a "positing-negating" movement which climaxes on Calvary. Christ is conceived, is born, grows, and develops; but in one and the same movement he is mortified in everything and dies to himself as a creature "made sinful flesh." Christ is not a man who is merely what he appears to be and nothing more. If he were, he would not be the Christ,; he would be a screen between us and God, whereas he is the revealer, the mediator. He is essentially self-negation: abnegation which establishes God and men in relationship. When this abnegation has gone to its bitter end, when Christ dies, he disappears, and it is then that he is fully for us what he is in himself: the Son of God. This must be comprehended, obviously, within the undivided unity of his life-death-resurrection-ascension. Then he reveals the Father to us absolutely and gives us the Spirit.

For one who is within the logic of Christ, for one who has faith, Christ reveals his mystery less at the transfiguration than at the cross, and less in the post-resurrection appearances than at the ascension. Obviously the *disappearing* (death, ascension) is revealing only as united with the *positing* movement (incarnation, birth, growth). The cross reveals the God of Jesus Christ only to the degree that it is comprehended as the end point of an earthly history which begins at the nativity. And this is why the cross is not the end point purely and simply, the end where everything stops, but on the contrary the end where everything begins in Truth made manifest: resurrection and birth of the Church.

Whoever does not comprehend Jesus Christ on the level of this negating movement, which is a thinking and a living, "gets no further than representations," and he risks living his faith merely within representations. To live within representations is to perceive mental images, external things, the words of the Bible, the events of salvation history, but without attaining by way of these representations the *meaning* which would lead one to live in conformity with Christ. In the Gospels we find all sorts of people who live within representations, such as Nicodemus when he comes to find Jesus by night (John 3). He poses questions to Jesus with a very good intention. But he is a man who has come to get information, to gather material; he is not on a level with Christ who interrupts him rather abruptly and shakes him completely. Nevertheless, Nicodemus profits from this encounter; he takes up Jesus' defense in the very name of the Law (John 7:51) and sees to the burial of him who has become his master (John 19:39). The Samaritan woman also comes with her representations, but she very quickly allows herself to be placed on the level of her interlocutor; she comprehends, is converted, and that very day becomes a disciple.

The crowds, the majority of those who hear the prophet from Galilee, get no further than representations. They include all those of whom Jesus said, "For those outside everything is in parables" (Mark 4:11). They hear the parables, and they even comprehend them on the level of the narrative. They are delighted with storytelling, but they do not grasp that the storytelling aims at calling them in question, that its meaning lies in asking: And you, where are you with regard to the kingdom of God? To go beyond the representation towards its meaning is to live on the level of this question and to work accordingly. The majority do not suspect this at all.

Still another example is Simon the Pharisee, who answers Jesus' questions very well (Luke 7:36-50). He is at the height of representation and he stays there. He did not comprehend that, after having answered correctly, the only thing left for him to do was to ask himself: Where am I in relation to him, in relation to the kingdom of God? On the other hand, the open sinner who threw herself at Jesus' feet had comprehended right away. The same is true of the rich man who asked the Lord, "What must I do to inherit eternal life?" and who said, "All these I have observed from my youth." When the Lord told him: "You lack one thing; go, sell what you have, and give to the poor...and come, follow me," he comprehended very well. With a silent refusal, he let himself go away sad; but he was not at all within the representation (Mark 10:17-22). These two incidents show us that it is important not to dwell within the framework of representations, but also that we transcend it only for better (conversion) or for worse (refusal). In short, the philosophical problem of the representation is very difficult, but it is simple enough to see what the issue is for faith and for life.

There is a danger that many people making the Spiritual Exercises get no further than representations. With a great deal of good will and fidelity, they fill their imagination with images, words, stories, and yet nothing or almost nothing happens. St. Ignatius was concerned with this problem in the sixth annotation, but he did not dwell on it at great length. For in such a case there is frequently nothing to do except to verify that the retreatant is not ready for the full Exercises. It is a serious problem. Those who remain within the representational framework will have made "a very good retreat," but it is ineffectual: it is not the conversion hoped for. On the whole, we do not know what to do with these persons, who often have good will. We realize that we are not in control—God is. We can only follow St. Ignatius' recommendation of thoroughly discerning who can or cannot make the Exercises. We must know how to bide our time.

One final remark is necessary. We must go beyond representations to arrive at the meaning.[25] But we can transcend the representation only by way of representations; the negative movement which allows us to go beyond them is internal to them. This is the case within revelation as much as elsewhere, if not more. And there this movement leads less to an intellectual comprehension than to the assent of a faith which bears fruit in works of charity. For that matter, it is inappropriate to oppose intellectual comprehension and faith. The important point we are stressing is that there is no question in the Gospels of turning our back on the man Jesus under the pretext of going right to the absolute meaning. Christ in his humanity is the way, the truth, and the life. Whoever does not attend to his words in the Gospels will never comprehend, for example, St. Paul's language of "Christ made sin." It is by passing through representations, through this Image which only unveils its internal negating movement little by little, that we arrive at the final truth. It is the roads of Galilee which lead to Jerusalem, and it is the initial contemplation of the externals of Calvary which leads to the heart of the redemption.

The present commentary on the First Week could be recapitulated now in light of these suggestions. The I that gradually arrives at the meaning which the *logical* language tries to convey clings unremittingly to the mediating representations. Whoever arrives at a spiritual existence on the level of 2 Cor. 5:21 ("For our sake he made him to be sin who knew no sin..."), whoever has dwelt

---

25 Taken absolutely, as it is here, the word *meaning* could be defined precisely as "the way, the truth, and the life."

in the depths of his own being through this identity of the Redeemer with sin, remains no less the beginner who gazes at Christ on the cross before him: "Imagine Christ our Lord present before you upon the cross." For everything starts from there and all is included there. I must begin by following the Gospels, representing to myself the historical event situated outside me, before it can truly dwell within me. The meaning, the reality as it is lived by the mystic, is the truth of the representation, but the representation is the body and utterly faithful guardian of this truth.[26]

---

26 This is all the more so since we are creatures (representations) and we can go beyond representations only in a very relative fashion. God alone is what he is absolutely, simply, and immediately. The creature, even as divinized, is what it is in God only at the price of a perpetual negating movement which never stops trying to overcome the difference between appearing and being. We are *images* of God.

Chapter 5

THE SECOND WEEK

Transition from the First to the Second Week

My reflection during the First Week is completed by the intense feeling (*sentiment*)[1] of the non-sense proper to sin, hell. By thus going to its ultimate conclusion, the non-sense of sin allowed the appearance of Christ made sin. The crucified Christ judges sin and uproots its deceitful existence, but at the same time he confirms the paths of sin as the avenue whereby Love becomes present in man's world. The sinful creature is not only a true creature but a creature *who has sinned*. And the Son of God makes the sinful creature his cradle and even his own body—so that what he does is also done by the creature. He saves the creature and the creature saves itself.

But why did this salvation, which comes to us by way of our own paths, have to proceed from Another, from the Son of God? Because our actions, for better and for worse, come from beyond us and extend beyond us. According to revelation, sin imbues the created world with a disorder whose dimensions are more than human; sin resists God's gift of himself and, so to speak, uses God against God. The sinner leans on God in order to position himself against God. The sinner does so without knowing what he is doing, but he does it. Since God gives him the power to be and to act in the very instant of his sin, the sinner compels God to collaborate with his deed while at the same time perverting and rejecting this collaboration.[2] Sin derives its power from this divine collaboration, but it also follows that the being necessary to negate sin is nothing

---

1 [Translator's Note. On the meaning of *sentiment*, see chapter 7, section IV, and the Note on the Application of the Senses at the end of chapter 5.]

2 God does not participate in the sin, but he does cause the existence of the sinner's freedom and all the things which his freedom uses.

less than God himself. God's intervention is all the more necessary because the sinful act, which grabs a power coming from God in order to posit itself, strikes God in himself: the God who gives me being and who gives himself in this gift.[3]

The I which has constituted itself for itself, by using God against God, can no longer get out of the situation it has brought on. Its deed oversteps itself; it is an act of godly dimensions, making the sinner a god in opposition to God. This is, at any rate, the nonsense of the sin that leads to hell. I am a sinner who is not yet in hell. But without Christ I am headed there by reason of a "logical" necessity I have brought upon myself and which I cannot escape. If I then find myself, at the end of my reflection, delivered from a sin "of godly dimensions," it is because I have been liberated from it by the very one from whom such power comes to me and who can say: "I am who I am" (Exod. 3:14).

Nevertheless, the rigor and glory of God's purposes also require that we, having sinned ourselves, should save ourselves. The power which saves us, therefore, will not remain outside us; it becomes present within the existence we have given ourselves, contravening us "from head to toe." But how can God become present within our existence, part and parcel of the finitude of the created world? If the infinite God becomes a creature,[4] he cannot undergo any action which would determine and establish him within the existence of a limited being. For he is absolute Freedom which nothing can determine.

It is God who determines himself, not by virtue of any internal necessity, but by a sovereign generosity, by an act of his own Freedom. God's Freedom comes into the world and becomes present there according to a logic which is unveiled for us in the fundamental meditations of the Second Week: the Kingdom, the Two Standards, and the Three Classes.

The preceding paragraph should not surprise us. The fundamental meditations of the Second Week are not merely pedagogical exercises enabling us to enter into the spirit of the gospel. They are rooted in the mystery of the Incarnation-Redemption. They show us what the Son of God does when he takes on flesh and completes this mystery in us and for us.

3 Theology states precisely for us that every sin is not only a fault against the order of creation, but even more against our relationship in Jesus Christ to God as Father, Son, and Spirit, the God who *gives himself* to us in Christ.

4 God becoming a creature is what is meant by his becoming present within our existence.

Consequently, our reflection has retraced the movement whereby Being becomes present in the world of non-being. The advent of Freedom into the sinful creature's world has not been deduced from sin as committed; instead, the advent of Freedom has been presented as the necessary condition for the existence of sin. Our reflection has gone back along human existence as it appears in the light of revelation: Sin, like every other act of man's freedom, transcends man. Sin presupposes a capability in the creature which is ascribable to God, for he does not put us in possession of ourselves without giving himself to us. Sin belongs to the supernatural order, and hence man cannot liberate himself from it. If man is saved from sin, it is through God becoming present within the existence where sin has been actualized. This salvation was announced even before the sin was fully revealed, for God was not caught short by our deeds. If he endowed us with such a capability, he did so in his Son, the firstborn of all creation, on behalf of his glory and in the interest of man. Adam precedes Jesus Christ in history, but in the realm of logic, the Incarnation is first—before sin, even before creation.[5]

The Choice between Good and Evil

Since we began reflecting in the First Week, our freedom has been engaged in authentically positing itself by itself. Now Christ will present himself to our freedom as the second term of an alternative whose first term is sin. "For do not forget that we are in the Before of a choice, and that at the end point of this second moment the opposition between good and evil is to *be represented* to consciousness."[6]

The creature is the one who introduced this opposition into the world at the very beginning, first by comparing itself with God and then by choosing itself in opposition to God. In this way evil, which God had neither created nor presented to the creature as the term of a possible choice, entered the world. But from then on evil developed its parasitic tentacles around the good, and our freedom must posit itself by way of a choice between good and evil. Our freedom is implicated in evil from the outset. The first effect of salvation for our freedom is that good be restored to it as a possibility; good is then present as the second term of an alternative.

5 [Translator's Note. On Ignatius' Pauline and Scotistic theology of the Incarnation, see Hugo Rahner, S.J., "The Christology of the Spiritual Exercises," in *Ignatius the Theologian*, trans. Michael Barry (New York: Herder and Herder, 1968), pp. 53-135.]
6 *Dialectique*, I, 52.

Our capacity to choose between good and evil at each moment is the work of God's Word in us, the Word who becomes flesh and liberates us. It is this concrete possibility, bestowed on sinful man from the beginning because of the New Adam, Jesus Christ, which is now presented in the Exercises, before the choice can take place. The Exercises actually unfold salvation history for us: first, the direction of our sins; then the existence of him who counterbalances their weight in us and who enables us to choose the good.[7]

Freedom will have to choose between the two possibilities of good or evil. But these two possibilities are very different from one another, since evil has, as it were, monopolized reality in advance. Before man even comes to the point of reflectively choosing between vice and virtue, he is already corrupted. He acquired knowledge of good and evil by laying aside his native innocence which had situated him on God's path as he came forth from the Creator's hands. By distancing himself from his Creator, man makes himself the second term of a false dilemma, "either Him or me." When anyone represents the situation to himself this way he has not yet sinned, for he can always choose God rather than himself; and yet he has already sinned by the simple fact that he compares himself with the Creator. Thus the I is corrupted from the beginning, down to its very manner of posing the problem of moral choice as an alternative between good and evil.[8]

The possibility of freedom, which even the sinful I retains, is not enough to counterbalance the I anew and compensate for the weight of its chains. For the I to have an *idea* of the good will not do —it needs the power of a *real* good. It needs a *concrete* freedom, an active presence. But, on the other hand, in order to come in contact with this I sunk in its sinful world and to accord it genuine initiative, Being (the Good, Freedom) must appear in a negative form,[9] not as a force constituted beside mine and joining mine, but as a power which has been emptied in my own powerlessness and, as such, is the source of my ability.

---

7 It would be a misunderstanding for anyone to imagine that, by attaching this possibility to the gift of Christ, we are contradicting the dogma that sinful man retains his reason and freedom. The sinner does in fact retain these powers but, without Christ, he only succeeds in freely choosing the evil which leads him to perdition. We are not defining an abstract human nature, which does imply reason and free choice, whatever sins may or may not have been committed in actual history. We are reflecting on man *within history*, that history which begins with sin.

8 We hope to tackle this difficult point in a theological work devoted to the main dogmas underlying the Exercises.

9 See *Dialectique*, I, 52.

We are speaking about Christ, who does leave us real initiative; he does not take our place, contrary to what we sometimes say without thinking sufficiently. Of course, he does expiate our sins and deliver us, but he does so in and through us—that is, to the degree that we let him live out in us the passion of love he warned us about by taking a sinful body. Christ's very presence therefore re-creates in us a real possibility of choosing the good, but this re-creating is done inside us, inside our freedoms. This nonviolent presence of Christ at the heart of our freedoms is only possible for God, for a God who empties himself in us. By this emptying of himself, God is *everything* in us, but under the form of *nothingness;* the power of Being, but under the form of the weakness of non-being; Freedom, but in the condition of a slave; Good, but reduced to the "sinful body." At this price and only at this price, we are—not strengthened by his divine power joining itself to our weakness—but rather re-created by him into really being able to choose and to do the good, that is, to become free for him.

Thus and not otherwise does God realize his bountiful purposes in us. Christ's humiliation or, as St. Paul says, his "emptying" is the essential condition for man's liberation which would be worthy of God and worthy of man. I cannot liberate myself alone, but I can do it in him who, by his power as Creator and his emptying as the incarnate Son of God, is more me than I myself am.

All conditions are perfectly fulfilled by this "Image" of Freedom, by him "who, though he was in the form of God,...emptied himself, taking the form of a slave, being born in the likeness of men" (Phil. 2:6-7).

The life of our Lord Jesus Christ, therefore, will constitute the antithesis of the history of our sins. Grace thus manifests itself sufficiently over against sin in order to counterbalance the weight of sin, but not enough to coerce freedom, so that choice remains real and necessary for freedom.

With the appearance of Grace/Freedom over against sin/slavery, therefore, we enter into the second moment of the Before. And just as sin knew a growth in time, grace must unfold now too; the positing of non-being must be matched by the negating of this positing.[10]

Two Men in Me

Our analysis of freedom as a choice between good and evil has

10 Ibid.

clarified the Second Week. With an eye to the choice I will have to make, the Second Week presents me with the Good, Christ, over against the evil in which my freedom has been implicated from the beginning. This analysis is precise, but insufficient; by deepening it, we will make our future progress easier.

The conflict between good and evil, vice and virtue, which we meet at every turn, reflects the ambiguity of our flesh-spirit condition. Either flesh or spirit is capable of becoming a path of temptation or a way of salvation. Without being incorrect, this description runs the risk of yielding to an illusion: fancying evil and good as two things placed before us, whereas all creatures are good in themselves, and they are indifferent to the morality of our deeds. None of them can make my choice good.

Besides, this analysis suffers "from a twofold defect: From the viewpoint of the object, the analysis portrays choice as an alternative between good and evil, whereas our concrete option is only made between the *less good* and the *better*.... And from the viewpoint of the moral subject, it does not express the total positing of self by self which is the essence of freedom."[11]

As a matter of fact, this analysis so far is merely a sketch. It indicates the boundaries, but it does not bring out the movements of opposed forces inside these boundaries: from the less good to the better, and from the better to the less good.[12]

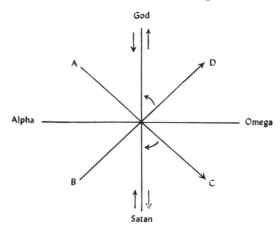

11 Ibid., 54.

12 [Translator's Note. The diagram here is based on Fessard's diagrams in a pullout at the end of *Dialectique*, I. Since Pousset's work does not include these very helpful tools for understanding the various "motions" within the person, grateful acknowledgement is here given to both Fessard and his publisher, Aubier, for their permission to reproduce them in our translation. Since Fessard's pullout is not paginated,

The movement from the less good to the better can be represented on the time line (Alpha-Omega) as an indefinite progression or at least as a tendency (B-D). A force in the opposite direction (A-C) restrains it or spurs it on, according to the choices of my freedom which yields or resists. Since the object that my improving or worsening choice immediately bears upon is particular, it limits the import of my choice. The dynamism of the I exerts itself in this choice, nonetheless, and the I tends to posit itself absolutely—at least by an intentionality inclining the I towards choices which will augment its tendency in the same direction. In this way my concrete option at a particular moment can combine the perfection of a total choice[13] with its indeterminate tendency towards the best. Something definitive or eternal is at stake in my options: being open or impervious to God. I can open myself to the absolute Good or I can close myself, ending in total evil.

These are the characteristics of my concrete decision which must be reexamined within the very general opposition between good and evil. Analysis is now going to show that within the I which I am, and which must choose between good and evil, two "I's" are concerned. In the first I, initially identified with the psychological tendencies of concupiscence, revelation enables me to perceive the "old man," the man of my past, Adam, who lets himself be seduced by the temptation of pure spirit. In the second I, initially identified with the light of my reason, the same revelation enables me to recognize the "new man," Christ, the Word of God who takes on sensuous flesh.[14]

In its essence, evil is not a tempting object, but a sensuous tendency struggling against my reason, which wrests me from myself, carrying me along in spite of myself, tending to grab every being.[15] But when all is said and done, beyond the real weakness and distress of a creature sucked down into sensuousness, evil is the attempt by reason ultimately to justify a behavior it may have secretly disowned in the beginning. Thus freedom, in power or weakness, prosperity or adversity, is tempted to posit itself by itself in an empty self-sufficiency.

we will refer to the number(s) of each figure. The diagram here is based on Fessard, figures 2 and 3.]

13 We refer to what was said about "cleavage points" or "Instants" in the First Week where something definitive is decided. What is possible in the direction of sin is equally and even more possible in the direction of the Good.

14 Note well these two contrary movements: from concupiscence to the temptation of pure spirit; from reason (*logos*) to sensuousness.

15 *Dialectique*, I, 54.

And what is the good? Reason, undoubtedly, which resists the sensuous tendency. But if my reason merely presented me with a sheer idea, it would be powerless to stop the tendency. How could a possibility (an idea) negate the existent (the power of concupiscence)? No, my reason portrays *me* to myself: the I which I already am and the I which I am not yet, the I which must build itself up by its deeds. The good is an I. It is not my former I (which gathers itself together and is concentrated in concupiscence), but a future, ideal, and absolute I. The good is an I which I *am* (it crops up in the present and counterbalances the concupiscence resulting from my past)—and yet which I *am not* (since, resisting my past, it has to build itself up)—but which I *ought to be* (uniting my former converted "I" and my approaching future "I").[16]

Going more deeply into the choice which is presented to me, I discover that I am split, not between two objects or even between two laws (that of my members and that of the Spirit), but between two I's. "I feel two men in me.... The first man is the I who, by compressing his whole *past* (the entire past of humanity) to the utmost peak of his tendencies, concentrates all his energy in the present moment when he becomes aware of his own sufficiency for being present in himself and for himself."[17] Sucked down into sensuousness at first, this I strives to extricate himself in the direction of pure thought by the struggle of his reason to interpret itself as the beginning and end of all things. His reason tries to explain everything on its own terms, in an effort to posit itself as the center of a universal coherence fabricated by itself.

"Contrariwise, the Absolute I, who was initially stationed at infinity from myself, offers to draw nearer."[18] To the degree that the covetous I retires into his shell, within his own self-sufficiency, the I·who comes from above, touching me at the fine point of spirit, unfolds himself outwardly. "The more the first I is inclined to become abstract in order to assume an angelic air, the more the second I tends to concretize himself to become incarnate spirit, a spiritual body which is *present* to me.... As a result of my deliberation, these two men (before me and within me) touch each other in their 'members.' The members of the earthly man are 'immorality, impurity, passion, evil desire, and covetousness' (Col. 3:5), while those of the heavenly man (1 Cor. 15:48) are 'compassion, kindness, lowliness, meekness, and patience,... [and]

16 Ibid., 54-55.
17 Ibid., 55.
18 Ibid.

love' (Col. 3:12-14). Their 'members,' like the words of people conversing, overlap, cross, and support one another so as to fashion only 'one body' (Eph. 4:4). They form one line: mounting from the good towards the best; rising from the present, containing the past, towards the future. For on one hand, if the man of the past in me is Adam, the 'old man,' he nevertheless always remains the one who prefigures the 'New Man'; Adam, in his very sin, is the figure of Christ. And on the other hand, if the New Man is Jesus, the Man of the Future, who appears in the 'fullness of time,' he is also 'the image of the invisible God, the first-born of all creation' (Col. 1:15), and consequently he who comes from the Origin, from my most remote past.

"In the 'carrying-on' of these two men, it is I who express myself in them. In Adam, perpetually tempted by pure spirit, I relive the dream of becoming like God, in order to posit myself at the limit of myself, a gift to myself. In Jesus, I continually hear the Father's command, the call to 'not count equality with God a thing to be grasped' (my own self-presence), but to 'empty myself' in order to await my being of the future when it will be bestowed on me. To hang onto, or to confine oneself to, a certain degree of good—or to surrender oneself unreservedly to the better as such: this opposition is just as categorical as that between evil and good. For the motive of my decision is either consciousness of my present self-sufficiency or else longing for a future increase. Under the species of the less good or the better, this opposition is the absolute antinomy between present pride (actually a ghost of the past which no longer exists) and faith in the future, the garment of the Absolute."[19]

The choice always bears on being, on a good, but it lends a negative or positive direction to being. The negative direction permeates the specific good I use in order to affirm myself and to retire into my shell in a self-sufficiency which gravitates toward sheer evil. The positive direction confers an added value on the particular good I use to open myself to the infinite. "Either I give birth to sin and augment the kingdom of death by assuming Adam's self-sufficient attitude, or else I 'put off the old man with his practices and...put on the new man who is being renewed in knowledge after the image of his creator' (Col. 3:9-10)."[20]

19 Ibid., 55-56.
20 Ibid., 56. [The RSV here has been slightly emended in accordance with the Greek and Fessard's text.] We quote Fessard's own footnote, ibid.: "This analysis allows us to explain some data from spiritual psychology: *Corruptio optimi pessima*, says

The law of the Incarnation is that, where sin abounds, grace abounds the more. While man is exploiting the sensuous realm in order to derive power for a more and more proud self-affirmation, and thus making himself an "angel," he who is of divine rank, but did not jealously hang onto his equality with God, immerses himself in the sensuous realm, taking on the body and form of a slave. It should not be surprising that the perspectives of the Incarnation irrupt within an analysis which began by presenting good and evil in terms of reason and sensuous tendencies within moral conscience. The individual person's I enjoys the dimensions of the history of humanity for better, as well as for worse; the least movements of this I towards the good bring into play the entire mystery of Christ, Lord of history and Spouse of humanity.

The discord within a person's consciousness ultimately has a significance as vast as the duel of the rebellious angel ("the I sheerly present for itself") with the Word made flesh. I take after both of them! I am these two I's at grips with each other, within the unity of a single consciousness.

The difficult point in this analysis of the two I's in me is to grasp clearly that they are at one and the same time myself and other than me. We must become familiar with a language which expresses not so much entities as systems of relationships. I am not Christ, and still less Satan or Adam; but I am defined by a twofold system of relations to one and the other. And this is what we mean when we speak of two I's in me.

The I of the past, which connives with Satan, wants to use

Scripture. For as the degree of objective good increases, the more violent becomes the conflict between the two men in us, and the more profound becomes the corrupting act of pride.

"While the saints are those who have only imperfections to reproach themselves with, 'as for example, if, having numerous supernatural lights about the same thing' they should follow the lower course because of spiritual weariness or thoughtlessness, (Louis Lallemant, S.J., *Doctrine spirituelle*, Collection Christus, no. 3 [Paris: Desclée de Brouwer], p. 216), they are the ones who best realize the conflict between grace and sin. While their salvation is 'morally infallible,' they also experience the greatest terror of God's judgments. For our ordinary, abstract, objective morality, not to choose the better is to be satisfied with the *lesser good*. On the contrary, for the concrete, deep-seated, subjective judgment of the saints, such an option becomes more and more choice of the *worse*." [Translator's Note. Thus far I have been unable to locate the phrase of Lallemant in the E glish translation, *The Spiritual Doctrine of Father Louis Lallemant of the Society of Jesus*, edited by Alan G. McDougall (Westminster, Md.: Newman, 1955).]

creatures for its egotistic ends and with an eye to its "ideal" of positing itself as a sheer gift to itself. When I slow down my progress or stop on the vector from the less good towards the better, where my conversion in the First Week placed me, I immediately fall back under the law of this proud I, and I risk taking a step towards the worse. Conversely, what never fails to further my progress towards the better is listening to the Father's command which is diametrically opposed to the satanic I's presumption, and which makes me participate in the mystery of the Incarnation with a view to authentic self-positing. His command, in short, is to "not hang covetously onto my equality with God." The command is addressed to the Son, Head and Spouse of humanity, but also to the faithful of Jesus Christ, and even to every person: Do not hang onto the ideal of self-affirmation and sheer self-presence, but lose yourself, while waiting and hoping for your being of the future when it will be bestowed on you.

We see how, in this analysis of freedom, the ideal of the positing of self by itself begins to be reversed into that of the positing of self through Another who is more me than I am. And it is in this way that man becomes like God. In wanting to be like God, the creature is utterly mistaken. God is not an I centered on itself and relating to itself. God is a Trinity of persons: three I's, each being only for the other, and finding its own being only in the other. Even the Father is Father only by his act of engendering the Son, communicating to him all that he is. When the Father charges us, in his Son, with "not covetously hanging onto our equality with God," he is simply asking us to renounce our false conception of divinity. He is asking us to renounce our unintelligent will to be self by itself, in order to embark upon the way that leads each of us towards really becoming ourselves by ourselves—that is, like the person of the Son, through Him who is more us than we are.

We do not have to take back anything from our initial definitions of freedom, but we must give up our immediate and one-sided way of comprehending them. That is, we must not hold out to ourselves the ideal of a self withdrawing into itself, to the exclusion of others. All these themes place us in the heart of the Second Week.

Panorama of the Second Week

The Second Week has us witness the development of Christ's presence in the sinful world, a presence which is the condition of our own act of freedom. Christ's presence is that of a freedom which posits itself. Freedom did not appear in the First Week, and it did not have to show itself: neither in us immersed in our sins (sin is the opposite of freedom), nor in Christ—as *represented* on the cross or as we *felt* him "made sin," but whom we have not yet contemplated in his historical becoming. In the First Week, the being of freedom was everywhere presupposed but it was nowhere posited, since only the non-being of freedom had been posited. The Second Week is totally different; now freedom appears as such, in the sinful world, of course, but in conformity with the truth of freedom—not as it exists in us, barely emerging from our sins and still subject to concupiscence—but as it is in Christ.

This authentic freedom shows through in the evangelical mysteries, but in a subdued light. The secret of its logic remains hidden from our eyes, the poorly trained eyes of scarcely repentant sinners. In the Second Week we are still like the disciples whom St. Mark depicts so well as seeing things from the outside; we lack the penetrating gaze of a St. John who sees into the heart of things. St. Ignatius enjoyed this penetrating gaze on our behalf, and he shares it with us in the fundamental meditations of the Kingdom, Two Standards, and Three Classes. These meditations point out to us the meaning of true life, along with the correct logic for the growth of freedom. They are not added onto the evangelical mysteries—they are a gaze which penetrates them, and this is why the Second Week is organized around them. But once this gaze has been acquired, they could be forgotten in favor of a very simple contemplation of the mysteries. The gospel mysteries bring about a gradual passage of Jesus' ideas and feelings into our own consciousness, and they thus begin to exert a negating influence in opposition to our sins.

Two points of view govern the Exercises and our mode of comprehending them: (1) the "logical" viewpoint[21] demanded by the principle governing the development of each Week; and (2) the viewpoint of consciousness, which sees the different exercises linked together in terms of the needs and awarenesses of "where the retreatant is at" (see *Exercises*, [4]), and therefore as not revealing their full significance.

The principle governing the Second Week is the Incarnation. There are two related consequences flowing from this principle. First, Freedom (the Word who IS) must grow in conformity with the laws governing every consciousness in this world. Thus Freedom

---

21 Recall that the *logical* viewpoint is that of the gaze which includes everything (beginning and end) at once; it sees the entire development in its principle, where beginning and end coalesce.

will present itself little by little. But as there is no freedom at all in this world—not even in God—which is not a freedom for another freedom, this presentation of Freedom-in-itself is simultaneously a presentation of Freedom to another freedom which it calls forth, attracts, and sets to growing simultaneously and proportionately with its own growth.

Secondly, the growth of Freedom is simultaneously growth of my own freedom, at first in the form of representations and feelings (I gradually acquire the ideas and inmost dispositions of authentic Freedom), followed by a deed uniting me to authentic Freedom, the Choice.

The two problems of Freedom and my freedom are really a single issue. The retreatant's consciousness, which glides along within this unity by living out the movement of the retreat, does not have to think in terms of two freedoms. But we, by contrast, have to comprehend the unifying movement of the Second Week in its fullness and on all its levels. Our task is to follow, distinctly but without separating, what is going on in Jesus Christ and what is going on in and for the retreatant's consciousness. As Jesus grows, there develops an interaction between him and the consciousness which contemplates and exercises itself: Freedom and my freedom do not follow two parallel pathways—the path is one.

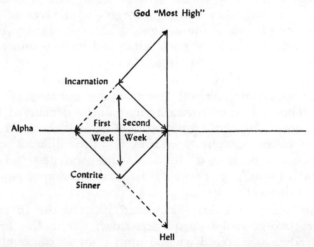

Consciousness, in its sins, was heading towards the bottom, hell.[22] Through forgiveness and contrition consciousness reversed its tendency and initiated a climb towards Freedom which, from

22 For the diagram of the first two Weeks, see *Dialectique*, I, fig. 4-5.

its side, comes down towards consciousness by following the vector of the Incarnation. On the threshold of the Second Week, the retreatant's consciousness and Christ's Freedom are still remote from one another; they are even at their maximum distance although they are no longer separated by sin. This remoteness is due to the condition of consciousness which, having emerged from its sin, still finds itself entirely outside the image of Freedom, carrying on a merely intentional relationship with it (consciousness is turned towards Christ rather than being united with him). This remoteness also corresponds to Freedom's positing in relation to me. In itself, this Freedom has always been coming down into the world (God had compassion on us from the beginning), and Freedom has even already appeared in history. But this history remains external to me—I have not yet actually comprehended what it is for me, to the point of living it out; I am only disposing myself to do that. Nevertheless, there is convergence in this external relationship which Christ and I have with one another; the descending line of the Incarnation and the rising line of my conversion are going to meet at the Choice. Hence there is only a single pathway for Christ and me: While Jesus (a subjective freedom) presents himself as (objective) Freedom, I allow myself to be carried towards this Freedom, until I become one with it.

The fundamental meditations of the Second Week, moreover, present the development of Freedom and my freedom in their mutual implications. This development is thoroughly paradoxical; it is at once an increase (Jesus Christ, through the mysteries of his life, discloses more and more what he is) and a decrease ("he emptied himself...unto death"). The trilogy of the Kingdom, Two Standards, and Three Classes lays bare the details of this twofold contrary movement. The retreatant's consciousness, on its side, will pass from the exaltation of the Kingdom to the "emptying" of the Three Classes and the Three Kinds of Humility.

"We have defined freedom from two opposed points of view: the positing of self by itself and the passage from non-being to being. But here the issue is precisely to unite these two definitions. Objective being (reached by passing from non-being to being) must appear, at the heart of the representation, as ultimately identical with the subject's self (positing itself by itself)."[23]

How is the impossible (a being positing itself by itself, while it is radically non-being) possible? What is impossible for the creature is possible for God, seeing that He became non-being (the

23 *Dialectique*, I, 57.

incarnate Word's emptying) without ceasing, even in the very depths of his emptying, to be God. He is; the creature is not. If infinite Being becomes non-being, then in Him the creature (who is not) can become being. The possible impossibility: such is the content of the Second Week. The possible impossibility is lived out by Christ, and in him, by me. The Second Week thus presents freedom from the viewpoint of its joint twofold definition: the positing of self by itself and the passage from non-being to being. Each fundamental meditation includes this twofold process of freedom's becoming.

The Kingdom

First point. On the horizon of consciousness, which is all eyes, dawns the perfect Freedom of Being. Freedom is wholly external to consciousness, but it is turned towards consciousness, addressing the latter and issuing a summons. Freedom, however, has no need of anyone, and what it issues is clearly not a call for help. Its summons flows not from need but from what it is: Freedom is. Its summons is identical with the movement by which Freedom posits itself; for Freedom, positing itself and addressing another is all one. But Freedom is wholly Being. At the beginning of its manifestation within the realm of non-being (where Freedom is *everything*, but appears initially as *nothing*), Freedom therefore posits itself by affirming an absolute right over everything and thus links up with its own mystery as the fullness of Being: "It is my will to conquer the whole world..." [95]. "Precisely because Christ is in fact still nothing, he must proclaim that he is the genuine proprietor and king and that his intention is to establish his kingdom in fact."[24]

Second point. From this declaration of right follows the fact: All who have heard this summons and "who have judgment and reason will offer themselves entirely for this work" [96], by passing from the good to the better.

Third point. In Jesus Christ, being sets to work in this world. Considering the Word of God, that is, Being (in its transcendence), however, we should say instead that passage to the fact has already (from all eternity) been accomplished by virtue of the intimacy of Jesus in his humanity with the Word of God; he is the very Person of the Word. From the moment of his appearance in the world, Jesus is already present *with* his (absolute) *Self*. This intimacy

24 Ibid., 58.

is effected by the mystery of the hypostatic union, and it summons another intimacy, that of me with Him. The Lord says "whoever wishes to join me...must be willing to labor *with me*" in the first point, and the third point indicates how this "with me" is realized.

Jesus is all in all by right (first point); he becomes all through work (second point); but in himself he already is all through his intimacy with the Word (third point).

This interpretation of the third point puts us quite far from the letter of the *Exercises*, where it is the offering of those "who wish to give greater proof of their love, and to distinguish themselves in whatever concerns the service of the eternal King" [97]. But the mystery of Jesus' intimacy with the Word presents itself precisely as an invitation to consciousness to offer itself for a type of life which will allow the retreatant to realize the greatest intimacy with the divine I. The intimacy of the divine I (the union of the human and divine natures in the Person of the incarnate Word of God) is a mystery of humility which is going to entail the humiliations of his life. Christ's humiliations flow directly from his humility and they are manifested in the existence where I myself live. According to the offering of the Kingdom, to bear "all wrongs and all abuse and all poverty" is to arrive at intimacy with the divine I.

There is thus a close relationship between Christ's invitation to be "with me" and the offering of the Kingdom, between the divine I and this offering. The "logical" viewpoint, which opens directly onto the mystery of the Incarnation, is thereby linked with the viewpoint "of consciousness," which perceives Christ's invitation to an offering "of greater value and of more importance."[25]

The Two Standards

The fundamental meditations of the Second Week are not stages of the Incarnation; they presuppose the latter and disclose its law. The Being who is rightfully the entirety appears in the representation at first as nothing. In this nothingness, he signifies what he is by first stating his purpose ("to conquer the whole world"), and

---

25 For consciousness, the Kingdom meditation is a summons to true freedom. Consciousness is able to perceive Christ's call insofar as it restores an evangelical content, a bit of Jesus' earthly past (see the first prelude, [91]), to the expressions of the parable. Thus it is memory which has to come into play first of all.

then by proposing it as an ideal to consciousness. These two steps are really one movement. Freedom thus presents itself according to its fullness. With the Kingdom we are still in the non-temporal realm; the mystery of the intimacy of the incarnate Word just begins to open up. The second point, however, suggests the direction of the Word's insertion in time. We enter that flow with the meditation on Two Standards, which presents the schema whereby Freedom actually grows in time.

Freedom is certainly the Being which has the right to come into possession of all, but its place is occupied beforehand by non-being: by the creature in sin and by concupiscence, which tends to grab and enslave. Consequently, Freedom is able to posit itself only by overcoming the radical opposition coming from the sinful world on the occasion of its contact with the things and people it needs in order to posit itself.

Freedom's alternative is either to go in the direction of the sinful world and to be trapped there, or else to go counter to the law of concupiscence: (1) to possess the world as an end or to make use of it as a means (riches as oppposed to poverty); (2) to subjugate others to itself or to submit to them (worldly honor as opposed to humiliations).

This twofold choice finally culminates in a positing of freedom for itself (a return to sin) or beyond itself (by opening itself to Another): pride or humility.[26]

Three Classes of Men

How can the opposition of sin to true freedom, this alternative of pride versus humility, be overcome? How can it be overcome to the point of suppressing the very opposition? How can freedom, by making choices, reach such fulfillment that it is no longer conditioned by choices? How can freedom go to its limit?—By becoming receptive to grace like Jesus Christ, who is sheer reception of the Father's will.

In the concrete, receptivity means *actual* detachment. This detachment can be understood (merely represented) and not really agreed to (first class); or it can be affirmed merely as a tendency—I agree to it, but without taking the real means to it

---

26 Through the Two Standards, consciousness becomes acquainted with the tactics of true and false freedom, which are radically opposed to each other. It is above all an exercise for the understanding, which must learn the rules for the spiritual struggle going on in life *now*.

(second class); or finally, detachment can be willed along with all the means—that is, affirmed as actual (third class). For consciousness, the meditation on the Three Classes is the moment of truth about the quality of its willing. Its will is turned towards the future, as love anticipates someone coming.

By a quick glance at the first two Weeks, we can grasp their meaning for consciousness. In the First Week, sin means the absolute sufficiency of the I in itself. The Second Week is the stripping away that results in the I's full receptivity to Being. The positing of self by itself is an ideal that reveals itself as the positing of self through Another.

By means of this movement Freedom reaches its objective being. The latter is nothing other than the universe of existing things and persons. The Freedom which at first dawns suddenly on the horizon of this universe as external to it (Christ at the moment of his entry into the world) will gradually pervade everything and everyone, communicating his own interiority, his own truth, to them; the I is all the while reaching the solidity of objective being. The Son of God, absolute freedom, becomes incarnate in the world, filling it, transforming it, and making it his own, so that the world becomes his world, his objective being—but an objective being which is at the same time wholly interior to him.

The Kingdom

First point: Being or totality

"It is my will to conquer the whole world...." There is more here than a summons inviting consciousness to share in the toil. This first point is Freedom's proposal for revealing what it rightfully is. On coming into this world (becoming nothing), Freedom manifests what it is by following the appropriate method for a this-worldly consciousness: setting a goal for itself as its end. But Christ already is this end which he says he wants to attain; from the outset his project covers the distance separating his apparent nothingness from the fullness of being. Jesus carried out his project by the words and deeds of his history, which expressed what he was and wanted: He receives worship from the great men of the world (episode of the Magi); he calls the apostles, "I will make you fishers of men," and he goes preaching through the *whole* of Galilee.

Second point: free positing of self

This mystery of totality which Christ already is (he is the Lord,

81

the firstborn of all creation) gains ground in the world through an activity. The enterprise cannot help but come to fruition since the transition from the fact (initial nothingness) to the right (fullness of being) is precontained in the mystery of the hypostatic union: Jesus is the Word of God. Freedom (first that of Jesus, then that of the consciousness which responds to his call) is therefore not facing the alternative of being/non-being, good/evil. Nevertheless, this Freedom follows the laws governing every freedom in the world; it must travel and make progress. Consequently, there is an alternative for this Freedom, one that defines its need to posit itself by choosing, like every created freedom. But its alternative is wholly within being or the good; it is the alternative between the less good and the better. Jesus' Freedom will always choose in the direction of the better, although it is exposed to the eventuality of the less good (there is room for temptation).

The consciousness which hears the call of the Kingdom is also beyond the alternative between good and evil, being and non-being. Consequently, it does not begin deliberating to learn if it will answer with a yes or a no; it offers itself. "Consider that all persons who have judgment and reason will offer themselves entirely for this work" [96]. Nevertheless, its journey will again present itself in the form of a choice between good and better: to continue in the direction of its first step, or to stop and risk going backwards.

Third point: with Self

The "logical" interpretation of this point seems, we have already noted, to keep us rather far from the letter of the *Exercises*. Actually, it points out the basis for the offering proposed to those who wish "to distinguish themselves" by emphasizing the close tie between Incarnation and Redemption. What Jesus actualizes by living out salvation history is what he already is in himself. What is he then? Absolute Freedom. But Freedom's Being is to be a self—that is, a world which has the objectivity of Being (everything that exists) and the free inwardness of consciousness; a world without inward distance, like self-consciousness which stays present to itself.

Christ's Freedom actualizes this perfection by following its own method appropriate for Freedom incarnated in finitude. It portrays its end to itself, which is already a way of becoming equal to its own mystery. And not only does Freedom portray its end to itself, but it embodies its end from the outset through the intimate union of humanity and divinity in the Person of Jesus. In Jesus, the Freedom that seems limited by the world where it is incarnated is already at its own limit. Rather, it overcomes every limit; it is the fullness of self-positing within the intimacy of one Person, an I.

Paradoxically, Christ does not cease living out this fullness by his continual and total emptying of himself, by renouncing his will before that of the Father. This humbling and renunciation weaves a secret network of ties binding his own I into a unity with every other I —even before the process of their accepting him unfolds in time. The intimacy of his I is thus an intimacy of Jesus with everyone, and he invites us to enter into that intimacy, "to labor *with me*."

Jesus' "with me" expresses his own mystery before being an invitation to companionship in history. "Those who wish...to distinguish themselves" grasp this very point. By their offering they straightaway transcend all outward life-styles with Jesus in order to unite themselves to the fullness of his mystery in the world: "all wrongs, all abuse and all poverty." "Christ Jesus,...though he was in the form of God, did not count equality with God a thing to be grasped, but emptied himself, taking the form of a slave" (Phil. 2:5-7).

The "logical" interpretation of this third point thus brings out the innermost mystery of Jesus in himself, and it thereby best accounts for the meaning of the offering made there. From its birth, faith puts us in touch with the mystery of Jesus, thus including a promise of familiarity with his I. Hope attends this promise and incipient charity actualizes it. In the offering of the third point, it is not a question of apostolic methods, but of intimacy with Jesus. The wrongs, abuse, and poverty are the very mode in which his I lives out the fullness of his mystery in this world; anyone who shares in them therefore enters into intimacy with him.

The image of Freedom, Jesus in the world, reveals the inner movement of his Freedom by his words, deeds, and behavior in the presence of things and persons: a free positing of himself that opts for the best by choosing to bear wrongs, abuse, and poverty. The call of the Kingdom to an apostolic life is rooted in the personal mystery of Jesus, who is everything even when he appears as nothing in the world. Any presentation of the Kingdom that would not be rooted in this mystery would be inadequate. And it is by reason of this rooting that the Kingdom announces and paves the way for the entire sequel: the Second, Third, and Fourth Weeks.

The Two Standards

The Kingdom sits astride the first two Weeks because, strictly speaking, the second moment being with the start of the objective growth of Freedom's image: Jesus' birth and hidden life. Jesus' history gradually discloses what true freedom is. Within the vagaries of Jesus' existence, a spiritual gaze discerns freedom's essential features; taken together, these features constitute a representation in which all the details of Jesus' history come and fall into line, clarifying one another.

In becoming incarnate, Freedom portrays itself, and the world furnishes the material for its representation. Freedom must actualize itself for everyone by using this world; and how it chooses to use the world makes it be what it is. Freedom's utilization of the world should be in conformity with its inner being, which is basically governed by an attitude of poverty. Poverty, both spiritual and actual, is the primary feature possessed by the presentation of Jesus' history.

But Jesus, on coming into the world, is no more neutral with regard to the world than the latter is with regard to him. Jesus in himself contains the "negating of the non-being that is sin"; and conversely, the world is the body which non-being seized at the outset. Nevertheless, it is within the world and even by means of the world that Freedom is to unfold and come into its fullness. Consequently, a confrontation will take place each time Jesus comes in contact with this world, that is, each time he has to exercise his Freedom. The opposition between the being of grace and the non-being of sin must appear at the root of every choice Freedom has to make.

Simply by reason of the Son of God's incarnation, forgiveness is granted to men, because the incarnation implicitly contains the entire development from the crib to the cross. The tendency of evil to get worse, even to the point of universal damnation, is turned around; non-being has lost all efficacy; it is negated. But the body which non-being has provided for itself remains, and the negation which already touches non-being must be inscribed in its body by the works and sufferings of Jesus' life. While true Freedom soars from the crib toward its fullness of existence, the realm of death, in which Freedom has become incarnate, offers it resistance. To the degree that true Freedom penetrates this realm or body of non-being, Freedom stirs up all available powers of opposition: Jesus collides with a growing hostility that wins him humiliations and sufferings. This is the second feature possessed by the representation of the Two Standards.

The enemy kingdom develops its opposition even within Jesus' subjective Freedom. As a matter of fact, all reality rightfully belongs to the domain of Freedom. The enemy has no other place to carve out his kingdom; he sows his tares in the field of the Father of the family. The enemy does not have his own territory; what is his has all been usurped.

Freedom's entry into the world unmasks non-being, sin and the prince of this world. Adam did not invent the act of absolute self-sufficiency; he is its first victim, and that is why he is both guilty and the figure of him who is to come. The antithesis of the God-man, of the true I, is the enemy, Satan, who is also a self, but in an eternal and depersonalizing contradiction.

In this vision of the world of the Incarnation and its ensuing dialectic, non-being (sin) is not a necessary moment through which Being must pass in order to posit itself. Instead, the creature (which is non-being) must renounce its sin of deadly self-sufficiency. If the creature becomes anchored in self-sufficiency, it will overtake the fate of Satan, the adversary whose worldly opposition most certainly affects the history of Being, but ultimately to no avail. The opposition characterizing the Second Week, therefore, is destined to be sublimated; nothing will remain of it except the "glorious mark of the wounds." True Freedom suffers and bears this opposition, but without negotiating with it. Freedom in the world thus lives out the mystery of God's infinite "weakness," indentical with his greatness: poverty, insults, humility. The adversary's opposition is useless, but the incarnate Son of God makes the insults and sufferings he earns so much his own, thereby achieving so completely what he is, that the opposition appears necessary. God in himself is humility and poverty; the adversary's opposition, consequently, does not prevent God from being himself (quite the contrary, if we can say so), but it adds to this manifestation of divine poverty and humility the terrible modality of redemptive sufferings.

Reading Jesus' history within this framework of the Two Standards teaches my freedom (whose ideal is the positing of self by itself) the truth of this ideal: namely, the positing of self through Another who is my authentic Self. It is this turning inside out which we must see brought to pass in the dialectic of the three steps of poverty, insults, and humility, culminating in the positing of self *outside oneself*, instead of the positing of self by and for oneself.

Poverty defines the self's new relationship to the world of things. Accepting *insults* defines the self's new relationship to persons. Freedom receives insults because of sin, but on any hypothesis, freedom renounces centering upon itself and demanding worship from others. By this route freedom ultimately attains *humility:* sharing in, and identifying with, the mystery of Being. Enlisting under the colors of the adversary means following the reverse tack: *riches* and worldly *honor*, whereby the I becomes its own focus and receives on behalf of itself the homage reserved to God; finally, it comes to overweening *pride*. These three steps are not essentially descriptions of methods; they express different ways of being: the personal mystery of the God-man, and the satanic dream of making oneself God.

The meditation on Two Standards presents the inner movement of the concept of freedom: renunciation of things through poverty; renunciation of oneself and any domination over others through accepting insults; and finally, the resultant humility whereby the self locates its authentic self in Another. This negative movement whereby Freedom negates its own non-being and arrives at Being is not that of a power triumphing over contradictions by dominating them. Rather, Freedom suffers these contradictions up to the cross, where truth manifests itself in a final renunciation; non-being is definitively rejected in its vanity and nothingness, and Being posits itself in the Resurrection.

Within this dialectic, moreover, sin is not treated as a purely external opposition. Through its poverty, suffering, and insults, the Self of true Freedom bears sin in its own depths—but without compromise —and it paves the way for eliminating sin. Everything within sin is thus taken up and accepted except sin itself, which is nothing. Through poverty and insults the God-man is made sin; but his identification with sin through suffering is simultaneously a judgment which sunders. At the end point, on the cross where Christ dies, there remains nothing more of our sins except the Son identified with them and the adversary who has been repulsed.

The themes of the Two Standards are thus already leading us into the full drama of the Passion. What distinguishes the Second from the Third Week is the position of consciousness in relation to true Freedom: Here, there is merely *represented* to consciousness what it will then live out *in union with* Freedom's image, transformed into the Man of Sorrows. Going beyond the representation will take place, we recall, not by a merely intellectual act, but by a decision of freedom uniting itself to Freedom: the Choice.

The union of the subjective I (the retreatant) and Freedom (Christ) is sealed only in the Choice. And though it is there that the I crosses the distance still separating it from what is portrayed about Freedom by these three meditations, the latter are nonetheless even now beginning to alter the retreatant's freedom. The summons to Being (the Kingdom) and the representation of true Freedom's authentic growing movement (the Two Standards) are paving the way for the decisive act of the Choice, and they are therefore already creating freedom. They are actually developing the attitude of the I which will posit itself in truth, the attitude of receptivity, diametrically opposed to self-sufficiency.

This attitude of receptivity is set forth in the three steps of poverty, insults, and humility. One final stage remains in order to render the retreatant totally receptive: that subjective freedom go to the limit. It is not a question of perfecting the portrayal of true Freedom's authentic movement; the Two Standards is enough for that, and there is nothing to add. It is merely necessary to specify the I's actual position with regard to this ideal as represented. The movement of the concept of freedom is not merely a matter of thinking; the I situates itself in relation to its world through both intellect and will. Therefore, the representation of Freedom will be ineffectual if the I subtly withdraws into an intellectualizing attitude. The I can thereby keep a real distance from Freedom's ideal which threatens its own non-being (if the I is still tied to its sin, it is hanging onto non-being as its being). Because the truth here is a concrete and total relationship of a subjective I to Freedom's I as represented, the subjective I must situate itself both through its intellect (which has been done now, since it accepts this portrayal of Freedom as the ideal) and through its will. Only through the joint operation of these two faculties will the I, in the Choice, emerge from its particularity, the source of self-sufficiency, in order to join the universality of Freedom.

If the intellect has now been extricated from the influence of non-being, since the ideal of Freedom has been presented and accepted by the understanding, the *will* may still be caught in the meshes of non-being. Insofar as the will has not been liberated from the influence of non-being, the unfurling of Freedom in the representation will not really counterbalance the non-being which was posited first. The latter can no longer gain a hold except on the affective level. For non-being has already been negated as a source of action, and likewise as real existence in the world, since the law of true Freedom has been substituted for it. Whatever existential reality non-being preserves in the midst of the world has been recognized as a deceit of the enemy: riches, worldly honors, pride. There is therefore nothing more except affectivity which can still be subtly (and illogically) caught in the seductions of non-being. The retreatant's affectivity will now be put to the test, *exercised*, in the Three Classes.

Three Classes of Men

The meditation on the Three Classes of Men is fundamental. This meditation illustrates that going beyond the representation to arrive at truth is neither a merely intellectual affair nor simply a matter of voluntary feeling. Going beyond the representation involves a synthesis of knowing and willing within the act of deciding. But the dialectic which leads to this decision passes through a phase in which one's affectivity comes to the fore. The affectivity in question is not the more or less superficial level of feelings, but the person's hidden center for voluntary options and very profound ties to some realm of reality. After the I has put its thoughts in order by subscribing to the teaching of true Freedom, it can, insofar as it is still attached to its irrational sinful past, take refuge in its affectivity, where its individuality is ultimately rooted. Then what the I professes is one thing and what it is is another; the meditation on the Three Classes serves to counter this split. This meditation is also the moment of truth—and sometimes a kind of agony—for the disciple who, in fact, has not yet followed the Lord...except on the level of representation.

In Freedom's image, no such split exists between representation (what it professes) and being (what it is); Freedom's image both is and carries out what it represents. In this sense, the meditation on the Three Classes of Men is connected with the logic of true Freedom: the latter would not know how to accept the cheating of the freedom it is summoning and calling forth.

This meditation proposes for our reflection three classes of men, each of whom has a different position regarding a good acquired "not entirely as they should have, for the love of God" [150]. But throughout this parable, it is a question of our taking a position, according to the teaching of the Two Standards, in relation to true Freedom's ideal as it should govern our subjective attitude regarding every good.

The First Class

"They would like to rid themselves of the attachment they

have to the sum acquired in order to find peace in God our Lord and assure their salvation, but the hour of death comes, and they have not made use of any means" [153].

The ideal of true Freedom remains a representation; and the I does not cross the distance dividing them. The I professes true opinions, but it does not actually subscribe to them, and its behavior proves they have no content. The objective unfolding of Freedom will not succeed in counterbalancing its burden of past sin. Contemplating as many evangelical mysteries as one would like will be secretly sterilized by a nonadherence. The I will never be in condition to posit itself in the manner of true Freedom.

The Second Class

"They want to rid themselves of the attachment, but they wish to do so in such a way that they retain what they have acquired, so that God is to come to what they desire, and they do not decide to give up the sum of money in order to go to God, though this would be the better way for them" [154].

For these men, the ideal of true Freedom is a representation they want to adhere to. This representation designates reality for them, and they have a clear understanding of how to treat it as such. Their freedom will aim at becoming equal to this ideal and, consequently, there is a sense in which they are ahead of the first class.

But their progress is all on the surface, and it runs the risk of hiding a situation even worse than the first group. Their good intentions are, in fact, secretly and subtly perverted by an unacknowledged attachment to self...to non-being. Indeed, the means for actualizing the ideal are not willed without ulterior motive. Instead of energetically matching true Freedom, their subjective freedom wants true Freedom to adjust to it: "so that God is to come to what they desire"! It is the worst of perversions, under the guise of good and good intentions—the case of all those who use the finest-sounding words to hide an underlying scheme of self-will and attachment to self.

The Third Class

"These want to rid themselves of the attachment, but they wish to do so in such a way that they desire neither to retain nor to relinquish the sum acquired..." [155].

Here there is not the least reservation in affirming the image of Freedom as my own ideal. By choosing Freedom's own means, I carry out what it portrays to me.

For going beyond the representation (see the Note at the end of the First Week), this meditation on the Three Classes of Men is basic. Transcending the representation calls for the meditation of profound affectivity and, later on, for freedom's decision (the Choice). It is not merely a question of evolution by which an initially defective knowing becomes adequate by emerging from forms of representation. Knowing has been adequate since the Two Standards.

From the viewpoint of knowledge, the Two Standards meditation covers all the evangelical mysteries of the Second Week, sketching their exact content and meaning. Within the realm of representational knowledge, the Two Standards is the entire Second Week; but within the realm of actual reality it is still nothing, if the I holds onto representational knowing. If the Two Standards is the *intellectual* focus of the Second Week, the Three Classes of Men constitutes the hub, the pivotal grace, by which the decisive movement towards the Choice and existential entry into true Freedom become *operative*. It is a crucial moment in which the mystery of the Third Week makes its proximity felt. St. Ignatius certainly felt it, for he proposes here the most solemn composition of place, the heavenly court; we will not come upon this setting again, except for the Contemplation to Attain the Love of God.

In the book of the *Exercises*, the meditation on the Three Classes of Men closes with the following note: "It should be noted that when we feel an attachment opposed to actual poverty or a repugnance to it, when we are not indifferent to poverty and riches, it will be very helpful in order to overcome the inordinate attachment, even though corrupt nature rebel against it, to beg our Lord in the colloquies to choose us to serve Him in actual poverty. We should insist that we desire it, beg for it, plead for it, provided, of course, that it be for the service and praise of the Divine Goodness" [157.]

Fessard comments on this note in a passage which we will simply quote:

> However great and however sincere its desire of matching Freedom's ideal may be, the I cannot help but feel at the same moment the weight of non-being that continues to hold it back and even to draw it in the opposite direction, preventing the choice of the better. The fruit of sin, attachment to the world, to its riches as to its power, can be conquered in principle, but

detachment is not yet actually attained. In the presence of the possible actuality of this stripping, freedom continues to experience a felt repugnance: "we feel an attachment opposed to actual poverty or a repugnance to it." At this farthest point of the Before, where the I ought to determine itself with all possible purity, there remains only one way "to overcome the inordinate attachment" and attain this "indifference" which will render it sensitive to the slightest motion of Freedom, "like a balance at equilibrium" [179]. Namely, the I must somehow *pre*-judge Freedom's choice, as if it *must be against* this felt repugnance, as if the choice had *already* transformed a merely possible actuality into a real actuality: "to beg our Lord in the colloquies to choose us to serve Him in actual poverty."

The affective detachment, which the meditation on the Three Classes has already brought to perfection, through this note thus finds itself posited at the point of being more-than-perfect. Not content with tending towards the limit of the Before in order to counterbalance the entire weight of non-being, the I proceeds further on its own, going beyond this limit in the direction of the After, anticipating the exclusion and rejection of non-being in a definitively dead past. Only one thing keeps the I from actually going from the Before to the After: It is still ignorant of Freedom's final determination, which alone can actualize its choice of the better. Hence the I is reserved in the presence of the end that it presently awaits: "provided, of course, that it be for the service and praise of the Divine Goodness."[27]

The Evangelical Mysteries

The three fundamental meditations of the Second Week (Kingdom, Two Standards, Three Classes) constitute the structure of this second moment in which the I learns to recognize its freedom as a summons to the totality of Being; then as a struggle against non-being with an eye to arriving at that totality; finally, as a need for actual and radical detachment. The evangelical mysteries accompany this outline in order to fill it with an appropriate content.[28]

Right at the outset, following the Kingdom and while this summons to the totality of Being could give birth to an enthusiasm not devoid of illusion in the disciple's heart, the *Exercises*

27 *Dialectique*, I, 62-63.
28 We are here following Fessard's text, ibid., pp. 63-64, very closely, sometimes even literally.

propose the mysteries of our Lord's birth and hidden life [101-134]. The humble appearances of the Annunciation, Visitation, Nativity, Circumcision, Magi, Purification and Presentation, Flight and Return from Egypt, Life at Nazareth [262-271] stand in opposition to the grandiose dreams which the call of the Kingdom could give rise to. This set of contemplations ends with Jesus going up to the temple at the age of twelve [272]. Here this adolescent appears capable of disregarding the dearest affections for the sake of serving his Father: a precedent which foretells the affective detachment in which the Second Week is to culminate (Three Classes).

After the Two Standards and Three Classes have accurately defined this end point, the I encounters the mysteries of Christ's public life [158-162]. Jesus' Baptism [273] shows the way open before the I. The Temptation in the desert [274], with the enemy's threefold summons to the senses ("command these stones to become loaves of bread") to the will for power (the devil "showed him all the kingdoms of the world and the glory of them; and he said to him, "All these I will give you..." "); and to spiritual pride ("If you are the Son of God, throw yourself down...") illustrate the problem posed to freedom in the Two Standards. Finally, the Vocation of the Apostles [275] renews and concretizes the Eternal King's initial call.

And as the I is henceforth no longer ignorant to what extent it must deny itself in its profound affectivity, the I finds the requisite illumination and support for its own decision in mysteries presenting various aspects of Christ's activity: *teachings*, setting forth the charter of perfect Freedom (Sermon on the Mount, [278]); *miracles* on behalf of bodies and souls, which furnish reasons for believing in him who provides these signs prefiguring the kingdom to be established (Marriage at Cana, [276]; Conversion of Magdalene, [282]; Calming the Storm, [279]; Feeding the Five Thousand, [283]; Raising of Lazarus, [285]; Transfiguration, [284]); finally, *decisions* which manifest the worldly forces opposed to incarnate Freedom's growth, and which teach the disciple what kind of responsibility this Freedom must assume in order to overcome them (Casting the Sellers from the Temple [277]; Sending of the Disciples, [281]; Supper at Bethany, [286]; Palm Sunday, [287]).

Contemplating the content of these mysteries in light of the three fundamental meditations, the I evaluates its own interior motions according to the Rules for the Discernment of Spirits.[29]

29 See chapter 10.

The I thus attains the end proper to this second moment: preparing itself for the Choice which will cause it to pass from Before (contemplating what is represented to it) to After (adhering to the mystery become present).

In order to put the finishing touches on this preparation and, at the same time, to serve as a backdrop for all the procedures of the Choice, St. Ignatius proposes a final exercise to the retreatant: "In order that we may be filled with love of the true doctrine of Christ our Lord, it will be very useful to consider attentively the following Three Kinds of Humility" [164].

Three Kinds of Humility

These three degrees of humility summarize the entire process beginning with the Principle and Foundation up to the culmination of the Second Week, the Three Classes of Men.

The *first kind* of humility consists in this: "As far as possible I so subject and humble myself as to obey the law of God our Lord in all things, so that not even were I made lord of all creation, or to save my life here on earth, would I *enter into deliberation*[30] about violating a commandment, whether divine or human, that binds me under pain of mortal sin" [165].

This first kind of humility remains within the relationship of obedience (the servant to his Lord) and it does not yet arrive at the relationship of love which creates equality. Nevertheless, within these limits, it goes to the utmost, excluding any possibility of deliberation: "I would not enter into deliberation." The first kind of humility thus goes beyond a certain conception of freedom which appeared in our initial analyses, before the conversion of the First Week: freedom as a choice between good and evil. Freedom originated in history with the formation of a problematic of the free act in terms of a choice between good and evil, and it was evil that had been fatally chosen (original sin). The divine forgiveness and repentance of the First Week have cleansed us of this evil. From now on, at the first degree of humility (which is also the first degree of freedom), I no longer juxtapose good and evil: "I

---

30 [Translator's Note. We are following Pousset's acceptance of the traditional translation of the Spanish "sea en *deliberar* de quebrantar" because his following paragraphs demand it. Puhl notes on p. 183 of his translation that Ignatius' use of *deliberar* means simply to choose, decide, consent, and not to "weigh reasons for and against" something. See Puhl's note for further references on this point.]

would not, at any price, enter into deliberation about violating a commandment which binds me under pain of mortal sin.''

The *second kind* of humility has the same dispositions as the first kind, but even regarding the least venial sin: "I neither desire nor am I inclined to have riches rather than poverty, to seek honor rather than dishonor, to desire a long life rather than a short life, provided only in either alternative I would promote equally the service of God our Lord and the salvation of my soul. Besides this indifference, this second kind of humility supposes that not for all creation, nor to save my life, would I enter into deliberation[31] about committing a venial sin" [166].

These are the dispositions mentioned in the Principle and Foundation: the indifference needed to begin deliberating for the Choice. But whereas the Principle and Foundation proposed these dispositions for my reflection, without my actually possessing them, they are now, at the end point of the second moment, acquired actual attitudes: "I would not enter into deliberation about committing a venial sin."

The *third kind* of humility "implies the I's wish for a total and irrational conformity to the image of Freedom."[32] It is the folly of love concerning what is for me no longer merely a representational image, but a Presence. "This is the most perfect kind of humility. It consists in this. If we suppose the first and second kind attained, then whenever the praise and glory of the Divine Majesty would be equally served, in order to imitate and be in reality more like Christ our Lord, I desire and choose poverty with Christ poor, rather than riches; insults with Christ loaded with them, rather than honors; I desire to be accounted as worthless and a fool for Christ, rather than to be esteemed as wise and prudent in this world. So Christ was treated before me" [167].

In relation to the I's project of becoming itself by itself, especially its one-sided way of understanding this ideal (characteristic of the sinner), the Two Standards—poverty regarding things, bearing insults from persons —represents an utter turnabout. The positing of oneself by oneself is, in fact, positing of oneself by stripping and not by possession, by openness and consent to Another and not by self-affirmation and self-sufficiency. This upheaval entails an element of the "irrational" which is the suprarationality of true love bursting forth in this third degree of humility. The

31 See the preceding note.
32 *Dialectique*, I, 65.

paradox of love will cast its fire on the deliberation for the Choice.

The irrationality of love is diametrically opposed to the irrationality of sin (and undoubtedly the latter could not be except for the former). When we lock freedom's ideal into positing oneself by oneself, we cannot avoid being preoccupied with the burden of unilaterally affirming ourselves. One-sided self-affirmation is overwhelming to human existence, and the severe ambiguities contained in this ideal of freedom are supported by contemporary philosophy.

The only way of living out this ideal of freedom and of keeping pace with contemporary philosophy, without renouncing the faith, is to acknowledge that freedom's destiny is played on the level of folly, the folly of love. Only within the domain of love which seeks to be identified with the beloved simply for the sake of identity itself does the relationship to another who is more myself than I am become sufficiently transparent and internal for this other to be in fact more myself than I am. Consequently, when my freedom is posited through the other in this kind of love, it is positing itself by itself. Short of this conformity, this compenetration by love, accepting Another at the root of my "I" and of my free act stays in the realm of a still outward obedience. It remains a domination/servitude relationship in which the ideal of positing oneself by oneself is, in fact, sacrificed and repressed by this obedience and hence liable to engender resentment. In any case, those who stay bound up with a one-sided understanding of this ideal reject obedience to another, and they do not recognize in obedience the very ideal of freedom. For, in fact, this ideal is not in their obedience unless the obedience is love to the point of folly.

The transition from Before to After is thus made ready by a "consideration" which, on one hand, gathers together all that went before (the first and second kinds of humility) and, on the other hand, anticipates what is about to follow (the third kind of humility). As a result, this consideration draws subjective freedom to its own limit in order to make it long for, and literally have a presentiment of, the transcending of its condition in the Before where its non-being has not yet been negated, except through an indeterminate project of Being. However, subjective freedom is not allowed to prejudge the concrete form of this transcending nor the real determinations of the project. This consideration thus arranges for the actual intervention of Freedom, which will render the I objectively free in its decision. And at the same time, by the way in which attending to this consideration stimulates the senses and summons the understanding to grasp what is going to take place, this consideration disposes the I to take immediate advantage of it in the After. That is the ultimate goal of the Three Kinds of Humility.[33]

The third degree of humility is already a sharing in Christ's passion through love. But the passion is present here only by way of anticipation: inclination towards, yearning, "if such were *now* the will" of Freedom for me. The choice will be preoccupied with Freedom's will for me, and it will take place in light of the third degree of humility. Whatever decision is made, it will involve some degree of loving participation in Christ's passion. That the most reasonable deliberation is carried out in light of such folly is fraught with significance: the paradox of the Christian mystery!

Note on the Application of the Senses

The beginning of the spiritual life coalesces with the course of man's existence in the world, and it is marked by a certain inner division, which has been hardened by sin. This division is a lived experience, rather than something native to man. It would not be impossible to show that the life of consciousness flows from a primordial unity. A human being feels divided in his relationships to the world, to others, and to himself only because he is basically *one*. This unity, however, must be promoted; it is not simply given, but it must be found by being fostered.

It is amidst his relationships to other persons (like the baby and its mother) that man awakens to a consciousness of the world. These human relationships remain constitutive of the person he is even when, in the development of his consciousness, he becomes occupied with perceiving things. Man's origin in human relationships is equivalent to his being radically constituted in a unity; and it is this oneness which enables him to progress towards greater coherence with himself and the world in a growing union of his body and spirit. Within a world of mere objects, without the presence of another person, a human consciousness would undoubtedly be restricted to what it perceived and there be frittered away.

Recognizing persons and perceiving things within *one* world presupposes an ability to step back from the reality in which I find myself and to step back from myself. That is, it presupposes an ability to negate reality and myself. *To negate* here does not mean

33 Ibid.

"to abolish," but to function so that reality is not something in which I am absorbed or ensnared, without that minimal distance which is the condition for being present to another and for knowing things.

This power to step back and negate, which belongs to consciousness and whose exercise constitutes consciousness, stems from the freedom of consciousness, a freedom which itself is rooted in a basic *desire*. Man, in fact, is universal and infinite desire—that is, a subject who is both present and absent to all that is. This presence/absence is the condition for desire: I would not be desirous unless what I desired were somehow already in me; but I would no longer desire it (I would be possessing and enjoying it) if it were actually in me.

A human being's desire shows the extent of his power, but it also measures his essential inner void. His unlimited power turns him towards the real, which he can always transcend towards more reality; his emptiness cannot be filled by any finite being, and as it accompanies him in all his undertakings, it sometimes tempts him to escape through the production of imaginary objects and even worlds. What do we mean by imaginary objects and worlds? And what is the imagination?

The imagination is born along with man's power to step back from the real and to negate it. But the imagination does not manufacture what is merely unreal. The imagination grafts itself onto sensory perceptions which it elaborates or transforms, and which it relates to thought. If we were nothing but bodily senses, we would be immersed in sensuous reality. If we were nothing but an abstract thinking activity, we would not be in touch with things or with persons, and our power of becoming every reality would exhaust itself in intellectual abstractions. The senses perceive concrete things, but in their particularity; thought conceives the universal, but in the abstract. The imagination exercises a mediating function between the two.[34]

The imagination produces schemata which highlight the structures of things and onto which conceptual thought grafts itself. The role of the imagination in this production is not so much to foster comprehension by furnishing thought with a support or

---

34 These brief remarks cannot take the place of a more subtle and developed analysis which would try to present our various faculties (intellect, will, imagination, bodily senses) as deriving from a single source. Such a primordial unity is presupposed by what we have just said and are about to say.

"concrete example" as it is to *make present* what thought conceives in an abstract, universal way. The imagination makes something present.

Unlike the perceived object, the imagined object has a rather considerable poverty; it does not have the lively colors of the former nor its wealth of concrete details. And we would break our heads trying to produce an imagined object which has the profusion of different qualities characteristic of each perceived object. We will have to bear this in mind.

The imagination does not merely fashion images for visualizing by a kind of inward look; the imagination is not simply a looking, but a sensing in all its forms. The imagination hears, touches, smells, and tastes in varying degrees, depending on the aptitudes proper to different individuals. It is by producing all sorts of images that man's power to step back and "negate" the real is exercised. But the imagination can go to the point of breaking away from the data of reality, transforming its schemata, and creating something new which no longer has any correspondence with the data.

The imagination, which plays a major role in the act of understanding by presenting to thought what must be understood, plays an equally important and even principal role in the act of creating. It may be the creation of a work of art, a new life-style, the conditions for a decision, or simply creating favorable circumstances for the unfolding of daily life. Without the imagination, thought is blind and impotent. And without imagination, sensuous reality "says nothing important" to the man who must reflect on his activity and decide in function of momentary data. Men of action, creative people in the arts or sciences, the saints—are all endowed with a powerful imagination. Therefore, we need not be surprised that the imagination plays a major role in the Exercises of St. Ignatius.

But this creative power is liable to degenerate and go astray in a proliferation of sterile fantasies. The individual overly affected by his inner void is tempted to escape in daydreams and to provide himself with imaginary satisfactions which alleviate, or at least compensate for, frustrations imposed on him by a reality "too hard to bear." Man's imagination can be a creative power turned towards the real, or it can be a way of escaping; it thus becomes a terrain on which some of freedom's most decisive battles are fought.

The affective life, which stems from man's very depths as his desire of becoming every reality, is unceasingly fed by sensory perceptions and by the imagination. It "circulates" between the senses and the imagination; it unfolds, is transformed, and is continually re-created under their influence and under the control (at least the moralists so advise) of reason. In the man who suffers from dissociations implanted in him by sin, his affective life can be ensnared in the senses (leading downwards) for want of a sufficient regulation by reason. In this case especially, the ever-creative imagination will beget and cultivate what are suitably called "disorderly passions." On the other hand, his affective life can escape into the abstractions of pure thought and become alienated in a totally cerebral intellectualism (being absorbed upwards). But a conversion going through the imagination manages to reverse these divisive inclinations and to establish a harmonious relationship within the converted sinner, from his senses up to his thinking and willing intellect. And this unifying relationship will go on becoming stronger until it comes to fruition in a spiritual existence within the bodily condition, a true anticipation of the resurrection. We can attain a *spiritual body* even now, as we will explain.

We have only too much experience of a certain division within ourselves.[35] In this situation we find ourselves with universal and abstract notions whose derivation we are hardly aware of, with images fashioned by an ever-active imagination, and with an infinity of sensory perceptions which result from our existence in the world. And these three activities/passivities of our thinking intellect, our imagination, and our senses lack coordination at the very least.

The Spiritual Exercises begin by accepting the retreatant in this state of inner division. They speak to his understanding by proposing revealed ideas (on creation, sin . . .) to him; they appeal to his imagination by presenting him with gospel "scenes" (although the Exercises employ the term *mysteries,* the word *scenes* undoubtedly corresponds better to the retreatant's initially rather external vision); and they even invoke his senses by suggesting he take advantage of his environment (the daylight, the darkness of a room with shutters closed. . .).

But from the outset these two extremes—my body, endowed with senses in a world which is its world; and my thinking and willing intellect, which appropriates the lofty ideas of salvation—are required to grow together, while waiting to be united in the

35 We recall that we do not consider this situation as intrinsic to man.

incipient *spiritual body* which we will here designate as the ensemble of the *spiritual senses*. (This latter term will be defined shortly.) This conjunction of body and intellect begins functioning by way of the imagination, which I am invited to use in my prayer. The imagination offers my awareness the content of the biblical or gospel "scenes" which present the events of salvation to me; and by resting in the poor and simple images of the imagination, I prolong this presence which I "taste interiorly."

This joining of the sensuous with the intelligible begins with the exercises for the first day of the First Week. The first and second exercises are largely intellectual, but the third and fourth ask that we "dwell upon those points in which we have experienced greater consolation or desolation or greater spiritual appreciation" [62].

The application of the senses to hell exercises the imagination by deriving from sense experience certain data which it enriches with symbols belonging to the language of faith: fire and the "weeping and gnashing of teeth" (to which the "wailing, the howling, cries, and blasphemies" in the second point of this exercise seem to refer). All this is done in order to make present to the retreatant who has reflected on sin the reality which sin engenders. Thus a unity of the sensuous and the intelligible is begun; its immediate fruit is conversion, and its further development will be the life of the new man reconciled with God, with the world, and with himself, in a body permeated by spirit.

It is within this perspective of a conjunction of faculties (intellect, will, imagination, and sensation) and of a unification of the new man, prelude of the resurrection, that we must comprehend and practice the application of the senses. Sin dissociates our faculties and confines each of them within its own self-satisfying activity. Thus the senses fill themselves with their own sensations, ensnaring us in sensuous reality. The imagination pursues its dreams (the connivance of the senses and imagination producing the *delectatio morosa* of the carnal man dragged "downwards"). As for the understanding, it sometimes becomes hardened and isolated in its own knowing. Consequently, it is a matter of breaking the circle of malicious enjoyment, or of a self-sufficient knowing, by an appropriate negating effort and then reestablishing the union of our faculties to serve the new man.

Thus the application of the senses to hell proposes images which evoke sensuous experiences diametrically opposed to the delight of the man given to malicious enjoyment. The contradiction will form the pivot about which the sinful man's "downward" inclinations will right themselves in an "upward" direction. Thanks to this corrective, the faculties will gradually arrive at their harmonious exercise under the auspices of reason (understanding and will), which is the faculty of the universal. The particular data from the senses will furnish their content to the universal concept of reason, while conversely, this universal will become embodied in the sensuous particular, their mutual exchange passing by way of the imagination. In this way our affective and intellectual life will go on unifying and simplifying itself until it becomes the life of a spiritual body, for which the concrete sensuous becomes spirit's flesh and the abstract universal becomes enfleshed spirit.

If we have not situated faith in this analysis, it is because faith does not play a particular role alongside our faculties; it permeates and animates all of them. The presence of faith becomes especially felt in the progressive stripping which is going to affect our sensations, images, and ideas. The process of stripping away begins with the first exercises.

The application of the senses which leads toward this unification and simplification of the new man becoming a "spiritual body" is a genuinely difficult exercise entailing some risks. First of all, it can give way to a misconception which must be avoided. It is not an exercise on the level of the five bodily senses, but rather on the level of the imagination differentiating itself after the manner of the five senses. When Ignatius alludes to the "vast fires,...the wailing, the howling,...the smoke, the sulphur..." he is not providing any sensory data, nor is he advising that retreatants provide such data for themselves. The mistake here could consist in confusing sensuous reality (of which there can be no question, since I am in my room and not in hell) with imaginary[36] reality, which is at issue. Anyone who becomes confused here would get involved in an artificial and even false exercise which would rack his brains. He would be struggling to provide himself with lively sensations, when it was suggested that he make use of images which can only be very poor and rather drab (we recall the remark made above about the poverty of representations furnished by the imagination). Moreover, as we will claim, this poverty is a necessary condition and sign of the truth of spiritual experience.

Consequently, it is not a matter of sensory data but of images. Another error, however, is possible. The imagination is a mediating and creative power which fashions simple and powerful images

---

36 *Imaginary* here includes what we will discriminate as "imaginary" and "symbolic."

aimed at sensuous, human, and hence social reality. These images combine the sensuous with the intelligible, that is, they unite man with himself, with nature, and with God. But the imagination always runs the risk of degenerating and proliferating images in a more or less anarchic, fanciful, and sterile manner. In the latter case, we are dealing with the imaginary (in the pejorative sense) and in the former, with the symbolic. When the imaginary proliferates, it is because the fantasizing individual is alone with himself, as before a mirror. He is experiencing his own interior emptiness, sometimes to the point of aberration, and he is seeking to fill it by an unending production of unreal objects. When something symbolic is uttered, it is because the individual, by the very act of producing the symbol, attains union with his fellow man within a community constituted precisely by the symbolic word. Thus the adolescent reaching puberty who daydreams by chasing more or less erotic images is within the realm of the imaginary. Whereas the man and woman who say "yes" to each other in marriage together establish themselves within a community by the symbolic word—and act—which they exchange.

When we liken the imagination to a more or less fanciful activity, we are really thinking of only one possible form of this activity; we forget the symbolic. The symbolizing function of the imagination is not at all fanciful, even if some fantasy is mixed in. The symbolizing function of the imagination is an act of social man, and it therefore constitutes and expresses the fundamental relationship on which human and religious communities are built. As such, the imagination is not at all the arbitrary function that rationalistic reason suspects. But it is indeed true that the imaginary can interfere with the symbolic and stifle it, for symbols do borrow their material from the flow produced by the imagination. It is a special exercise of spontaneous or reflective reason which discerns the symbolic element in the midst of what is merely imaginary. In generating great religious and social symbolisms (forming religions, founding familial and political human communities), this process of discernment is unconscious and entirely immanent. If it should stop or get out of kilter within a religious or human community, it spells decline and decadence for that society, which disintegrates into the imaginary (for example, the religion of ancient Rome). Within a secondary social or religious activity, such as philosophy (which emerged from reflection on myths and symbols), or the elaboration of a juridical code, prayer, and so on, critical reason must intervene explicitly, sorting out the symbolic and the everrenascent imaginary element. It opts resolutely in favor of the symbolic, which fosters reason, action, and communion; whereas the imaginary is an escape and an empty affirmation of subjectivity running after itself, sometimes to the point of frenzy.

This discernment must take place in the application of the senses, or else the imaginary is in danger of overcoming the symbolic.[37] This would be a fatal error! As a matter of fact, Ignatius' allusions—the vast fires, howling, sulphur, and so on—run the risk of stirring up mere imagination in the retreatant who is inexperienced and still engulfed in his senses, whereas they should rather be directed towards the *whole* man (body and soul) contemplating the symbols which revelation uses to present ultimate reality to us: the kingdom of God, or here its contrary, hell. In order to make hell present, revelation resorts to symbols of fire, "weeping and gnashing of teeth," the "worm of conscience"; these are strong images which simultaneously (must) remain very simple as to their representational content.

Symbolic images are not intended to fill up our inner void, as fanciful imagination seeks to do, but rather they serve to make reality present to the man of desire. This reality can become mine only if I renounce the entire phenomenal or sensuous realm and agree to rest in a void that will even go on hollowing itself out, but which will be receiving that Presence which cannot be reduced to its own symbols. We will explain this shortly.

In the case of the application of the senses to hell, the reality is rather the converse of reality, the non-sense of sin. It is this non-sense which the images make present to me, and the exercise consists in letting myself be permeated by this proximity of non-sense. If non-sense has been experienced in my flesh, so to speak, it cannot but bring about the reversal which is the beginning of my conversion—a reversal which is not merely thought or willed, but actually inscribed in my being which, for the moment, is more flesh than spirit. The patience (if it were a question of the application of the senses during the Second Week, we would speak of *repose*) for enduring this weight of felt non-sense is a form of prayer which is very simple and, for this reason, very elevated. It is not

---

37 Of course, this discernment is not merely the business of critical reflection; it is rooted in the bearing of the whole person towards reality. It presupposes a certain conversion which frees us from disordered passions, from self-will, from illusion—in short, from everything that would divert us from reality and attach us to unfounded daydreams. Would not the principal obstacle to the exercise of the application of the senses be an insufficient conversion to the will of God, that is, to reality?

within our reach; we can gently dispose ourselves for it by having a try at applying the imaginative senses without forcing it, and especially without attempting to compensate for the lack of presence by vain imaginary outputs. As a matter of fact, the inner unification of the whole person must already be quite advanced in order for the symbols to make the reality they represent somewhat present at the heart of the person's corporeal-spiritual being.

Thus we see that, even in the First Week, the application of the senses activates the inner unification of the repentant sinner. This exercise simultaneously aims at the sinner's integration and presupposes it; it brings about his unification while being the body in which the harmonization takes place (= manifests itself).

If the application of the senses has this unifying role, we can understand why Ignatius placed it at the end of the day: (1) when the retreatant, through reflection and more intellectual contemplation, has already become quite familiar with the subject matter of the exercise, for then the imagination will more easily be able to make the material present deep within him by way of simple and impoverished symbols; (2) when the evening is inviting him to relaxation and repose, the very medium in which this exercise of unifying the self with itself and with reality ought to unfold.

The application of the senses during the Second Week takes place, as in the First Week, at the end of the day. When the retreatant has become familiar with the "mysteries" by contemplating and assimilating their message, he pauses to gather the fruit of his effort. The conversion of the First Week has laid the foundations of a reconciliation of the whole person (body and soul) with himself, with the world, and with God. Even in the First Week this exercise was an initial step in reconciliation: I patiently let reality penetrate all the way to my core, by way of the symbols that portrayed it to me. In the Second Week this inner reconciliation goes on, thanks to the presence of the *image* of the invisible God, Jesus Christ our Lord. This image is the basic symbol around which all the other symbols contained in historical revelation revolve, from which they radiate, and to which they return. The Gospels and the entire Bible are woven with these symbols: the particular representations suggested to us by the persons, by the words they exchange, and by images of all kinds that contribute to our perceiving what they are and what the kingdom of God is to which they belong. By allowing these symbols to reach him through his imagination, the converted sinner dies to his inner divisions; he is strengthened in the unity of his flesh and spirit; he is simplified, and thus he is already advancing towards the resurrection: towards being a spiritual body, a body animated by senses which have become spiritual—that is, which perceive not merely the intelligible dimension proper to the sensuous world, but which perceive the very reality of the kingdom of God.

Of course, the application of the senses can be sustained with the help of particular images which the praying retreatant fashions on his own, for example, imagining the behavior of the persons, the conversation they are considered to carry on, and so forth. But this activity runs the risk of going astray into the imaginary (daydreaming, the interior and whimsical "movie theater"), where all prayer would dissolve while faith becomes attached to some representations, rather than to God. The retreatant must take advantage of Ignatius' sober suggestions and realize that biblical symbols, as found in the scriptural texts, are the privileged, and ultimately the only authentic, subject matter for the contemplative imagination. More generally, it is helpful to recall that the objects of the imagination, even in the natural order, are quite poor in comparison with the objects directly perceived in the sensuous world, and that it is not necessary to try to compensate for this poverty. For it puts us on the track of the essential poverty which governs the birth, growth, and existence of the Son of man up to his death.

The images which make present to us the realities of the kingdom of God revealed in Jesus Christ are already poor in themselves, but they must undergo in us the same gradual stripping which marks the earthly existence of the *image* of the invisible God. From the crib to the cross, the existence of Jesus Christ is a growing self-renunciation all the way up to the absolute denuding in death which reveals him to the eyes of the believer as the Son of God equal to the Father (the truth of the image). Likewise, the images produced by the praying person's imagination must gradually grow poorer and more simple until, as a result of grace, they disappear in the interior silence and night which place the person in immediate contact with the reality of God and his kingdom. Is it not, in fact, a question of seeing God whom no man can see without dying, of hearing those "words which man is not permitted to repeat," and of perceiving "the infinite fragrance and sweetness of the divinity" which surpass all perception? Consequently, the production of symbols which are already so sober and simple in Scripture must, in one and the same movement, be their negation—even to the *imperceptible perception* of Presence.

This negating is obviously not a simple psychological operation (the ascetic practice of suspending the course of our thoughts, and of remaining recollected without the support of any image). It is essentially the fact of the conversion of the whole person, which continues to be deepened by the Choice and what follows. Hence this negating process is the movement of a freedom becoming converted, deciding, and giving itself by dying to itself, with the hope of rising in Jesus Christ. The gradual extinction of images in the praying consciousness is only one consequence of this movement. Therefore, this negation of images is not accomplished solely within the context of the Second Week; it is rather the (often delayed) fruit of a spiritual existence lived out in the rhythm of the four Weeks, that is, of the entire Christian mystery.

The imperceptible perception of Presence can affect a person, in the restored unity of his body and soul, by way of a touching, a smelling, or a tasting, according to various temperaments. It would be rather useless to analyze the experience by trying to discern what was owing to each of the five spiritual senses. Is it a seeing? But it's night! A hearing? But all is silence! Smelling, tasting, touching? Yes, perhaps and more probably, for these three senses are all blind and deaf. Tasting ("to taste the infinite sweetness of the divinity"), which no longer has anything sensuous in this simplifying utter negation, would be like a fusion of the creature in its Creator. Touching, on the contrary, would maintain a kind of externality between them, which some would find more suitable for the absolute difference between the creature and the "Divine Majesty." But these various nuances do not prevent one from saying—at least after the event, when the person recalls it—that there is an extreme simplicity to this imperceptible perception onto which the application of the senses will one day open.

Meister Eckhart writes:

> Here now speaks the bride [that is, the soul] in the Canticles: "I have traversed all mountains and the capacities of my being, and have reached the dark power of the Father." Observe now what she means when she says that she has traversed all mountains. She means thereby a transcending of all reasoning which she can achieve by her own power, and that she has reached the dark power of the Father, where all reason finds its end. Then I heard without sound, saw without light, smelt where nothing wafted, tasted what was not there, received what had disappeared. After this my heart became an abyss, my soul

knew no more love, my spirit was formless, my nature lost its being.... To hear without sound is an interior perception, when one experiences the First Cause, where all reasoning has its end. To see without light is a naked and dark perceiving in the midst of nothing. Then I smelt where nothing wafted: that is, I received the impression of that oneness in which all things are at rest. I tasted what was not there: that is, the tranquil, dark oneness hovers above all sensation. And I received what had disappeared: I sensed the mystery of that Being which, while remaining unalloyed by all creatures, dwells in all beings. After this my heart became an abyss: that is to say, the wonder at all wonders exceeded all my capacities. And my soul knew no more love: that is, I was robbed of all my strength and all my senses. And my spirit became formless: that is, the compressing of my spirit into the unformed form and image which is God.[38]

The simplicity of the imperceptible perception borders on the simplicity of God, and it is that simplicity which ends by unifying man in himself, and which has him taste, in this world, something of the joy of the Resurrection. Body and soul are one, and from now on there is no more journey. Prayer no longer follows a method; it merges with love itself which goes, comes, rests or leaps, works or sleeps, suffers and rejoices, parts company with itself to go wherever a sin is committed and becomes reunited with itself by embracing the world.

A result of God's presence in us—who brings forth faith, hope, and charity—the spiritual senses allow the disciple to see, hear, and perceive, in the things of this world, the humble Jesus of Nazareth, Lord of glory, Creator of heaven and earth.

Jerónimo Nadal, the companion of St. Ignatius, writes: "The spiritual senses are the effect of the three theological virtues. From constancy of faith comes the power to hear. From insight into faith comes the power of vision. From hope comes the power to smell. From union in love comes the power to touch. From the enjoyment of love comes the power to taste. This activation of the spiritual senses helps us receive ever greater graces. The helps of grace which Jesus Christ our Lord gives to those whom he loves. He who possesses them will know what this means."[39]

38 Text cited by Hugo Rahner, S.J., *Ignatius the Theologian*, trans. Michael Barry (New York: Herder and Herder, 1968), ch. 5, "The Application of the Senses," pp. 202-203. This essay by Rahner also drew our attention to the next two texts we will cite.
39 *Monumenta Nadal*, IV (Madrid, 1905), pp. 677-678, as cited by Rahner, p. 205.

St. Augustine alluded to this knowledge of God through the spiritual senses when he wrote:

But what do I love when I love my God? Not material beauty or beauty of a temporal order; not the brilliance of earthly light, so welcome to our eyes; not the sweet melody of harmony and song; not the fragrance of flowers, perfumes, and spices; not manna or honey; not limbs such as the body delights to embrace. It is not these that I love when I love my God. And yet, when I love him, it is true that I love a light of a certain kind, a voice, a perfume, a food, an embrace; but they are of the kind that I love in my inner self, when my soul is bathed in light that is not bound by space; when it listens to sound that never dies away; when it breathes fragrance that is not borne away on the wind; when it tastes food that is never consumed by the eating; when it clings to an embrace from which it is not severed by fulfilment of desire. This is what I love when I love my God.[40]

Practically speaking . . .

How can we begin applying our senses in prayer? More precisely, how can we distinguish between the imaginary and the symbolic, when all our senses have been alerted? How can we perceive whether our prayer, after having begun with the symbols of Scripture, is not creeping towards the imaginary? The mere worry of keeping oneself from "flights of fancy" can compromise the relaxed atmosphere needed for this exercise and paralyze one's prayer. Therefore, one point is essential: not to have too much concern, or be too preoccupied with discerning. It is enough to have a global preference for the images and words of Scripture, and a certain restraint, if one is imaginative. And what does it matter if we most often remain halfway between the imaginary and the symbolic? The key point is to gently strive for a simple prayer which is nourished by a meditative word in the Scriptures, and which is content with an image unifying the attention, without letting it drift and yet without constraining it either. To gently strive for this simplicity and . . . to give oneself some time. In general, a person cannot succeed quickly in this exercise, for the simple reason that a person does not achieve simplicity quickly, and because the unity of a living person is a work of patience, a gift of the Spirit.

40 *Confessions*, X, 6, 8, trans. R. S. Pine-Coffin (Baltimore, Md.: Penguin Books, 1961), pp. 211-212.

The best criterion for judging whether this exercise has succeeded, whatever percentage of imaginary and symbolic elements are necessarily mixed together, is serenity: the tranquillity of sensuousness, a feeling of interior freedom which issues from the docility of the flesh to the Spirit, and which creates this peace of the faculties all ordered to their end in the harmony willed by the Creator.

Whoever wends his way thus, yielding and letting this peace come to him, will receive in silence and almost imperceptible joy greater graces which are less felt.

Chapter 6

THE CHOICE

In its sinful past, the creature has given itself a false reality, that of an I which withdraws and wills itself as the beginning and end of its action and being, instead of confidently accepting him who entrusts the creature to itself, God its Creator and Lord. The I, having abandoned its error and been forgiven, finds itself as subjective freedom, that is, as called to freedom, but without its own content, for it has not yet made a decision. In the Second Week, the presence of the *image* of the invisible God counterbalances the weight of the sin which persists through its consequences in the I. But the I is still on the threshold, close to the moment when its freedom is going "to determine itself at the same time that it will only be determined by God."[1] We are now arriving at this moment: Following the logic of the Two Standards, freedom is going to posit itself by agreeing to poverty and insults, thereby arriving at humility, the path whereby God becomes more myself than I am. This act of freedom cannot be represented, because all is from God and all is through me.

Like all interventions of divine Freedom into the physical, social, and religious world, this action of God in and through me cannot be grasped directly, even if it took place in some extraordinary way which would break the flow of things and consciousness. "Nothing is more dissimilar than the Before and After of the Choice. But the Instant of transition eludes every conceptualization, precisely because it is not a question of a *thing* but of an *act*, not of a *fact* but of a *fiat*, not of a *given* but of a *giving*."[2]

1 *Dialectique*, I, 69.
2 Ibid.

God's action varies in intensity according to whether it touches the I in the Instant and enraptures its faculties, or whether it leaves the I to itself for a more reflective and voluntary collaboration.[3] "To the degree that this intensity decreases, reflection will surround the 'phenomenon' with precautions, formalities, and rites intended to provide for God's action, to verify it, and to record it with the least possible error."[4] St. Ignatius therefore presents a set of rules in paragraphs [169-189], devoted to making a Choice of a Way of Life. We will go over them.

Introduction to Making a Choice of a Way of Life

In every good choice, as far as depends on us, our intention must be simple. I must consider only the end for which I am created, that is, for the praise of God our Lord and for the salvation of my soul. Hence, whatever I choose must help me to this end for which I am created.

I must not subject and fit the end to the means, but the means to the end. . . [169].

For freedom, the transition from Before to After comes as the middle between beginning and end. Freedom does not coincide with this transition alone. Freedom is not merely a streak of lightning which flashes for an instant; the preliminary avenues of approach and the consequences of the decision also embody it. But it is quite true that freedom tends to be concentrated in the Instant which concludes the Before and directs the sequel. Freedom thus appears essentially as transition, middle, and mediation.

In the definition of freedom as the positing of self by itself, the I appears as its own beginning and end: it is itself (end) which it posits by itself (beginning). Sin has hardened this representation by giving it a false actualization. But the dialectic of repentance and forgiveness revealed to the I that its true beginning is God, Being, who creates and calls the I; in the course of the Second Week, this same Being appeared to the I as its final end. From that moment on, the I is the midpoint between the originating Being, God the Creator who sends his Son, and the final Being, the Son who has been sent and who leads the I back to the Father.

---

3 These are different modes of union (Ignatius speaks of three "times" for making a correct and good Choice), but they are essentially identical. It is always a question of my freedom determining itself at the same time as it is being determined only by God.

4 *Dialectique*, I, 69.

Between one and the other, who are one and the same God, is situated the choice of the means intended to unite the I to its end by an action proceeding from its true beginning. This "shrinking" of the I, which initially made itself the beginning and end, in keeping with its overweening pride, does not render freedom's ideal (positing of self by itself) null and void; instead, it allows freedom's sole authentic actualization. The path of this actualization is a descent through the stages of poverty and insults all the way to the humility which is true life. This path will have brought me to its end point when I am completely conformed to the image of Freedom, which also goes from Being, the Father who sends his image, to Being, the Father who exalts the Son and divinizes us in him. At that end point, my outwardness in relation to Christ will be overcome; and in being determined through Another, my freedom will be determined by itself as well. That union of beginning and end is the paradox of love, by which I recognize my Creator and Lord as being more me than I am, the one who reinforces me in myself.

This recognition is reserved for one who throws himself into the search for a "total and irrational identity" with the image of Freedom, an identity desired, but not yet actualized, in the Three Kinds of Humility. Hence, for the moment, my beginning and end remain as though outside me. By virtue of this outwardness, I head for freedom only by beginning to submit to my end and obey my true beginning. This submission is the essential rule for the Choice. It consists in a reverence for order: beginning, middle, and end; in which the middle, freedom which passes over to Being by making a choice, conforms itself to the end and rejects every subtle temptation to subject the end to itself.

Inverting this sequence would bring in a more refined and worse perversion than that of the forgiven sin; freedom would be choosing this object and that plan for themselves, subjecting the end to that choice as a means for confirming and conferring value on the choice. This is called trying to win God over to my own will. The logic of such an inversion would amount to elevating a particular disordered will into an absolute. It would confine freedom to what it desires, instead of opening freedom to welcome God, who comes to us through the things of the world when we use them correctly. One who first chooses a profession and secondarily the service of God in it secretly attaches himself to the means elevated into the end, and he thoroughly perverts this inversion by thereby pretending to serve God. Attached to this particular means rather than united to God, he becomes its slave. And if he sinks deeper into this attitude, he will go from one thing to another, seeking...and finding his own will, that is, emptiness. He will experience the contradiction of always being brought back to his own self by that very dynamic which is supposed to make him know the joy of going beyond himself towards God. For man is the void that is filled with emptiness as long as he devours things instead of letting himself be led by them to the Other, from whom all comes and to whom all is obliged to return.

The weariness and exasperation that sometimes result from this contradiction show in many a face. Nevertheless, the least flower could bring me to the verge of bliss if I preferred to the flower the One "who gives the growth." "So neither he who plants nor he who waters is anything, but only God who gives the growth" (1 Cor. 3:7). The goods that I seize are some emptiness to fill my void. But if I preferred to these goods the One who is present in them, they would lead me at once to the joy of his presence, the One who uses them to raise me to himself, them in him and him in me.

But our choices are most often vitiated by greed, which takes away from us with one hand what it proffers with the other. Freedom dissolves in the pursuit of particular things which it devours without being satiated, since nothing created can, of itself, match freedom's desire. Freedom thus remains a prisoner of successive instants of this vain pursuit and a victim of their dividedness. Once things are exalted into an end, they become jaded or lose their charm insofar as freedom takes possession of them. Freedom is then thrust towards a new choice that is just as thoroughly vitiated as the first one, and it does not realize any progress towards its true end, the Eternal One, who comes before us in time.

Action consistent with a rational choice, such that the means is ordered to the end and not the reverse, produces an incipient union of time (where created freedom unfolds) and eternity. I use things, and I find in them a flavor which comes to me from the Creator. Things have more flavor when one has the soul of Francis of Assisi than if one is a profligate. I live with others, and in communicating with them I find myself in the presence of Him who gathers us together. A man and woman are well aware of this, if they prefer the beloved to possessing the beloved, for they find in their union a joy that extends beyond what each can expect from the other. And a Don Juan, in his own way, witnesses unintentionally to the truth; he does not find God or the woman in his women, and thus what he desperately gropes for forever eludes his grasp. He is the image of the freedom which, taking the means for the end, fragments itself in time, frittering itself away in things, without attaining anything of the end which would enable it to overcome the dividedness of time and to posit itself.

The end sought by freedom is the Infinite, the positing of its self through its Self, which definitively overcomes the dividedness of time. The means as such is a transition from nothingness to Being, through Before and After. To invert the basic relation between the means and the end is, therefore, to want the Infinite to be at the service of the transition and to prolong the division of Before and After, instead of overcoming it. Those who first choose a state of life (marriage, an ecclesiastical position...), and secondarily propose to serve God in this state, "do not go directly to God, but want God to conform wholly to their inordinate attachments." True Infinity escapes them, and they can only attain the "false infinity."[5]

The "false infinity" is an unending movement which passes from one thing to another, forever rediscovering their inevitable limits, and never being able to overcome them; it is "an insoluble, perpetually present contradiction. The circle freedom enters into by inverting end and means is no longer one which is to lead it, at the end point of its becoming, to posit its Self in a perfect unity of Before and After; instead, it is a circle whose endless gyrations can only perpetuate the conflict of freedom's divisions."[6]

Matters about Which a Choice Should Be Made

"It is necessary that all matters of which we wish to make a choice be either indifferent or good in themselves, and such that they are lawful within our Holy Mother, the hierarchical Church, and not bad or opposed to her" [170]. St. Ignatius then distinguishes two cases: that of an "unchangeable choice," such as the priesthood or marriage; and others "with regard to which our choice may be changed" [171]. In the first case, the commitment is definitive, whether or not it was made according to a correct choice. In the other cases, I can reconsider the matter if my first choice was not made correctly.

---

5 Ibid., 71. [Translator's Note. The "false" or negative infinity of an endless progression is taken from Hegel's logic. See *The Logic of Hegel*, translated from *The Encyclopaedia of the Philosophical Sciences* by William Wallace, 2nd ed. (New York: Oxford University Press, 1963, reprinting of 1892 edition), paragraph 94, pp. 174-175.]

6 *Dialectique*, I, 71.

After an unchangeable choice, "since it cannot be undone, no further choice is possible. Only this is to be noted. If the choice has not been made as it should have been, and with due order, that is, if it was not made without inordinate attachments, one should be sorry for this, and take care to live well in the life he has chosen. Since such a choice was inordinate and awry, it does not seem to be a vocation from God, as many erroneously believe. They make a divine call out of a perverse and wicked choice"[172].

This sober language is a warning to us. Not everyone who wants to make a choice does so. We are not always in a position which allows us to discern a divine vocation for ourselves, either because we have committed ourselves according to a choice which was awry, or because we end up discovering that a divine vocation is being reexamined.

Let us stress this latter case, which is not directly envisaged by Ignatius, but which is in order here. It can happen that our direction leads to an impasse; it becomes impossible to continue on the path we had entered according to a seemingly divine vocation. In such a case, it is advisable not to reread one's own past in an entirely new way and to fancy that one is free for a new choice. We do not emerge from the impasse by "discerning," according to the rules for a correct choice, a "new" divine vocation. I can merely *verify* what is now the case, because of my own will, and go courageously from there in search of a divine will that I have forced to go through mine.

Salvation comes through sinful paths; this is the universal rule of redemption. Therefore, I can hope for salvation and even a joyful life. But it is not the joy which would, here and now, crown the recognition of a divine vocation; rather, it is a joy which will come slowly and by some painful paths, in a penitential patience.

Israel, which lost a decisive opportunity (Num. 14), learned that there is a cost for following God by paths that one has picked for oneself. "And for many days we went about Mount Seir" (Deut. 2:1). "And the time from our leaving Kadesh-barnea until we crossed the brook Zered was thirty-eight years..." (Deut. 2:14-16).

But a day came when Israel discovered that its time in the desert was also a time of betrothal. "I remember the devotion of your youth, your love as a bride, how you followed me in the wilderness" (Jer. 2:2).

For all is grace.

115

Three Times When a Correct and Good Choice of a Way of Life May Be Made

These three "times" designate three ways of making a choice, according to the various forms of God's action in the consciousness which lives in time. The choice is the act by which divine Freedom and mine are united. This union can be brought about according to a first form in which God so moves and sovereignly attracts "the will that a devout soul without hesitation, or the possibility of hesitation, follows what has been manifested to it" [175]. This is the *first time:* My freedom undergoes the simple and sovereign action of God. Conversely, the choice can be made according to a temporal and discursive form in which my freedom weighs the matter and then comes to a decision, while the divine Freedom remains almost imperceptible. This is the *third time:* My freedom makes a move without experiencing that it is moved. Between these two extremes is an intermediate time in which freedom feels that it is moved, but according to very delicate promptings that belong to the flow and alternations of consciousness. This is the *second time.*[7]

First Time

"When God our Lord so moves and attracts the will that a devout soul without hesitation, or the possibility of hesitation, follows what has been manifested to it. St. Paul and St. Matthew acted thus in following Christ our Lord" [175].

It is interesting to put this description side by side with that of the "consolation without previous cause" in the second and eighth rules for the discernment of spirits for the Second Week: "God alone can give consolation[8] to the soul without any previous

---

7 "If we did not know that Ignatius' main concern is to discover how freedom can insert itself within historical existence, his choice of the word *time* could appear strange. For what he really designates here are three *states of the soul,* corresponding to three *degrees* of the divine call. Undoubtedly, these "times" are independent of one another: one person is called in the manner of the "first time," another is called in the manner of the second, and still another in that of the third. But he does not preclude these "three times" from being intimately connected to one another, so that Ignatius' analysis of them is going to make us delve deeply into his conception of freedom within historical existence" (*Dialectique,* I, 73-74).

8 In the *Exercises,* St. Ignatius gives this general definition of *consolation:* "Finally, I call consolation every increase of faith, hope, and love, and all interior joy that invites and attracts to what is heavenly and to the salvation of one's soul by filling it with peace and quiet in its Creator and Lord" [316].

cause. It belongs solely to the Creator to come into a soul, to leave it, to act upon it, to draw it wholly to the love of His Divine Majesty. I said without previous cause, that is, without any preceding perception or knowledge of any subject by which a soul might be led to such a consolation through its own acts of intellect and will" [330].[9]

"Just as this 'consolation without previous cause' is the pattern and even ideal of consolation, so the Choice in this first time that leaves no room for any deliberation or hesitation is the pattern and ideal of freedom. And we can say without exaggerating that there is not a line in the *Exercises* which is not aimed at disposing the I to perceive this summons of the Instant and to respond to it generously."[10]

Such an Instant is mutual presence, and even contact, of God and the creature. It is a lived experience, but the flow of consciousness within the Instant is nearly suspended in a duration without consecutive instants. St. Ignatius here is therefore claiming that the divine action is not merely believed and affirmed by the creature because of its faith in God in general, but that the divine action is experienced, and that it establishes a perceived contact between the creature and God. The creature feels and recognizes God's presence, although God does not become an *object* in this experience; he remains the Elusive One, even as he becomes present. Feeling does nothing but touch him, and only to the degree that feeling tends to disappear in the "non-feeling" of pure faith. We will come back to this experience. For the moment, we are satisfied with affirming, following St. Ignatius, that it exists.

The spiritual life is literally a life, an experience. It does not belong to the realm of an *idea about* God or *about* Christ which would merely be a guide for the human subject's own moral agency, even if he professes—in his head—that all comes from God. Spiritual experience can take the form of a complete passivity to God's sovereign action. The example of St. Paul here could run the risk of sidetracking us, as if the divine action necessarily had to take place in this first "time" by way of a thunderbolt, with something of the extraordinary and miraculous about it. St. Matthew's call, likewise mentioned by St. Ignatius, makes any such confusion impossible. It involved nothing extraordinary, although the Lord's intervention was no less sovereign or decisive

9 These rules for discernment will be explained in chapter 10.
10 *Dialectique*, I, 74.

than for Paul on the road to Damascus. "He said to him, 'Follow me.' And he rose and followed him" (Matt. 9:9). To characterize this first "time" as extraordinary would be defining the essential through the accidental and giving to understand that God rarely acts in this way. In fact, if the spiritual life is union with God, why be surprised if the Creator and Lord manifests himself there as he pleases, according to his sovereign power and generosity? However that may be, whether this first time is more frequent or more seldom, it is the one to which the others are to be referred since it seems to situate them. For in the first time the divine Freedom manifests itself in an unveiled way, as it were, and "the choice which takes place in this way, without leaving room for any deliberation or hesitation, is the pattern and ideal of freedom."[11]

Second Time

"When much light and understanding are derived through experience of desolations and consolations and discernment of diverse spirits" [176].

The Instant when the eternal strikes in time can remain veiled amidst the fluctuations of consciousness. The divine action, always so sovereign in itself, no longer makes itself felt as such. It joins the alternations and discontinuities of this consciousness, which has been left more to its own fluctuations; and the divine action even finds itself, like the Word becoming incarnate, mingled with some elements from elsewhere: from man's nature, his history, or even his enemy. The present moment of consciousness, which was an eternal Instant without dividedness or succession in the "first time," is now split in two directions: upward motions (God drawing it to himself) and downward motions (our less good or worse elements trying to drag it down). But their conflict only clarifies the meaning of the transition from Before to After, that is, what I ought to do, and what I do.

Determined by God, who moves and gently draws it to himself, freedom determines itself by discerning these motions and letting itself be carried in God's direction. It is a very simple movement that makes it do what it ought to do, namely, decide. This self-determination cannot be articulated, and yet it lends itself to analysis. It cannot be articulated, for the motions originate from a source that consciousness does not control. At the same time, it

11 See the Note at the end of this chapter for a further reflection on this first time of making a choice.

lends itself to analysis in that the motions produce states that can be reviewed and recognized according to the Rules for the Discernment of Spirits. These rules will show in greater detail how my freedom and divine Freedom unite.

This second time is the mystical life in the duration and dullness of the everyday; it is time with Christ, the Son of God, man and redeemer. Being fashioned after Christ is conducive to establishing one's entire life within the sphere of this second time. It is advisable to try to make one's choice in this manner before going to the third time, which will be employed especially as a control. Besides, the third time is permeated by the second, and it even tends toward the first time, according to what follows from the hints given by St. Ignatius.[12]

At the moment of making his choice according to the second time, the retreatant uses his memory to gather together all the indications contained in his successive experiences of motions that "come from above" or that "come from below." He will see the former motions concentrating themselves vertically above the present moment, with the latter clustering below. Of course, in this case the enlightenment and attraction from above will not have the clarity and power that the direct call of the "first time" has. But, although this call of the "second time" becomes present partly through the use of one's memory, it is nevertheless of the same nature as that of the first time. And the direct intensity which it lacks is made up for by the opposition coming from my sinful body or from the enemy (motions coming from below, desolations). The "middle" is neatly defined between the "above" and the "below," and the I will no longer run the risk of taking the end for the means and the means for the end.[13]

Third Time

In the "third time,"[14] a time of tranquillity, the eternal Instant is spread out in the delicate continuity of consciousness. It is present

---

12 See the following note of François Courel, S.J., from p. 99 of his French translation of the *Spiritual Exercises* (Paris: Desclée de Brouwer, 1960): "It is through this second time that the experience proposed in the Exercises and especially in the discernment of spirits is fully realized. It is therefore fundamental to foster its success before resorting to the third time." [Quotation supplied by translator.]

13 This paragraph, with some modifications, is taken from *Dialectique*, I, 76.

14 In our analysis we are going from one "time" to another, as if they were connected in experience. That is not the case at all; the choice is made, and it is sufficient that it be made, according to one "time" or another. It is merely our analysis which,

there in the form of *indifference*, now an acquired indifference with regard to all worldly things and all beings, to the point where freedom knows and sees clearly what God wants for it. It is this state of indifference that constitutes this "time of tranquillity" for consciousness; it does not exclude the vicissitudes of a laborious search.

In a still indeterminate form, this balance of indifference attains a union with God analogous to that of the first time. What this union lacks is merely a *determination:* knowing what God wants for me now and deciding according to his will.

"If a choice...has not been made in the first and second time, below are given two ways of making a choice...in the third time" [178]. In this simple phrase, is it not significant that Ignatius combines the first two times and opposes them to the third? He considers that the second time can provide a certitude equivalent to that of the first. But, on the other hand, why imagine that a choice, even if it is made in the greatest possible tranquillity, cannot have recourse to the criterion which defines the second time, the discernment of motions caused in the soul?[15] It is impossible to enter into the process of the Exercises without being immediately subjected to the movements of consolation and desolation, as proved by the various recommendations contained in the introductory Annotations [1-20].

Consequently, one must not have understood anything of Ignatius' method to suppose that he imagines a choice in which these spiritual movements would not have been taken into consideration. In the "time of tranquillity" they are simply much less perceptible.

in the framework of objective structures, isolates some relationships between the three "times." Isolating these relationships is important for a correct understanding of the spiritual experience which, in a concrete choice, unfolds according to one or another "time." But this does not at all imply that we have to go through all these "times." Not only are the first two entirely independent of us, but the third time does not have to intervene if the choice has been made according to one of the first two. We must not confuse theoretical analysis, which isolates some relationships between all these "times," and the concrete approach, which by no means has to go through all of them.

15 The importance and role of motions, even in this third time, is seen very clearly in such notations as these: "I should beg God our Lord to deign to move my will, and to bring to my mind what I ought to do..." [180]; "offer Him his choice that the Divine Majesty may deign to accept and *confirm* it" [183]; "the love that moves and causes one to choose must descend from above..." [184].

Two Ways of Making a Choice of a Way of Life in the Third Time

"The first of these two ways analyzes in six points the genesis of the free act that is made in the sole light of reason. The second proposes four complementary rules for controlling the result obtained through the first way. The one is a discussion in which the I deliberates within itself in order to make the better decision; the other is more like a consultation in which the I becomes someone else in order to evaluate objectively, from outside, the value of the alternatives proposed for its choice. But what is common to both ways is the effort to go beyond the purely rational and to recognize even in this time of tranquillity the 'motion and attraction' that comes from above."[16]

First Way: In Six Points [178-183]

The *first point* asks the I to place itself before the matter that is the object of its choice. What is it all about?

The *second point* defines the initial attitude of consciousness before this object: *indifference.* "It is necessary to keep as my aim the end for which I am created, that is, the praise of God our Lord and the salvation of my soul. Besides this, I must be indifferent, without any inordinate attachment, so that I am not more inclined or disposed to accept the object in question than to relinquish it, nor to give it up than to accept it. I should be like a balance at equilibrium, without leaning to either side, that I might be ready to follow whatever I perceive is more for the glory and praise of God our Lord and for the salvation of my soul" [179].

The Introduction to Making a Choice of a Way of Life [169] had already recalled this attitude by relating it to its source, considering the end, and being indifferent to the means, which is simply a corollary of the Principle and Foundation [23]. But Ignatius now says, "I must *be* indifferent," and no longer "*make* ourselves indifferent," as in the Principle and Foundation. The difference between the two verbs measures the gap between the outset of the First Week and the end of the Second. At the outset, indifference is still only a simple proposal of the will. Now, the I must *be* indifferent, like a disposition that has already been acquired and somewhat rooted in the I's affectivity. Likewise, Ignatius characterizes this indifference both by the twofold participle, "I am *not more inclined or disposed,*" and by its objective result, the

16 *Dialectique,* I, 78.

balance at equilibrium between two alternatives whose four terms he is not afraid to enumerate.[17]

The equilibrium of a balance beam! By recalling this image of the balance,[18] Ignatius recovers the fundamental representation of his dialectic, balancing Before and After in search of the Instant that vertically unites time and eternity. The horizontal equilibrium and the possibility of the I's wavering between the two terms of the alternative define a state which is simply awaiting its determination (= what God wants) and is thus leading to union. One hopes to receive this determination by *feeling* whatever "is more for the glory and praise of God" (second point, [179]); next, one asks God to settle it himself by his *motion* (*third point*, [180]). It is only afterwards that one resorts to rational reflection (fourth point, [181]).

"With mathematical rigor, the *fourth point* describes the framework of the investigation, wherein the I is to exerts its own activity. Like the two equal arms of the balance beam, the alternative

---

17 See ibid., 79.

18 "In this second point, where Ignatius wants to bring out the relation between the free (and, hypothetically, purely rational) act and God's Freedom, it is evident that the image of the balance allows him to recover the vertical element of the call from above (the 'first time'). As a matter of fact, the indifference symbolized by the equilibrium of the balance beam is still only a preliminary step that is to lead to the decision, the choice of the means. Now, immediately after having recalled this image, see how Ignatius, following the same comparison, expresses the way in which my decision will be confirmed: Starting from this indifference, it will suffice, 'to follow whatever I perceive is more for the glory and praise of God our Lord and for the salvation of my soul' [179]. After the equilibrium, it is hence the 'sensitivity' of the balance that induces me to 'perceive' the weight from above inclining me in the direction of the divine Freedom.

"By means of this mechanical symbol, do we not see the reversal operative in the whole analysis of these 'three times' of the Choice? The first supposed a decisive vertical intervention of Freedom in the 'now' of consciousness, determining the means and causing the I to immediately cross the midpoint between Before and After. In the 'second time' this pole of Being was toned down, but there simultaneously irrupted that of non-being (motions coming from below, desolations), so that the tension between above and below is enough to define the midpoint. Hypothetically, the 'third time' suppresses this tension in order to leave the I with the entire initiative of choosing the means for pursuing its horizontal becoming. . . .But the mere description of the state in which the I is so 'indifferent' is a warning that it should seek anew to *perceive* what is *more conducive* to the end. In other words, through the balance we are first of all reminded of the conflict between below and above, hence of the 'second time'; and thereby we are reminded of the 'attraction and movement which come from above' as the determining principle of the free act, in short, of the very essence of the 'first time' " (ibid., 80-81).

proposed to freedom has two terms: to take or not to take this means. For each of the two contrary solutions, it is necessary to determine the advantages and disadvantages in function of the end, the positive and negative reasons for taking or not taking this means. As in examining an equation, we can arrange the reasons in four columns, alternating plus (+) and minus (—) signs. To view the problem under these four aspects that oppose one another in pairs, like the four quadrants of the circumference of a circle in geometry, is obviously to close the circle of reflection!...The result of the deliberation, the decision, should be generated from the quasi-algebraic summation of the various motives.

"The *fifth point* says it explicitly: 'After I have gone over and pondered in this way every aspect of the matter in question, I will consider which alternative appears more reasonable' [182].

"The I's activity thus consists in a rational disquisition, going through all the aspects of the question, which amount to four. But, like the activity of a physicist who has arranged the weights, counterbalance, and objects for weighing on the scales of his balance, it stops there. The result no longer depends on him; he only has to see it, to read it on the dial where it is registered.

"Likewise for the free act, it is no longer the I that must choose; it is 'reason' that must 'incline' its will. 'Then I must come to a decision in the matter under deliberation because of weightier motives presented to my reason, and not because of any sensual inclination' [182]. Rational objectivity is here equivalent to the divine 'motion' of the other two times, and the sole concern of the I must be not to confuse it with any sensuous motion whatever."[19]

St. Ignatius here evinces resolute confidence in reason, and Fessard stresses this boldness when he writes: "Rational objectivity is here equivalent to the divine 'motion' of the other two times." Can an operation of human reason then be equivalent to God's sovereign action in his creature? Yes. For the reason which operates uprightly throughout (as here, by viewing the four aspects of a problem, thus closing "the circle of reflection") is both an *activity* of the *subject* and a *passivity* of this same subject to the *object*. In a deliberation, it is the subject who, in a sense, elaborates his motives by constructing the ideas and reasonings which express them. From this angle, reason is an activity.

Ordinarily, some scarcely rational impulses are intermingled with reason. But the indifference presupposed here, and the patient

19 Ibid., 81-82.

efforts at objectivity which reason exerts by going through the four quadrants of the deliberation, do their utmost to curtail the non-rational. The force which these impulses give to this or that motive, enunciated in abstract and general terms (how could it be otherwise?), is gradually replaced by the force of rational objectivity. How does that work? By the interplay of the positive and negative reasons in the direction of one or another option. Taken separately, these reasons are all general propositions, unable to bring about the decision. But their cross-examining, through convergence and opposition, succeeds in effecting a determination. The abstract generality of reasons taken one by one changes into a concrete determination; or at least it tends to. To the degree that the I, which is deliberating by actively elaborating motives, submits to the cross-examining dynamic, it becomes passive to objectivity; thus reason's activity becomes passivity. It is then that the rational motion can be called equivalent to the divine motion; it is no longer really the I that determines itself by the reasons it alleges; it is the object that determines the I, through the cross-examining which is set up among the reasons. The object is undoubtedly the matter for decision, but, more precisely, it is this matter *appearing to me with a certitude that does not come from me.* For St. Ignatius, this objective certitude must come from him who moves and gives being to all that is, God our Creator and Lord.

In the finite and composite creature that we are, certitude cannot be produced by the sole play of rationality. And if certitude ultimately comes from God, it is by way of some conjunction between theoretical reason and affectivity. Of itself, the abstract generality of reasons merely tends to turn into a concrete determination; it does not simply become such a determination. The most stringent cross-examining of reasons does not succeed, by itself alone, in effecting sudden certitude about what God wants for me now. Man, in the best of hypotheses, is not pure reason coinciding with concrete reality; he remains composed of reason (clear and universal, but always more or less abstract) and affectivity (blind and particular, but in touch with the concrete).

Ultimately, certitude is there only because of an affectivity dragging along the weight of reasons. My affectivity always runs the risk of being deflected by a remnant of my inordinate desires, instead of being moved by God alone. This is why the choice, according to St. Ignatius, does not terminate with reading some objective result of the deliberation. It is still necessary to check whence comes the inevitable impulse provided by affectivity.

Even the most objective deliberation, one that has led to the most obvious conclusion, must be extended in a prayer that offers the choice to God "that the Divine Majesty may deign to accept and confirm it" (*sixth point*, [183]). To "confirm it" is to make consciousness *feel* that this is indeed actually His divine will. St. Ignatius here returns to the way of making a choice according to the "second time": "...turn with great diligence to prayer in the presence of God our Lord, and offer Him his choice that the Divine Majesty may deign to accept and confirm it if it is for His greater service and praise" [183].

"Through this movement of prayer and offering, the I turns anew towards the end which, from the outset, has inspired all its steps. And by asking that its choice be accepted and confirmed, at least if it is for the greater service of God, the I shows that, in making this major transition from Before to After, it remains guided by the same end and ready to follow its course according to the essential rhythm that has led it up to now."[20]

Second Way: In Four Rules[21] *[184-188]*

The first way of making a choice contains an antinomy which only a divine communication can overcome. Through its choice, the I should go out of itself in order to go to God by the aid of its chosen means, for example, a way of life. But the first way of making a choice remains centered on the I; the arms of the balance oscillate about the I, and it is the I which goes through the four aspects of the alternative presented. The motion of reason directs the I towards getting outside itself, but this motion does not immediately bear the mark of its divine origin. Only something coming from God and recognized as such, however, will be able to uproot the I from itself. In the sixth point of the preceding way of making a choice, the I wants to assure itself of this divine origin when it diligently goes to prayer.

The second way of making a choice will establish an awareness of this divine origin. The initial stage is now no longer indifference. It is preference for some object, whether this preference results from the first way of making a choice, or however else it is found in consciousness.

---

20 Ibid., 82.
21 [Translator's Note. Here and in several other places in this section, Pousset speaks of four "points," but I have followed Ignatius' Spanish (*reglas*) and Puhl's translation of these as four "rules."]

Thus we see that St. Ignatius does not conceive of our being able to get no further than a wholly intellectual determination, by a simple summation of motives. Our summation and ensuing decision must always be accompanied by an affective perception, that is, by a love. So long as the initial indifference has not been changed into a felt preference, the second way of making a choice cannot take place. Presupposing this felt preference, the proper role of the second way is to discern whether this preference is not secretly vitiated by sensuality.[22]

It is noteworthy that the end point of the process is always the same: to "turn with great diligence to prayer in the presence of God our Lord" [183, 188]. The choice cannot be concluded without God's *felt* response.

Therefore, the starting point is now "the greater or lesser love experienced by the I towards the chosen means."[23] The four rules are designed to decide whether the origin of this love is a disordered affectivity or God, the source of all love.

First rule: "He should perceive that the greater or less attachment for the object of his choice is solely because of His Creator and Lord" [184]. Since the "rational motion" takes the place of the divine motion, it is necessary to be assured that it is indeed rational. Accordingly, St. Ignatius now no longer asks the person merely to sum up his motives in order to perceive what side reason is leaning towards, but to seek to recognize the divine nature of this rational inclination. And he gives two signs for this: The apparently quite rational weight is, in fact, affective, it is a love; and it descends "from above." "The love that moves and causes one to choose must descend from above, that is, from the love of God" [184]. This affective criterion tends, even more than the preceding deliberation, to make the choice pass from the "third time, in which it is hypothetically always situated, into the second time."[24]

22 *Sensuality*, for St. Ignatius, designates the lower appetites [Pousset's term: *affectivité inférieure*] in general.
23 *Dialectique*, I, 84.
24 Ibid. It is worthwhile to point out how Ignatius, by a reflection on time, binds this affective criterion to the rational criterion (used in the first way of making a choice). First, I go out of myself (out of my sensuality) in *the present*, by supposing that I am dealing with the matter for someone other than myself [185]. Next, I place myself mentally at the extreme end point of my temporal life, *the hour of my death*, and I consider "what procedure and norm of action I would wish to have followed in making the present choice" [186]. Finally, I "picture and consider myself as

Let us now examine more closely the method suggested by Ignatius for our discerning whether the felt preference for the chosen comes from above or not, and for conforming our preference completely to the love of God.

It is the I's subjectivity which runs the risk of being a source of error within rational thought; thus Ignatius begins by eliminating subjectivity as far as it can be done. "*Second Rule.* I should represent to myself a man whom I have never seen or known, and whom I would like to see practice all perfection. Then I should consider what I would tell him to do and choose for the greater glory of God our Lord and the greater perfection of his soul. I will do the same, and keep the rule I propose to others" [185].

Hence I ought to get rid of my inwardness, placing myself in the position of a stranger whom I have met for the first time but for whom I desire the uprightness and perfection that I am aiming at myself. In short, I am invited to become another in relation to myself.

This is good psychological advice; no one is ever good judge in his own affairs. But there is more here; I am being invited to consider my present situation by means of an existential reflection that encompasses the whole period of my life. What distinguishes such a reflection from psychology? Psychology is an empirical science that is interested in subjective reactions and behaviors without considering them under the aspect of the final and total meaning of existence. Existential reflection, on the contrary, is concerned with freedom's decisions in time and with their reference to an ultimate meaning. That St. Ignatius is inspired by this kind of reflection is revealed by the fact that, in the third and fourth rules, he will consider the end of the individual's history and of all history, death and the last judgment.

Out of myself, I will encompass the period of my life from the outside; in the present moment, I will anticipate the hour of my death and the judgment that will reveal the *reality* of the present. "God searches mind and heart."

"*Third Rule.* This is to consider what procedure and norm of action I would wish to have followed in making the present choice

standing in the presence of my judge on the last day" [187], *the end of all time.*

It is by a similar reflection on time in the rules for the discernment of spirits that St. Ignatius will connect both the intellectual and affective criteria. We will take up this topic again.

if I were at the moment of death. I will guide myself by this and make my decision entirely in conformity with it" [186].

Death is the end point of my subjective time and of every objective time for me that is based on it. Death clarifies and reveals the present in a non-temporal light wherein is dissipated the secret of the future. Within time, the future hides from me the innermost reality of what I want and do. The presence of death places before my consciousness the end which I ought to regard in first place, and it dissipates the deceits which tempt me regarding choice of the means. To align myself with the hour of my death is a sure way of discerning exactly, between my past and this ultimate "After," the "midpoint" that the present moment bids me cross.

But death is not merely the end that suppresses time; a transition, it opens onto the eternal, onto the judgment which brings all time to a close. *"Fourth Rule.* Let me picture and consider myself as standing in the presence of my judge on the last day, and reflect what decision in the present matter I would then wish to have made. I will choose now the rule of life that I would then wish to have observed, that on the day of judgment I may be filled with happiness and joy" [187].[25]

To weigh the motives of my decision in this light of judgment is to evaluate them with God's very eyes, which preserve me from every deceptive subjectivity and bid me coincide with what I truly am. To follow today the "rule of life that I would then wish to have observed" is to identify my present instant with the Instant of eternity, to rid myself of every subjectivity that seeks to hide, and to agree to this sovereign action coming from above, as in a choice according to the first time.

And in fact Ignatius does lead us back to the first time; the "happiness and joy" which I hope to have on judgment day recall the "consolation without previous cause." "The final words of this entire analysis of the Choice and especially of this second way of making a correct and good choice, a supreme effort at objectivity, lead us back quite naturally to the starting point of this whole process, that is, to the instantaneous Choice according to the first time."[26]

25 Some Scripture texts could help in this consideration, such as Ps. 139; Matt. 25:31-46; John 12:44-50.
26 *Dialectique*, I, 87.

Summary

In the choice according to the first time, my temporal present is joined, in the Instant, to the totality of the eternal that is contemporaneous with all times. In the second time there appears the conflict between the above (whence comes consolation) and the below (which drags into desolation); between the two is situated the present of my freedom. The third time is that of consciousness left to the free play of its discursive faculties, in the equilibrium of indifference. The latter is a time of tranquillity in which the Instant is not merely broken into two conflicting polarities, as in the second time, but is diffracted and spread out in the duration of consciousness. It is a precarious tranquillity which can be confirmed by the union of my finitude to God's infinity, if I arrange the means/end relationship correctly, but which can likewise be lost in an indefinite pursuit of earthly things, if I invert the relationship of means and end.

It is then that the two ways of making a choice in this third time intervene as two complementary ways of leading to the initial unity of the first time. The first way begins with the situation characteristic of every freedom attracted by the alternative of one or other choice; and it rediscovers, in "rational motion," the simplicity and verticality of the Instant: what God wants of me now becomes clear to me.

The other way posits as a principle that the "rational motion" must be love that comes from God, and it thus distinguishes this motion from every motion coming from sensuality (*first rule*, [184]). It separates the I from its own subjectivity in the next step by having it consider itself as another person: I am to imagine a man whom I have never seen and whom I do not know (*second rule*, [185]); then as becoming totally other at the moment of death (*third rule*, [186]); and finally, as judged by God (*fourth rule*, [187]).

By degrees the authentic presence of the I to itself is thus realized, the objectivity necessary for true rational motion to appear. This self-presence which, in the objectivity gained, is subjectivity fulfilled, is ordinarily obscured by an unauthentic and deceptive subjectivity. The I is consequently stripped of the latter. The self's distance from itself, which is introduced by considering oneself as another, stretches away into the uttermost future, death, and then it goes to the limit of time altogether. Thus my gaze becomes fully objective in relation to myself. This objectivity is me before God, who, in this ultimate self-emergence, makes me reach the innermost depths of what I truly am, a creature that rejoins

God as its own principle because it wants to and does what it wants. "Rational motion" and divine Freedom are now recognized as identical: I in God and God in me. The choice is ratified, and I find myself within the peace of an "Instant of eternity."

Universalizing the Ways of Making a Choice

St. Ignatius envisages this universalizing in the Directions for the Amendment and Reformation of One's Way of Living in His State of Life [189]. In his eyes the Exercises, and especially the ways of making a choice, have an absolutely universal bearing. They are valid not merely for the macro-decision that involves an entire life, nor even merely for the decision of moderate magnitude that plans a reform. They are also suited for directing the multitude of choices implied in the running of a household, the carrying out of a profession, and all our relationships with others, even if it is only a question of saying or not saying a *word*. In short, there is no micro-decision in our daily life, however tiny it may be, that does not fall within their competence.

Thus, according to [189], the *Exercises'* methods need to be universalized in a twofold way. First, in scope, their structure permits them to be adapted little by little in order to serve the sanctification and conversion of all men, however average they may be. Next, in depth, their general principles are supposed to determine the least choices of a person who has assimilated them.

Immediately after having said that the ways of making a choice ought to guide all the decisions implied in the running of a household or the distribution of income, Ignatius adds: "Let him desire and seek nothing except the greater praise and glory of God our Lord as the aim of all he does."

Thus, after getting down to the individuality of everyday actions, he leaps back to the summit, to the universal. And this is in order to announce, perhaps more strongly and more clearly than anywhere else, the general principle governing the entire analysis stretched out in the four Weeks and the multitude of minute details contained therein: "For every one must keep in mind that in all that concerns the spiritual life his progress will be in proportion to his surrender of self-love and of his own will and interests."

"Every one must keep in mind" (it is consequently clearly a question of a principle for the understanding) "that in all that concerns the spiritual life his progress" (both in all kinds of virtues and, when the opportunity presents itself, in all the choices in which the rules for making a choice can be applied) "will be in proportion to his surrender" (that is, he will be stripped) "of self-love and of his own will and interests." The proportion measuring spiritual progress echoes the Principle and Foundation: "in as far as" (*tantum...quantum*). But here the transformation that the initial indifference regarding the means must undergo in order to assure maximum progress is also spelled out. As freedom's progress consists in receiving each and every one of its determinations from God's love that descends from above [184], the means for its ever greater union with divine Freedom is a surrender of self. It is a surrendering of self-love, of its own will, and of its selfish interests, all three of which are at the opposite pole from the love that comes to us from God. These expressions allude at once to the three stages distinguished in the Two Standards, to the dispositions of the Three Classes, and especially to the Three Kinds of Humility.

We can bring out these allusions by first adopting the reverse of Ignatius' order, even if we then explain his order in the sequel:

1. In opposition to the desire for riches [142] and even to the mere attachment to the sum acquired which prevents making use of the means for salvation [153], one should abandon all his own interests, and thus guarantee the first kind of humility, which consists in so subjecting and humbling oneself before the law of God that one would not consider violating a commandment binding under pain of mortal sin [165].

2. In opposition to seeking the empty honors of this world [142] and the attitude of a freedom that places conditions so that God is to come to what it desires [154], one should strip away all self-will, and thus establish the I in so profound a humility that it can no longer envisage the possibility of committing a venial sin [166].

3. At the opposite pole from pride [142] is the "surrender of self-love" to the point that from now on the heart abandons everything in order to will only as God our Lord inspires it, for the greater service and praise of God [155]. This desire is even carried to the perfection of the Third Kind of Humility: "Whenever the praise and glory of the Divine Majesty would be equally served, in order to imitate and be in reality more like Christ our Lord, I desire and choose poverty with Christ poor, rather than riches; insults with Christ loaded with them, rather than honors; I desire to be accounted as worthless and a fool for Christ, rather than to be esteemed as wise and prudent in this world. So Christ was treated before me" [167].

131

In short, the more profound the subjection of my freedom is, the more God's love will descend from above in order to unite me intimately with his Freedom. As Ignatius is here [189] bent on making this opposition between above and below stand out, he mentions the "surrender of self-love" first because that is what governs and measures the renunciation of one's "own will and interests."

We have just followed the reverse order, corresponding to the advance of spiritual asceticism from the most external renunciations to the most deep-seated detachment. Self-surrender governs all spiritual progress, from the least sacrifice to the uprooting of one's entire will and the death of self-love. The self-surrender recommended here by St. Ignatius implictly refers to the Third Kind of Humility, where an appeal is made to imitating Christ poor and humiliated, and it thus belongs to the very logic of the Incarnation: "Have this mind among yourselves, which you have in Christ Jesus, who, though he was in the form of God, did not count equality with God a thing to be grasped, but emptied himself, taking the form of a slave, being born in the likeness of men.... He humbled himself and became obedient unto death, even death on a cross. Therefore God has highly exalted him..." (Phil. 2:5-9). And since this humbling and emptying of self proceeds from the love that is Father, Son, and Spirit, we can say that Ignatius' dialectic refers to the life of the Trinity as its perfect exemplar.[27]

Note on the Immediate Relation between God and the Creature (*Concerning the First Time for Making a Choice*)

"It belongs solely to the Creator to come into a soul, to leave it, to act upon it, to draw it wholly to the love of His Divine Majesty" [330]. This is a decisive sentence of St. Ignatius, who affirms the possibility of an immediate, spiritually experienced relation of the Creator with his creature. This immediate relation is based precisely on creation and the Incarnation.

The difference between the creature and the Creator consists in the fact that God is Being by himself and from himself (a deficient formula, for God is—he is not "from..."), whereas the creature is by itself from Another, who is God. It is the Creator who, in creating, posits the difference; without the creative act, nothingness is nothing at all, and there is no difference between God and

---

27 Our exposition relating to paragraph [189] of the *Exercises* has reproduced several passages from *Dialectique*, I, 89 and 102-103.

whatever might be (nothingness!); God is there (a deficient formula) in his absolute identity. The difference between the nothingness that comes to be (the creature) and God who is both inevitable and willed. It is inevitable because God is and nothingness is not, and yet nothingness becomes something. It is willed, and willed for itself, because creation is a work of love, and love wills the difference in order to consummate union. In love, difference becomes the path for the union which brings about unity.

In relation to us, God is totally other, beyond any possible measure with us. God is more than incommensurable (incommensurability still indicates some proportion between the two terms), not limited by us in his otherness and, by this very fact, immanent and present in our finitude. God's transcendence is the reason for his immanence: "It belongs solely to the Creator to come into a soul...."

The Incarnation particularizes God's presence in the world; it does not increase it. But by clothing himself in flesh and thus agreeing to undergo all the passivities which his creatures can impose on him, God makes us present to his presence and he transforms us in it. Without the Incarnation, we remain partial strangers to the truth, which is the transcendent God's presence to beings. Through the Incarnation, we creatures become sons who have access to the trinitarian mystery buried at creation in the heart of the world.

God freely crosses over the infinite distance (the non-relation) that separates the creature from him; he makes himself present to the creature and moves its freedom from within. God is more me than I am; he is more my freedom than my freedom is itself. To begin with, there is a structure of the basic ontological relation between creature and Creator, and it is this structure that we designate when we say that God is the act that causes my act of being to be. As such, God first establishes my difference from him; and according to this difference, my being is not his being; my freedom is not his Freedom. But from this difference is constituted a relationship which, through the Incarnation, tends toward union. To the degree that this relationship develops, the creature experiences this very fact: God is more myself than I am. By such a formula we signify that the basic ontological structure(=God, the act that actuates my act of being) becomes experience, experience for consciousness itself and for freedom. God does not always deal with his creature according to the totality of aspects that constitute this ontological structure, and this is why my basic ontological dependence is not always felt as the sovereign and active presence of an I who is more myself than I am.

That God is the act of my act of being can be realized in two modes internal to each other, but which are distinct and even somewhat spread out in time: (1) God causes my act of being to exist—he is creative act; this act grounds my full autonomy before him, and it bestows me on myself in the freedom that he causes to exist (thus this freedom that God causes to exist will, nevertheless, be an act of becoming itself). (2) At the same time, God is the heart of my act of being, and my autonomy in relationship to him is nothing but my full conformity to what he does in me. These two modes should not be separated (although they can be disjoined in the contradiction of hell), but their distinction marks the time of my historical freedom. The time in which I live is the place where they gradually come closer together for me, time in which my freedom, which initially understands itself as the positing of itself by itself in collaboration with God, winds up by discovering itself as that which is dedicated to dying and rising in this Other— in Him.

Sin can harden the distinction between these two modes to the point of opposition or even the definitive contradiction of hell, where the autonomy that God causes to exist in me ceases, and even refuses, to be faithful to what he does in me.

What I ordinarily experience is my autonomy left to itself. That God is simultaneously the heart of my act of being and of my freedom remains in the realm of reality that is believed, but not experienced; and this reality is, moreover, partially challenged or denied or even annihilated by sin. Ordinary experience— even in the spiritual life—is that of *active* freedom. The fact that freedom *moved* by God is still freedom, and moreover a much better freedom, remains for consciousness a paradox that it does not realize at all. But God sometimes acts *for* consciousness according to the fullness of his prerogatives as Creator, and, for consciousness' greater happiness, God causes it to feel his motion. God's action becomes experiential for consciousness (in a way that we are going to specify). At that moment, freedom can feel itself entirely submissive; yet there is no forced entry of God into its place because God is more my freedom than my freedom is itself, and God indicates this to my freedom by the feeling of bliss attached to such an experience.[28]

28 This divine action on freedom's very center can be declared by others to be an intrusion destructive of freedom, a "violation" or constraint. In fact, this action is

Why doesn't God enter into our freedoms all the time in order to thereby bring about our own work? That is a mystery of Freedom. The full measure of this mystery is predestination. When God thus enters into freedom and works there immediately, freedom correlatively finds itself in a passive state, but this passivity is the summit of its activity. Created freedom cannot not cleave to God, while simultaneously there remains the possibility of a worse sin afterwards than the sin of one who has not known this grace. As long as freedom, because of its imperfections or past sins, has not fully consented to divine Freedom in such a state, this passivity can be experienced in physical or psychic tensions of which the ecstatic state is an especially intense form.

It is this type of immediate relationship to God that Fessard calls the "ideal and type of freedom." The discursive and deliberative form that gives my freedom the feeling of its own autonomy is transcended here for immediate union with divine Freedom. This is a zenith of the positing of self by self, God being recognized here, in varying degrees, as more myself than I am: positing of self by Self.

This Experience and Time

This sovereign entry of the Creator into the freedom of his creature brings about for the latter an experience which always exceeds the capacities of reflective consciousness. Such an experience is undergone, lived; it cannot be immediately integrated nor adequately expressed by the ideas and feelings of reflecting consciousness. This is why, at the root of such an experience, there is above all the feeling of something vast and elusive. In the Instant of the consolation without cause, consciousness is experiencing, but, strictly speaking, it does not fully know what is going on. This Instant is an emergence of time outside time, an instant of existence in which the distinction of past/present/future is suppressed, but to which there can correspond a variable psychological duration, usually quite brief. In other respects, this Instant forms one body with time. And this is why it is followed by a second time in which

---

the fulfillment of created freedom that acquiesces with love. Such a fulfillment leaves created freedom entirely free in the banal sense of the word (free to do what it wants), if not in the instant of this union of love (created freedom then does not want anything else than what happens to it), at least afterwards. If anyone is worried about freedom here, he need not be; freedom retains full latitude to damn itself, if it likes! It can do so even more "freely" than another.

the ineffable experience spreads out into reflective consciousness and begins there to be embodied in ideas and feelings.

St. Ignatius has very precisely noted both times: "A spiritual person who has received such a consolation must consider it very attentively, and must cautiously distinguish the actual time of the consolation from the period which follows it. At such a time the soul is still fervent and favored with the grace and aftereffects of the consolation which has passed" [336].

To a reflecting consciousness God is present above all in the mode of *having been* present, and the Instant of the consolation without cause cannot be apprehended by consciousness except as a past Instant. Yahweh was there and I did not know it, says Jacob. Moses does not see the divine glory except from the back. This is, moreover, the classical doctrine according to which God is grasped in his effects and not in himself.

Between the Instant and the period which follows it, there is both rupture and continuity. In the fervent feeling and abiding favor, I am still in touch with God himself and the Instant; at the same time, this feeling and favor are effects which are not God himself. Even independently of the fact that there are mingled some ideas and feelings having nothing to do with the experience of the Instant (and which come from me or the enemy), these effects continue to act as mediators, but there are some intermediaries that can become obstacles.

At the very heart of the immediate relationship to God we are not freed of our historical conditionings, and it is the latter that become felt as soon as consciousness has emerged from the ineffable Instant. It is even necessary to say that this Instant is not expressed in and by reflective consciousness except by means of psychic material proper to the human being. The person can be purified or freed from some contingencies, but he can likewise be, and at least partially is, weighed down by these contingencies. A mystical experience, even a very authentic one, is always reflectively lived and interpreted according to a culture and in the setting of a particular age. This fact explains why the saints remain people of their age and why they sometimes espouse its prejudices and aberrations, even when they have opened out onto the eternal at the growing edge of themselves.

In the time that follows the Instant, therefore, an antinomy of the uncreated and the created (ideas, feelings) comes into play; and this antinomy is complicated by the intrusion of sin and error. ...What saves us from this antinomy and its complications is the

Incarnation and Redemption. Thanks to the Incarnation, the period that follows and endures, in which our Instants of contact with God are embodied, becomes and remains the locus of an authentic mediation between the created and the uncreated. This mediation is primarily the Word of God: this man of history is God; this man who is God saves us from the aberrations of history or even simply from its lacunae. If within this "period which follows," as I live it, my ideas and feelings become one with the incarnate Word, they are authentic mediators. This means having the thoughts and feelings of Jesus Christ and expressing them, as far as possible, in the very words of Scripture. If the period which follows the Instant is thus a time with Jesus Christ, through him it will be a time with God, as in the Instant.

The ambiguity of time and creatures is that they are both mediators and obstacles between God and man. But the ambiguity is removed in Jesus Christ, God and man: In him time and finitude are mediators; without him, they become obstacles. The discontinuity of the eternal and the temporal is taken up in him, and he becomes, for us, the uninterrupted path of man's presence to God who makes himself present. In the Instant of *immediate* contact with God, we remain caught in our finitude and in time; in this Instant, therefore, it is only in Jesus Christ that we are really present to the presence of God. Christ's mediation operates even in the Instant of immediate union. But then his mediacy is present in its immediacy; its temporal thickness is as though suppressed, and the sacred humanity of Christ is there in its supreme destiny— which is not to be abolished but to give way in the most profound contact that it makes possible. In the Instant the persistence of time poses no problem, since God has all the initiative and he is sovereignly shaping us to his Son. As a result of this immediate action of God that touches us in Jesus Christ, time and finitude inevitably exercise their mediation, for they are, in us, the time and finitude of Jesus Christ. It is no longer the same situation in the "period which follows," and it is then that discernment and voluntary conformity to the incarnate Word must intervene.

Thus Creation and Incarnation ground man's immediate relationship with God, at the heart of an experience. This experience can be subtle or intense, which are merely questions of degree, but its structure remains the same. The lowest form of this experience is already infinitely precious, and it is less rare than we often imagine. We must have reflected on it and believe in it, in order that, when it does occur, it is not left crushed under the stream of impressions, ideas, and feelings of consciousness.

Chapter 7

THE THIRD WEEK

I. *After the Choice: Logical Summary of the Third and Fourth Weeks*

Divine Freedom as such does not manifest itself in the world independently of human freedom; it is visible through our act of faith, or it is obscured and suffers from our lack of faith. Divine Freedom is not like a thing in the world—it is an act that transcends every sensuous reality. In the sensuous realm, even in the humanity of Christ, it begins by disappearing. It manifests itself in Christ's humanity only insofar as his freedom is exercised: when Christ speaks and acts.

But one freedom does not exist except for, and even through, another freedom. This is true, first and foremost, of the Blessed Trinity; there each of the Persons is for the other two. This is likewise true of the Son of God made man, as it is for every man. Christ's freedom in the world does not exist except in and through his relationships with other freedoms, those of other men.[1] Therefore, if no one accepts his word, if no one believes in him, the divine Freedom in Christ remains repressed. And since it took on flesh only in order to express and give itself, it begins to suffer a passion.

The developments that follow will be poorly understood if this fact is not kept clearly in mind: Divine Freedom neither posits nor manifests itself in the world except insofar as someone—even

---

1 Since we are considering the *manifestation* of divine Freedom in the world, we do not have to take directly into account here Christ's personal relationships with his Father and the Holy Spirit. The latter can only be manifested through Christ's relationships with men. Without the apostles, the Son's relationship to the Father as it bursts forth in St. John's Gospel would not have existed *for us*.

if it be only one person—comprehends and welcomes it.[2] Strictly speaking, every act by which a human freedom opens itself, at least in faith, is a manifestation of divine Freedom; the divine act manifests itself in and through the human act. In the world, as in the Blessed Trinity, freedom's existence is always that of one relating to another: sign and call, gift offered and received. This is why the Choice that just occurred in the course of the Exercises is not merely the act of a human freedom; it is even more the act of divine Freedom manifesting itself. It is two acts that already make only one act, even if this unity still has to perfect itself in a history. With each act of human freedom that goes in the direction of God's will, Christ's incarnation becomes a little more complete. Therefore, a formula like the following must be taken strictly: "The Before (of the Choice) developed the conditions of free choice; the After must manifest its consequences. The main thing is to make apparent, by the very change that the choice brings about, *Freedom in its absolute self-positing.*"[3]

The Freedom designated here is divine Freedom, but, in the world where it is incarnated, it is itself only by calling forth a human freedom and making it posit itself. Freedom is; this is the trinitarian mystery. But Freedom does *not appear* (that is, does not exist in our world) except in and through created freedom. Even if the I which has made its choice does not realize it fully, because the consequences of its act have not yet unfolded for it, its act is already an act of Freedom.

Having appeared in the world, being embodied in it "by the change that the choice brings about," Freedom (and I in it) is going to unfold what it is. That is, Freedom is going to actualize itself by developing its network of relationships with the universe of men. From now on the I (*Moi*)—or the Self (*Soi*)[4]—is simply

2 At two essential moments, the Virgin Mary had this role of being the only one to comprehend and welcome the divine Freedom: at the Annunciation and on Calvary.

3 *Dialectique*, I, 107; emphasis added.

4 In these pages the expression *Self*, or *absolute Self*, will recur several times. It designates God not as he is in himself, but insofar as he permeates, spiritualizes, unifies, and makes his own the universe of human beings and even of things: namely, the Son of God and his body, forming only one reality. This *Self* is not merely the body of Christ (Mystical Body) as distinct from me, who am a member of it, but it is this same body having become mine through my union with Christ. This is precisely what a St. John of the Cross expresses: "The world is mine, Christ is mine. ..." Why have recourse to this concept of *Self*? Because it refers to the notion—and the reality—of *self*-consciousness. A human subject is self-consciousness. In such an expression, the word *self* denotes the human subject as the content of his own consciousness. This

God and I. The Choice certainly appears as my act, and it is this act, in a sense, that leads to the union of God in me and I in him. But this act is even more God's act in me, that is, Christ's act who, on the eve of his death, made his own Choice and in whom I, in turn, decide. Christ's Choice is the gift of himself that he ratifies and accomplishes by instituting the Eucharist. This is why the Eucharist is at the juncture of the Second and Third Weeks. There exists a very close relationship between my Choice and the Eucharist. We will come back to this point.

Thanks to the change brought about by my conversion and choice, the divine Freedom that became manifest in Christ now enters into, and appears in, my own history. There Freedom is about to unfold. The After of the Choice sets forth this change, developing the stages by which Freedom's act, posited in principle at the institution of the Eucharist, is carried out in history, my history and that of all men. This act unfolds in the voluntary suffering of the Passion and in the Resurrection, and it constitutes the new universe proper to Freedom. We have just explained (in note 4) the meaning of the term *Self*, pointing out the characteristics of this new universe: It is the world established in Christ, a world endowed with the inwardness and self-presence of consciousness, a human-divine community. For us this community is the Church in the world, the germ of the reality re-created in and by Christ, the seed of the kingdom of God.

We will develop these three points: (1) the change; (2) actual formation of Freedom; (3) the new universe proper to this Freedom.

1. The Change

The change is a conversion. A conversion does not destroy what

content is himself (the subject) with the set of images and ideas that he has of the world, that is, himself with the world as images and ideas in himself. In this relationship to self (self-consciousness), the content is immediately present in relation to the subject; it has the inwardness of the subject to himself, and it is this characteristic that we preserve here. For Christ who has made his choice, and who dies and rises as a result, the world (the natural and human universe)—in its very reality, and not merely as images and ideas—has become the content of his own freedom. Christ, from now on the universal Lord, is the sovereign of the heaven and earth which he contains within himself and which are thus, in the strict sense, founded on him. Reality, present to him within him, is his own Self.

As for the I (*Moi*), it is the subject who has the Self for its content. Hence it is primarily Christ and then, in him, the man (I) who through his Choice participates in the mystery of death-resurrection. Quite often the I will denote the human subject, but as united to Christ, the man who has made his Choice.

has been; it transforms values. Life's content after the Choice, as before, is still sin and grace. But from now on sin is excluded as a positive reality; it subsists merely as a possibility.

As for grace, it is no longer merely something that comes to me from outside: Christ, the image of the invisible God, who came into the world, but external to me. Grace is now one with me and I with it. Sin is excluded; it is therefore marked by a minus sign (−). Grace permeates me, animates me, and thus posits itself in and through me (Christ in me); it is therefore marked by a plus sign (+). It was just the reverse before the Choice.

We must see the fundamental reality behind this reversal of signs and algebraic play, namely, that we will never be separated from our past; it survives in us, but as transformed and converted. Sin is destroyed in that, as sin that has been forgiven, it becomes the path of God in me. And my human nature stops being a sinful principle in order to become, in the stripping away of self, receptivity to the Lord. As for grace, it is Christ personally becoming one with me. The original externality of grace survives solely in the fact that I must always welcome grace precisely as something that is gratuitously given. This kind of reversal constitutes a more radical transformation than a pure and simple canceling of sin that would be replaced by grace. Our sins are destroyed more effectively when they become the path of God and thanksgiving than if they were "wiped out" and we would then set off as if nothing had happened! Conversion is forming a new man, beginning from what has been.

2. *Actual Formation of Freedom*

The Freedom that comes by virtue of the Choice is divine Freedom, but in the sense that we have mentioned: a unity in which human freedom and divine Freedom merge, the latter being the basis of the former, and the former the path by which the latter is manifested in the world. The content of freedom is, in the most general terms, the passing from non-being to being; freedom's extent is no less than the totality of being. My choice remains particular, and it is not a passage to the entirety of being; but it implies a complete change of attitude regarding non-being as well as being, the entirety of being. My choice thus excludes any return to the past; through it something happened. Even if I go back on my choice through a total inconsistency, I could not simply go back to the previous situation, as if a free act could be annulled. A choice creates a bit of freedom; or rather, a choice is a bit of freedom that creates itself. This is doubly so because, within the act, it is God's act that constitutes freedom.

In life, our choices do not always effect irreversible options. The decision does not always make a categorical break with sin. Correlatively, neither does grace establish itself in us in a definitive way. Nevertheless, with each free decision, something happens; what was not from now on exists, either as an improvement or as a regression. I strengthen my step, or on the contrary I worsen the conditions for future choices. A decision is never a time for nothing. It settles me in the better, or it undermines my situation towards the worse.

A good and correct choice settles me in the better; it makes me enter into the movement of Christ who decides to hand himself over, condemning himself to death for the life of the world. Each time that some freedom appears in the world, it is the mystery of Christ's death and resurrection extending itself.

3. The New Universe Proper to this Freedom. The Church

The new universe is not merely the creature's being, the totality of I's in the world. It is the being that God allots himself in all beings. This being is not a thing among things, nor an I among I's. It is the being of beings. It is ourselves, not in ourselves over against God, but insofar as we, together with God, make "neither one nor two." That is to say, the new universe is likewise God, but as gathering us all in his Son, establishing us in him, causing us to be through him. It is not God in himself, in his incommensurable difference from us. This difference is presupposed; it is the very principle that makes us be "neither one nor two" with him. This consummation in unity will be completed at the end of time, but it starts happening with the Choice, and it is already fully actualized for Christ by virtue of his death and resurrection. The new universe proper to Freedom is the natural and human world drawn together and constituted in the risen Christ. We have already designated this unity of everything in Christ by using the notion of *Self*: in the resurrection, for Christ (the I) the proper content of his consciousness and Freedom is the natural and human universe, his Self.

This unification in Christ develops, in the course of human history, according to the laws that the Second Week sets forth in its "basic meditations": the Kingdom, the Two Standards, and the Three Classes. These meditations present the law of true freedom, according to which the world of things and human beings becomes the

"Self" of Christ in his death and resurrection. After the Choice, this law of genuine freedom no longer has to be represented *apart* from the concrete realities it animates. In the Third and Fourth Weeks, there are no more "basic meditations" constituting a distinct framework. Why? Because the I, by its Choice, has made this law its own. From now on, the I no longer contemplates this law outside itself; the law animates the I from within. The I's freedom has become embodied in an option that unites it to the divine I. There begins a life of union, the unitive way. Along this way, some particular suggestions are offered to help the person who has made his Choice go to the heart of the reality. These are mentioned in new and "special points" which are proper to the Third and Fourth Weeks, but which are found in the very body of the contemplation of the mysteries.[5]

By objectifying itself in the Choice, subjective freedom became embodied. The being that it thus acquired is not a new being but rather a conscious identity between this I (whose free, self-determining Choice was also determined by grace) and the absolute Self (Christ who, dead and risen, contains in himself all that is).

Far from producing a new element that would be added to the representations of the Second Week, the conversion resulting from the Choice abolishes an opposition, that between the I and Christ as an image coming from without. It was this opposition in the Second Week that had necessitated the distinction between true freedom's *image* contemplated in the gospel mysteries and its *law* presented in the fundamental meditations. But after the I has been called to union and freedom (the Kingdom), and has been shown how to answer the call (the Two Standards and Three Classes), grace joins and actually frees the I. This is why the prior opposition, and consequently the distinction, between the image and the law of the I's true freedom disappears. Union must no longer be sought in representations; it must be lived according to the decision by which freedom emerged from its body of sin and attained its body of grace. In the resolution taken, which is my new converted

5 The three points for the Third Week are: "to consider what Christ our Lord suffers in His human nature, or...what he desires to suffer" [195]; "to consider how the divinity hides itself...[and] leaves the most sacred humanity to suffer so cruelly" [196]; "to consider that Christ suffers all this for my sins" [197]. The two points for the Fourth Week are: "to consider the divinity, which seemed to hide itself during the passion, now appearing and manifesting itself" [223]; "Consider the office of consoler that Christ our Lord exercises" [224].

body after the Choice, the absolute Self (creating me a second time) and I (freely co-creating myself) are intimately united.[6]

The absolute Self that appears in the Choice is Christ, the universal Lord of heaven and earth, and I, who am converted and resolute, in him. This new being, Christ in me and I in him, is a single, concrete, and universal I, whose real content is already the whole universe. My Choice began to place me in a true relationship to the universe, which is destined to become as present to me as my thoughts are, and that is why we have designated it by the notion of a "Self." This I which we are, Christ in me and I in him, is not one more element to be added onto what has already been present from the beginning: the world, the sinful I, and the image of the invisible God coming into the world. It is rather the very union of these three components, which had been external to one another until this point.

The Exercises, where what happens from Week to Week is expressed, should now indicate that the union is actualized. And this is what they do in placing the Eucharist, as the very principle of all the mysteries that follow, at the juncture of the Second and Third Weeks. In the Eucharist Christ actually possesses a new presence to the world and to men: that which he acquires by the thanksgiving in which he exchanges his body of sin for a body of grace, his eucharistic body. In this exchange is accomplished and sealed the union which is an I, namely, Christ who dies and who, by rising, arrives at universal Lordship, and I in him from now on.[7] Christ's eucharistic presence is the beginning of the conversion of the natural and sinful human world into a spiritual world, the suppression of the breach that sin had opened up between God and his creature.

If it is true[8] that the Exercises lay out the structure of the free act and analyze it as we have just shown, one of the first and not least consequences of Ignatian reflection is to enhance the eucharistic mystery, to the point of designating it as the central point where everything comes together and whence everything flows.

6 These last two paragraphs, with some changes, are taken from *Dialectique*, I, 109-110.
7 In the Third and Fourth Weeks, it is always a matter of this I: hence, primarily Christ, and I in him. Everything which is true of one is true of the other by virtue of the sealed union. It goes without saying that this concrete I does not abolish the absolute difference between the divine Being and the being which I am. Rather, it clearly presupposes such a difference, which is the principle and condition of reciprocal love and union.
8 The final paragraphs of this section are taken from *Dialectique*, I, 110-111.

A more objective and less profound view accords more importance to Christ's birth and death. According to this view, these events are two moments easily depicted in space and time, and they mark off the boundaries within which Jesus' span of life unfolds like that of every other man, while at the same time his words at the Last Supper do not appear especially different from his other words and deeds. As a result of this view, the continuity of Jesus' span of life tends to blur both the moment of the Choice and the central role of the Eucharist.

According to the perspective proposed here, Christ's birth and death appear, on the contrary, as intimately dependent on the intention revealed in "This is my body," and as ways of manifesting this intention. The eucharistic *This* marks, so to speak, the utmost point of divine Freedom's self-surrender, whose two intermediate stages on the way have been the Creation and the Incarnation, and whose two return stages will be the Redemption and the sending of the Spirit (the new creation). From this point of view, the eucharistic *This* becomes the hinge round which occurs the wrenching, the conversion, that the whole of Christ's life makes the world undergo.

II. The Third Week

In the period *before* the Choice, the development of subjective freedom led to setting up an equilibrium between the tendencies consequent upon sin that held me back, or even drew me downwards, and the call that comes from above and draws me upwards. It was an equilibrium that was broken as soon as it was achieved; I did not stay in a state of indifference, but I chose in the direction of the call from above. In the unity of the same act, at the very moment in which the I "takes on the sentiments" of the Image,[9] a determination is posited in the I (an effect of divine Freedom), and the I makes a resolution. In the Christian, as in Christ, man and God have no more than one and the same act.[10]

---

9 Thus, in the Three Kinds of Humility: "I desire and choose poverty with Christ poor, rather than riches; insults with Christ loaded with them,...I desire to be accounted as worthless and a fool for Christ....So Christ was treated before me" [167].

10 At the moment of the Choice, the unity of the act between the I and God is not yet fully actual. It is already partially actual, since I ask God to place in my will what it should do and to ratify and accept my decision. This unity is thus already constituted in itself, and the basis is laid for a new existence (the life of union).

The Choice closes with an offering: "offer Him his choice that the Divine Majesty may deign to accept and confirm it" [183]. This offering is a *present*: a gift that is fulfilled in the present where the synthesis of past and future must be actualized. What I have been, now converted, opens onto the future that is coming towards me. The converted past and the future that is becoming present are Christ, who clothed himself in a sinful body by taking on flesh, and who is now making this world pass to his Father. My decision, as we said, is an act of his freedom in me; Christ himself makes a choice in my choice, and he offers himself through my offering. His offering is the full objectivity, reality, and principle of my own. His offering has been presented *once and for all* in history, and it is presented *anew every time* that a decision is taken in the direction of God's will. It is the offering of the Last Supper, in which the conversion of his body of sin into a body of grace takes place, and on which is based my own conversion from sin to grace.

This eucharistic conversion (and mine in it) is to make the future, containing Freedom's new being, a present reality; and correlatively, the sinful body, the past that still veils the presence of this future, is to be given up to death. This twofold movement is accomplished by the Last Supper, and it is reproduced by every personal conversion, whose meaning is precisely to be united with this mystery. The Eucharist is there, at the juncture of the Second and Third Weeks, as the objective reality reached by the subjective conversion effected through the Choice. It is in the eucharistic conversion of bread and wine into Christ's body and blood that every personal conversion takes on its full significance.

First Contemplation: The Last Supper

In its offering motion, the freedom that makes a decision links its present choice to the act that is its absolute significance, Christ's offering at the Last Supper. Like Christ, freedom says: This (the resolution taken) is my body (from now on my freedom has no other body than this resolution...and this sacrifice) which is given up for you (the decision makes the individual come out of his narrow confines and leads him into the universal, into a community for which he sacrifices himself; this is the ecclesial import of every choice).

"For freedom, making a decision is in fact to choose a pivotal point within the natural and human world about which the conversion, the total reversal of the initial situation, is to take place: Non-being becomes unreal (death of the old man), Being becomes real (birth of the new man). The choice for me, like the words at the Supper for Christ, contains a death sentence for the individual (the man of the sinful past) and a seed of resurrection into a community."[11]

Seed of Resurrection

In positing itself, freedom takes on the body of grace, the eucharistic body. Freedom's determination is not a simple accidental change that stays on the I's surface. Although none of our acts immediately recapture all that we are, and every act leaves "behind" in us many things unchanged that we also are, the Choice, as an act in which I strive to posit myself entirely by letting Christ unite me to his own choice, begins effecting a re-creating of my being; it touches the substance of what I am. The substance of the old man is converted into that of the new Man.[12]

Before this conversion, grace was only an accident (that which *happens* to me from without); it came from above into an I whose whole substance was primarily constituted in a rejection of God, heading towards every evil. After this conversion, it is just the reverse. The new man that I am from now on, body and soul, is re-created by grace, and it is sin that becomes an accident (that which can still occasionally happen to me). St. John of the Cross, speaking of the final phase of this re-creation, says, "God is substantiated in the soul."

The summons to freedom came from without (the Kingdom) and penetrated into the depths of the I (Three Classes of Men, Three Kinds of Humility). The response, on the contrary, comes from within freedom; it is conceived all at once interiorly (the Choice, the Last Supper) and then moves little by little outwards.

Death Sentence

To take on the body of grace is, for freedom, simultaneously to forgo its body of sin. The decision cuts off everything that had being in my life up to this point—inclinations, habits, motives permeated by sin—as soon as it comes in contact with them.

---

11 *Dialectique,* I, 113, with some modifications.
12 Taken no longer on the level of my subjective freedom, but on that of the Freedom of Christ making an offering of himself that changes the universe, this formula is absolutely verified. Christ, made a body of sin and thereby connected to the entire being of the universe, changes this being of the universe (symbolized by the bread and wine) into his own body, the body of the new Man, the body of grace—*transsubstantiation.*

"Freedom manifests its supreme activity by subjecting its objective being, its body, to a supreme passivity."[13] Freedom's objective being, its sinful body, was the ensemble of relationships that it had set up with the natural and human world before its conversion. It is this ensemble that is called into question again and radically smitten by the decision. The resolution thus entails a passion in which freedom undergoes the gradual cutting away of what it had been, and opens onto the transformation of its former relationships into a body of new relationships. This is a "supreme passivity" for freedom, because God himself is much more the agent of this abnegation.

By my free decision the future becomes present, and insofar as the present is a result of the past, it is condemned and reduced to nothingness. Under the action of the future that is becoming present (the new Man), the present (the old man produced by the past) moves into the past. This transition is a real passion, entailing the death of the old man on behalf of the appearance of the future Man.[14]

The passion of Christ, as well as our own, is governed by conversion. The latter takes place in an instant, while the passion, in which the conversion externalizes itself, is actualized in time.

The conversion effected by Christ changes some earthly elements into his body (transsubstantiation) in order that his body, assimilated by us, may transform us into him, and that, from being God's enemies, we may become sons animated by his Son's life and members of his body. But in order for Christ really to become our food, he must pass through death—just like any natural product that only becomes human food by being cut off from life and transformed. Wheat becomes bread only if it is harvested, threshed, ground, and so on. Thus, in saying, "This is my body," Christ is committing himself to the death that alone makes such a conversion possible and brings it about; he is going to his passion. In the passion, Christ fulfills what he said; he surrenders himself and gives his life for all men. He renounces himself and becomes sustenance for all; he becomes all to all.

The Eucharist thus starts Christ's death; we must even say that it presupposes it. If in the instituting of the Eucharist the end (the transforming of the world into Chrit's body) appears before the means (Christ's death) has been brought to bear, it follows

13 *Dialectique*, I, 113.
14 Ibid.

necessarily that Christ must die. But this necessity draws its entire force from the free gift of himself that Christ agreed to. "No one takes it from me, but I lay it down of my own accord" (John 10:18).

If the Eucharist precedes the passion, it is because the passion is only the material execution, necessary to be sure, but secondarily, of a spiritual dynamic that ends in "This is my body." Without the self-surrender of Christ's freedom that is expressed in this word, no passion is possible.[15]

The analysis of a human choice will make this relationship between the Eucharist and the Passion apparent. Take, for example, the choice of a young man who, in the course of the Exercises, decides in favor of religious life: "This type of religious life is my body." The opposition betweeen the grace that called him and his will, involved in his sinful body and its disordered inclinations, has been resolved. His true freedom has just been created and is creating itself by taking on a body of grace. As for his sensuous being, the body of grace is still only a resolution, a word, that has in view living out a particular kind of life. He has considered, desired, and even willed a new existence within a community of men, but his new existence is not yet actual.

The Eucharist at the Last Supper is also only "This is my body" applied to what we call bread; it is not yet the Mystical Body that gathers all men into the community of God's sons. But just as the Eucharist, in its profound and authentic being, is the movement of transformation into God that believers coming in touch with it will undergo, by virtue of their faith, in the course of time; likewise, the resolution "I will be a religious" contains within it a movement of transformation into God which this young man's being will gradually undergo, to the degree that religious life will permeate him, and which he begins to undergo from now on.

In both cases this movement has the same starting point, the exodus of a naturally egoistic and limited individual, and the same objective, entry into a universal community. "This is my body given up *for you and for the many*," says Christ. And the young man is also drawn to his sacrifice by love of other I's (the poor, sinners, pagans, children, and so on, according to his vocation) and through these I's (which are his *you*) by love for *the many*, where God is objectified for him.

15 Beginning with this paragraph, the rest of the material in this section on the Lord's Supper is taken directly from ibid., 114-115.

Finally, it is the presence of this transforming movement in him that is going to bring about his death to the world. On his coming out of retreat nothing has changed externally. But little by little the resolution, the body of grace, will erode the casing that still hides it, the body of sin. For example, this young man had envisaged this career, these studies, those trips.... When these projects are now presented to his consciousness to be actualized, they will collide with his resolution, which will neatly sever these desires of nature to allow only the desires of grace to be fulfilled. In a matter of time his "death" will be apparent to everyone by his religious profession, which is also the beginning of a life with a "glorified body."

Second Contemplation: The Agony

The Choice brings about an instantaneous interior conversion. But the latter must be actualized externally in a passion where the exclusion of all sin (death of the old man), prelude to the positing of Being (resurrection), is carried out. This passion is the fruit of freedom, and it begins from within, with the soul's agony.

The Freedom that just joined my freedom strikes at the root of the egoistic and carnal individual. This individual is myself—and all of us who constitute Christ's sinful body. Consequently, it is preeminently Christ himself who, because he is without sin, bears all our sins.

In positing itself by a *No*, our will unleashed an unlimited power that tends to survive into a present born of the past. Hence two wills still confront one another within the converted sinner, and specifically within Christ in his agony, who bears the sins of the world. There is the will that comes from the past (the will of Christ who experiences in himself all our refractory wills) and the will that comes from the future (Christ's same will as totally acquiescent to the Father). Their struggle and the option that sacrifices the former will to the latter stand recorded, in the After of Christ's choice, in the form of a conditional wish: "Father, if thou art willing, remove this cup from me" (Luke 22:42).

This wish expresses a certain resistance in the face of the absolute Freedom that is making itself present and which is already a "Thou" for the "I" that is agonizing. Nevertheless, this resistance only expresses itself in order to die. As a matter of fact, this "I" is not constituted by our refractory wills; it experiences them as its own, but it only experiences them in the act of negating them. The latter act lasts as long as Christ's agony: "not my will" (ibid.).

Not my will. By this *Not*, this struggle (his agony is a struggle), Christ identifies himself with the "Thou" in whom he has his origin and beginning in a communion of nature: "but thine, be done" (ibid.). "Father, thy will be done!"

In his soul's agony Christ lives out the opposition of the sinner's will to God's will. But for Christ God is not an external being with whom he has a merely intentional relationship; God is a *Thou*, the Thou of his trinitarian relation. In the act of sinning, human freedom opposes itself to God, but it does not live out this opposition at the depths of an intimacy with God. Instead, human freedom is quite external to the One whom it thus resists. This is why the sinner's opposition to God is not immediately painful for him. In Christ's agony, on the other hand, the malice of sin is oppressive within the face-to-face intimacy of the Trinity. Christ bore the world's sins under the gaze of God.

As one of the Trinity, the Son's individuality is complete openness to the Father and his will, open avenue to the will which is identically the substance that begets him. But in his condition as a man clothed with the world's sins, Christ knows the limitation of the creature and the resistance of our refractory wills that tend to set the creature over against the Father. The creature wants to be itself next to God, nay, even in place of God. Sin in the creature is resistance to him who is the Other. But as Christ in his human condition is no less the Son, sheer openness and acquiescence to the Father, he negates this limitation and resistance during the very time in which he is constituted in them. This negating of his individual I identified with ours is his identifying with the *Thou* in whom his "I" has its origin and beginning. In the agony, he is the Father's Son in and through the very act by which he becomes one with us and negates our sin. It is through this act that he lives out his identity as Son and yet remains one with the Father.

But what is bliss for him within the eternal intimacy of the Blessed Trinity is infinite suffering within the intimacy of the agony, where he lives out his being as Son in the condition of a creature burdened with the world's sins. It is suffering in the very measure that he is Son —hence absolutely, beyond measure.

In this situation, Christ in his agony has nothing to look forward to, either from God, if we can speak this way, or from men. He is the Just One, and hence unjust men are working for his destruction or are in a dazed condition (his friends). He is bearing the world's sins, and hence the holiness and justice of God weigh heavy on him.

Are we to say that Christ on the cross, if not in his agony, was made sin to the point of incurring condemnation? Yes, perhaps, if someone receives this light from God, he is obliged to confess that Christ was made sin, the world's sin, down to losing faith, hope, and charity—down to condemnation. Nevertheless, the Father recognized in this outcast his Son, the sin that negates sin. The Father sees only our sins in him—God's justice weighs heavy on him; but he sees only his Son in our sins—mercy forgives us. In Jesus Christ, since he is the Just One, God's justice and mercy coincide; we are saved by mercy, that is, justified. This is what the "Man of Sorrows," in the depths of his misery, obtained from the Father.

It sometimes happens that Christ's agony is not merely contemplated from without, but that, in accordance with the profound logic of the Choice, it is somehow shared by the repentant sinner who reaches this point of the Exercises. Then the principle of this Third Week is completely verified: What is true of Christ is true of his disciple. This can only happen to the sinner who is already forgiven, repentant, and freed from his sin. He must be (relatively) just in order to participate in the agony of the Just One; and God alone knows what this means and when it can happen.

What then takes place is a radical negating of sin, its exclusion. God personally is the direct cause of it. Sin, already disowned by the human freedom that repents, is then uprooted and destroyed by divine Freedom that, thanks to the Choice, has inserted itself at the deepest level of human freedom and thus predisposes it to be reborn in the risen Christ.

The agony is a mystery of divine intimacy; God there presents himself to the I as its personal Thou. Such intimacy becomes possible only when the I's own will has deliberately forgone every right to exist; then God uproots it. For God alone can bring about the actual death of this will, the death that provides passage to Life. This is the soul's agony and passion, and its passion is suffering and death. From the soul the passion extends to the body, which must also know suffering and death.

After the soul's passion, it is the body's turn to come to an end, to be negated. The "body" is the bundle of inclinations where the will to be, the I's initial positing, has settled itself; and this bundle's tie is the will to perpetuate its own kind—that is, the concupiscent desire that constitutes us, fastening together what we are, and whereby carnal life begets carnal life. The negating of each of these inclinations is suffering, and the negating of their tie is death.[16]

These inclinations, however, are really the willing of a creature that has sinned, a creature that, in seeking to be, has instead committed itself to *not being*, has negated itself, and has fallen. Suffering, insofar as it results from a free choice (Christ *"desires* to suffer" [195]), is the negating of this degradation, negating of a negation. It acts against concupiscence, and as concupiscence ends in generation that begets death, suffering is fulfilled in the death that leads to Life.

The Three Special Points of the Third Week

"Having been defined in its growth (sorrow and passion) and end point (death), the Third Moment, like the Second, is actualized through the portrayal of a real history in its contingent details, the history of Christ's passion. Over and above the already defined framework, we must reduce each of these details, in its very particularity, to the center whence it proceeds and which it exhibits: divine Freedom. Just as the meditations on the Kingdom, Two Standards, and Three Classes had the goal of providing the *meaning* of Christ's history, the special points[17] of the Third and Fourth Weeks are supposed to allow us to connect each of the details of those Weeks to the very entirety of the dialectic."[18]

These details, the various episodes of the Passion, are all related to the divine Freedom that is the principal cause of what takes place here. How is this relation defined? What does it consist in? In what sense can and ought we say that God is expressing himself and acting in Judas' betrayal, the ill treatment accorded Jesus, the Sanhedrin's condemnation...? These questions are answered by the three special points of the contemplations of the Third Week. They are no longer, like the basic meditations of the Second Week, representations for a consciousness still outside the mystery. They are the mystery itself, and for us they are the act of getting in touch with the mystery, beyond appearances.

After the Choice, consciousness has kept within the representation; we continue living in history. But at the same time, consciousness goes beyond the representation to join the reality, God made man effecting our salvation. Appearances[19] do, of course, continue

16 Ibid., 116.
17 These points have already been indicated in note 5.
18 *Dialectique*, I, 117.
19 *Appearance* here does not have the pejorative meaning of a *misleading and changeable* appearance; it designates whatever is appearing, the *reality* appearing, history.

to exist. They offer a contingent history that hides God's action beneath human initiatives; from without, the events of this history are ascribable to men. But at the same time, consciousness can intuit by faith what is truly going on: God (Father, Son, and Spirit) is at work; and consciousness can let itself be joined to this impenetrable mystery. The special points accompanying each contemplation invite and aid consciousness toward this loving attention that sees further than its eyes. In this way I will draw close to the Reality as it appears in its contingency and as it is in its mystery: living the passion as Christ lived it. What is involved here is not the emotion of pity, but a faith that adores the God of majesty in the most divine of his works.

The Origin of the Passion

"*Fourth Point.* This will be to consider what Christ our Lord suffers in His human nature, or...what he desires to suffer..." [195].

Pain by itself has no meaning; it is valuable only insofar as God thereby destroys sin in us. But pain never has this value independently of human freedom's conversion, a decision that chooses to will what God wills and accepts his action. If God has not been chosen and accepted, pain cannot be related to him as its true principle; it remains an accident bereft of meaning, an especially absurd form of our contingency.

To be redemptive, pain must include a connection with the will of the one in whom it exists and who wills whatever God wills. But the will proportional to this redemptive value can only be that of Christ, aware of all consciousnesses. "Christ suffers and desires to suffer."

But pain is pain only because there remains, in the one suffering, a reality that feels loathing for suffering and for what God wills and does. Body and soul, I am this kind of reluctance, and my pain is at the juncture of this reluctance and the divine action. Thus Christ, the Son of God burdened with the world's sins, is at once someone who desires to suffer and who feels loathing at suffering such a passion. Our wills are constituted as individualities closed in on themselves; his pain, the avenue of transition from the particular (the individual sinner that I was) to the universal (the new man that I am becoming in him), "bursts the enclosure where the I had shut itself up."[20]

20 *Dialectique* I, 117.

The Unfolding of the Passion

"*Fifth Point*. This is to consider how the divinity hides itself; for example, it...leaves the most sacred humanity to suffer so cruelly" [196].

Christ's will cleaving to the Father's will is at the origin of his suffering; Christ positively willed it as the negating of sin and "transition from the particular to the universal." But whatever the case may be concerning his will asserting itself and holding out in agony, his suffering seems to be the result of events, of human wills; and it actually does stem from them, since Jesus' enemies acted freely. We have said why it is this way: The Choice, even that of Christ, does not suppress history; it merely causes a power of conversion and salvation to enter into history, the power of God that is, of course, already at the beginning of history. This power is exerted in the form of *not interfering*. It is the weakness of God, which is rather his supreme power, in the service of Life for all men. God alone does what he wants by letting men do what they want; he does it precisely through his Son's passion and cross.

Man was created in innocence, that is, in an essential relationship to God that was already movement towards God, without a Yes to God requiring a No to himself. But man's congenital weakness is being able to understand himself as God's antithesis: "either God or me." This is the bitter fruit of the tree of the knowledge of good and evil, when man picks it *on his own*. Created in innocence, man provides himself with the knowledge of good and evil by inventing this antithetical dilemma: either God or me. God wants to save man from this weakness, and he gives him the command that puts him on guard: "Of the tree of the knowledge of good and evil you shall not eat" (Gen. 2:17). But man simply made this precept the occasion for a suspicion and trial of God's intention by situating himself precisely within the perspectives that the command was to protect him from. Man imparts his trust to the tempter instead of to God: "You will not die. For God knows that when you eat of it your eyes will be opened, and you will be like gods" (Gen. 3:4-5). It is the greatness of man to be *for* God in the midst of having to go through the danger of willing himself, at any cost, for himself. Man's weakness does not outweigh his greatness, but it is precisely this greatness of his that marks him as one who is not himself except by an Other; and his destiny assumes that he give this Other credit in the hour of decision. Is it then so impossible to give God credit? It appears so.

Then God forgives. He goes to the bitter end of his bounty by exposing himself to man's distrust, by letting man operate according to his own will. He whom man is unwilling to trust can only undergo mistrust and die from it. To be mistrusting is to confer death. In death, mistrust reaches its end; it fixes itself in ultimate non-sense, unless in death the one who went to the bitter end of his bounty thereby proves that he is the Living One beyond life and death, the source of Life that can restore life. In doing what he wants, man ends by encountering this power. And it is by God's thus not interfering that God does what he wants; he completes his generosity with forgiveness, bestowing Life.

To whom should we ascribe this non-interference? Not to Christ, who wills to suffer the pain and expresses himself completely in this will. Nor to the Father, who positively wills this suffering and "orders" the Son to accept it. We must instead attribute this non-interfering to the divinity that conditions everything and that is common to both Father and Son. There is in God a positive will for redemptive suffering because that is the means for God to do what he wants (to save us) by letting us do what we want.

It is this positive salvific will that appears at the Passion's origin, in the Agony that is precisely not a mystery left to the contingency of human willing. At that time the Father's plan, accepted by the Son, is fulfilled as is fitting for God—by letting men do what they wish. The mystery unfolds in history beneath the sign of contingent human wills, while "the divinity *hides itself*... [and] *leaves* the most sacred humanity to suffer so cruelly" [196]. Under this veil hiding the divinity, there unfolds, in fact, the Blessed Trinity's action that appeared momentarily during the Agony, and which men (the sleeping disciples) did not know how to recognize. The Father's willing, the Son's acceptance, all within the Spirit's unity, bring about true Freedom; they will and create Freedom: that of man joined to God's, especially that of the Man of Sorrows, in whom all freedom is re-created.

This distinction between the divine *Persons* who will the redemptive passion and the *divinity* that hides itself and lets it happen can seem artificial, since the Persons are the divinity and the divinity is the unity of the three Persons. However, let us admit that for us this identity breaks down within our language as soon as we try to express the contrary aspects either of God's being or of his action in history. Following this linguistic necessity, we here attribute the positive willing to the Persons, and to the divinity (whereby we designate the Persons' impenetrable nature) we ascribe what is for us the most mysterious aspect of God's action, namely, precisely that he does what he wants by letting us do what we want. According to this mystery, God's sovereign power that acts is identical with the patience that submits; strength unfolds in and through weakness; majesty shines forth in lowliness; God manifests himself by hiding himself.

For the I that is contemplating the mystery of salvation and that grasps, in the night of faith, what is truly taking place, the divine willing (the positive will to suffer) and the non-interfering (the contingency where sinful man unleashes himself) are one. Taken separately, they are the two moments of the representation; lived together, they are the very mystery that I let myself join.

The End

"*Sixth Point.* This is to consider that Christ suffers all this for my sins, and what I ought to do and suffer for Him" [197].

The divine will to suffer and not to interfere are the two objective sides of the mystery. The I penetrates this mystery insofar as it relates the mystery to itself: "all this for my sins." Without this final reflection, the contemplation of the mystery would remain wholly extrinsic. Thanks to this reflection, it appears to me that the mystery takes the very path of my sins and that the latter become the path of Love. Such is the reality.

The sins are done away with one by one in suffering.[21] At the end point, there is only union: "what I ought to do and suffer for Him."

Just as the initial positing of sin was concretized in an evolution of sins (all the world's sins, all the sins of my life [51, 56]), the exclusion of these sins is concretized in an exactly opposite

---

21 Suffering presents itself as a non-interfering by God. Under this guise, the hand of God is not always easily recognized. In those who are sufficiently converted, suffering sometimes takes a form close to Christ's agony; this spiritual suffering is a mystical grace. It is the converted sinner's very close union with God that purifies him, the contact of sin's residue in me with the love and holiness of God. In this type of face-to-face encounter, the soul bears the weight of its own past sins or those of others. It can happen that consciousness feels hostile to God without in any way being hostile—quite the contrary. That is a result of Love's touching the very source whence sins formerly sprang.

God is never the direct cause of suffering. Suffering comes from the encounter between God's holiness and the imperfect creature marked by sin that I am. God does not cause suffering; he purifies, that is, he shares his holiness with us; it is this purgation that causes suffering, Holiness' encounter with what we are.

evolution of sufferings. Insofar as the sphere of these sufferings widens, the sphere of sins diminishes. Through concrete suffering, sin loses its reality; it is "remitted" to its own position and there finds its truth, the truth "of that which should not be."

After this negating has grown commensurate with sin through the mysteries of the Passion, non-being's will-to-be is promptly stifled. The death of the Man of Sorrows is the annihilation of sin: *Consummatum est.* The objective existence of sin is finally past: *Passus est.*[22]

III. Transition from the Third to the Fourth Moment: Christ's Three Days in the Tomb

Human freedom, the I, joins the mysteries of the Passion insofar as this grace is granted it. These mysteries take place, however, in a history where there remains a certain distance between Christ and me. This difference becomes obvious in the mystery of death: Christ dies; I am not yet dying.

There could be an utterly objective way of discussing the mystery of Christ's death that would leave aside the I. This objective viewpoint is not consistent with the logic of the present dialectic, according to which whatever occurs in Christ also happens for me (not merely through contemplation, but through an at least incipient union or participation). Consequently, we must examine the mystery of Christ's death in close connection with the I, with my freedom. What is Christ's death, in itself and for me, for us who do not die at the same time he does?

In this mystery of death and then of the resurrection, the sole being that was equal to the event was the Virgin Mary. She therefore occupies an eminent spot in our present reflection, corresponding to the position she held during the event. It is in her that the event is lived and perceived by human I's, because she alone fully lived it out in the moment itself. It is then through her that my contemplation joins me to this mystery. It is through her that I can reflect, while including my situation within my reflection, that is, while participating. In this way we can comprehend why St. Ignatius, on the sixth day of the Third Week, proposes the following topic for contemplation: "from the burial inclusive to the house to which our Lady retired after the burial of her Son" [208].

---

22 *Dialectique*, I, 118.

"As Mary, at the outset of the second moment, had been the site of the appearance of the Image of Being (virginal Annunciation, Nativity), she is now also the site of its transformation from a simple presence in this world, here and now, into a glorious manifestation, a perpetual and universal presence, 'to the close of the age' (Matt. 28:20); from a simple external passing (Christ walking among us) into an interior dwelling of the Spirit. It is in Mary's solitude that there takes place the transition from sorrowful memories (tied to Christ's existence in this world) to triumphant hopes."[23]

Why is the death-resurrection transition not immediate, as some would have it? It is quite true that the Father, in the very instant that he sees his Son dead, exalts him. St. Paul has expressed the death-resurrection transition from God's point of view, as it were, in his epistle to the Philippians: "...he humbled himself and became obedient unto death, even death on a cross. Therefore God has highly exalted him..." (2:8-9).[24] But what is unified and instantaneous for God in his eternity happens for us in time; for us time is a very condition of the reality of events.

The sin that is non-being does not beget a history by itself; it is a parasite that becomes embedded in history and merely alters the modalities of history. Thus we meditated, in the First Week, on a "history" of sin that was, for us, made up merely of representations (the sins of the angels, Adam,...). This is why the end of the dialectic of sin consisted in a reversal, a turnabout—that of conversion —immediately giving access to the Being underlying the whole dialectic of sin.

At the end of the Third Week, we no longer have merely the denouement of a thoroughly individual and subjective dialectic, but the end of a real history that is at once individual (Jesus' history) and social. What happened to Jesus must also be for us. How can we participate in the death of someone when we do not die ourselves? By observing it, and by experiencing the emptiness that it costs us. This presupposes a certain lapse of time. We must live without him.

For a death to be truly a death not merely for the one who dies, but especially for those remaining, it must leave an absence, an absence that lasts. For us, therefore, Jesus' resurrection could not

23 Ibid., 122.
24 See the analyses of Xavier Léon-Dufour in his book, *Resurrection and the Message of Easter*, trans. R. N. Wilson (New York: Holt, Rinehart and Winston, 1975), especially chap. 2, "Jesus, Lord of Glory."

occur at the very instant of his death. The disproportion between the individual and social dimensions (Jesus dies, but we are not yet dying) is clarified by the time intervening between death and resurrection. And it is this disproportion that makes death not merely a transition for the one who dies, but also a condition that endures for those who remain.[25]

IV. Recapitulation of the First Three Weeks

The spiritual experiences that are linked together within the Exercises are knowledge through understanding, desire, decision, and finally the *affections*. We could even say that the Exercises are a schooling of basic spiritual feelings that enable faith, hope, and charity to flourish in a converted sinner's consciousness.

We define *feeling* as follows: "For the individual, feeling is that whereby his I relates vitally to his own species in nature before this feeling is reflected, purified, and transformed through the word, causing the I to relate to everyone through the Spirit."[26]

This definition is not concerned merely with an interior psychological emotion confined to the individual; it denotes the individual's relating, on the sensuous level, to what is not himself. At first, this communication is lived out on the level of immediate (non-reflective and quasi-animal) sensuousness; man is spirit, of course, but at first he is nature. The newborn child lives its spiritual being primarily in the mode of rudimentary vitality; it is an ensemble of biological feelings. But a development starts at once; in its rudimentary vitality appear the first signs of thought; the baby recognizes its mother and smiles at her. This development goes on throughout the child's upbringing, especially by way of language (the word).

To the degree that reflective thought frees itself from the feelings that put it in touch with concrete things and beings, it becomes abstract. To go through abstraction is necessary, but to stop there would be disastrous. Beyond the opposition between sensuousness and thought, they can and should permeate each other. Then sensations are no longer a given that is still entirely biologicals and thought is no longer merely abstraction. Their union in feeling, of higher affectivity is a blend of the warmth and concrete immediacy of the sensations with the clarity and universality of thought.

---

25 We will come back to this problem of death in another book dealing with the main dogmas structuring the Exercises. For now, see *Dialectique*, I, 119-122.

26 *Dialectique*, I, 123.

As such, this higher feeling is still not the *spiritual* feeling wherein shine faith, hope, and charity, but it can become the latter if God's word (the Word) finishes the work of human language here, bringing the person to faith and leading him into divine life.

Springing from elemental affectivity, feelings are at first thoroughly sensuous; they are nourished by sensations coming through the five senses and elaborated by the imagination. They are gradually transformed by the contemplation of some revealed mysteries (understanding), and by the desires and decisions that are formed by contact with the Word of God. Thus a higher affectivity develops, whose important role we saw in the Choice, and which is ultimately the authentic arena for encounter with God. The characteristic of this higher affectivity is to unite the sensuous and the intelligible, welcoming and transforming the sensuality of the former, and making the latter surrender its own abstraction. It is on the level of this higher affectivity that there expands within consciousness the life of God in us: faith, hope, and charity. From then on, feeling as "reflected, purified, and transformed through the word (human and divine), causes each one to relate to everyone through the Spirit."

The logic of the Exercises' four Weeks can be presented in function of these basic spiritual feelings, as follows.[27]

The First Week had as its fruit and end point the awakening and development of a feeling of abhorrence and sorrow in the presence of sin: contrition. Born of the sense of hell and the feeling of absolute separation from God, this contrition allows the principle that arouses and sustains it to appear: faith in Him who creates a bond between God and us that is even more absolute than our separation. Contrition and faith in Christ dead on the cross are the reverse sides of the same reality. My freedom begins to be re-created by going from sin to contrition (negative side); it discovers the principle of this re-creating, Christ, to whom it cleaves through faith (positive side). As a result, contrition and faith are internal to one another, like the reflection on sin and the colloquy of mercy throughout the First Week.

In the Second Week, faith has grown, but still without becoming internalized into a participation in the mystery of Christ dying on the cross. Faith has been at work, but after the fashion of a spiritual prompting that barely counterbalances one's sensuous

---

27 The following paragraphs on the logic of the four Weeks follow quite closely ibid., 124-125.

impulses, the concupiscence that sin produced and that contrition did not abolish. For us who have gone to the end of the Exercises and comprehend their unfolding from the viewpoint of their true principle (Christ and the Father who sends the Son), the historical and contingent happening narrated by the Gospels is the direct expression of the mystery, the work of the Spirit. In the gospel portrayals we perceive the mystery of the incarnate Word, the Redeemer. But for the consciousness that lives out the Second Week from day to day and does not yet see the mysteries in their ultimate truth, its faith is not yet a participating in the latter, but rather an intending that lets itself be drawn by an end, undoubtedly its final end, but as still external and distant. Faith brings about in this consciousness an understanding that directs the will, but it does so by offering it an Exemplar to imitate, rather than by introducing it to a Being that would develop within consciousness itself. And this is why consciousness, at the end of the Second Week, remains truly free in the most common meaning of the word, free to choose.

But in passing from the Second to the Third Week through the Choice, faith becomes deeper and welcomes into itself the reality that it was still cleaving to from without. Faith becomes internal to this reality, and from simple consent to a rather external representation (Christ as *image*), it becomes voluntary participation in the reality of this image. The movement by which the individual freely surrenders himself, renouncing his egoistic subsistence to the point that the world simultaneously loses its standing and allurements for him, is also the movement by which faith is welcomed into the Reality it believes in, and secures its own present reality.

The following is the result. Instead of faith appearing, as in the Before, as the *ideal negating* of the false existence of sin (the exchange that substitutes evangelical feelings and representations for the feelings and representations of sinful consciousness), faith operates, in the After, as a really destructive power, mortifying sensuous impulses, consuming the casing of sin. This negative action of faith presupposes the following positive aspect. Just as contrition abolished sin and allowed its own true principle to appear (faith in Christ as the Lord who calls us), so here compassion destroys the consequences of sin and is about to manifest that which makes compassion possible and confirms it: not merely faith, but living faith, that is, hope, the Spirit's response that sustains and rewards the faithfulness of freedom in its ordeal.

Hope has not been absent from the preceding stages. From the first summons that arouses faith in a coming Kingdom, hope is there as the bond of the representations that make the Kingdom present to us. Hope is present above all as the soul of the movement which, in the course of the Third Week, destroys and consumes the body of sin. It is hope that ultimately provides the ability to endure the ordeal of the Passion. This active presence that has been previously invisible is due now to manifest itself.

Resurrection! The resurrection of Christ is the manifestation and fulfillment of our hope. Hope is first aroused through the apparitions, the signs that the risen Christ gives his disciples. But when the disciples are steadfast in their faith, he finally disappears from their eyes and thus leads them into the mystery of charity. Charity that lives on pure faith no longer needs particular signs to recognize the Lord, because everything becomes a sign of his presence.

Chapter 8

THE FOURTH WEEK

"I lay down my life, that I may take it again.
No one takes it from me,
but I lay it down of my own accord.
I have power to lay it down, and
I have power to take it again;
  this charge I have received from my Father" (John 10:17-18).

In the Passion, the passivity of Christ derives from a positive, will to suffer; it is an initiative. God does not interfere; this is his sovereign way of actualizing what he wants. The divinity hides itself, but faith recognizes in this self-effacement the absolute revelation of the power of God. The Resurrection, therefore, happens as the manifestation of the hidden, but operative, reality. "In this way the death of God, the fruit of sin, has the effect of allowing the life of God to appear, grace visible and sensuous as such—no longer merely as *Image*, but as *Word of Life*."[1]

Through his incarnation, the Son becomes the Image of God; this Image is God, but God as separated from himself and placed outside his natural element, so to speak. Through death, this separation is abolished, and through the resurrection, the Image rejoins the reality that it represented and which remained hidden in it. The Image disappears (Christ no longer belongs to this world), but for faith this disappearance is the arrival of the truth; from now on Christ is acknowledged as Lord and Word of Life. This life of God is grace as visible and sensuous; at first with a particular import and for a time (the risen Christ manifests himself to his disciples); then with a universal import and for all times (Christ

1 *Dialectique*, I, 126.

is present in the Church, and he acts through her, especially through his word and the sacraments).

In order that this life of God appear as such in Jesus Christ, it is necessary for it to come in contact with the very booty that death acquired for itself and took from Jesus: Christ rises in his body; he emerges from the tomb.[2]

Through the Resurrection, Christ enters into his glory. This glory cannot be spoken of in itself; the life of God is ineffable. But his glory is not merely in itself; it is likewise turned toward us. In this latter respect, Christ's glory is his universal Lordship, as the letter of St. Paul to the Colossians, for example, proclaims (1:15-20). From this point of view it can be said that the natural and human universe is his world from now on. Christ is no longer contained by the universe, as in the time of his mortal life; rather, he contains the universe, as our own consciousness contains images and thoughts of the world: "In him all things hold together" (Col. 1:17). According to the terminology that we have explained, the universe is his Self, without any distance or opposition in relation to him, its Lord.[3]

Through his incarnation, the Son of God (his 'I') became a being amidst the beings of the world, situated in space and time, outside other beings and limited by them. He took upon himself all the oppositions that sin hardens between us and ourselves, us and others; he clothed himself in sinful flesh. But his sufferings and death were a renunciation of existence, the negating of sin and its consequences. The outwardness characteristic of our condition has been overcome, and the resistances brought into our condition by sin have been abolished. The risen Christ is a being who freely posits himself as absolute Freedom, permeating the universe and reigning over it even better than consciousness permeates its own thoughts and rules over them.

The body of Christ rises. This particular thing, wherein spirit became determinate at the beginning (incarnation), is not dissolved in the universe, but is taken up again in its truth, which is to be a "universe-body," the content of his I. We rightly call it a "universe-body" (*corps-univers*). Even now in its mortal condition, the body is a center of relationships that extend by degrees to the

---

2 We will come back to the value of the gospel witness concerning the empty tomb and the meaning of this assertion in our second book, in the chapter on the Resurrection. See our article, "La résurrection," in *Nouvelle Revue Théologique*, 91 (1969), 1009-1044.

3 [Translator's Note. See above, chapter 7, note 4.]

limits of the world. My "body" is not merely my own physical body, but likewise the objects I need, the means of transportation that I employ, the tools I use, and so on. As a result, we can truly say that our "body" extends to the stars. In the resurrection, this universality of our body is fully attained. The body of the risen Christ is thus, in a strict sense, the entire universe, but individualized by his particular body. And this body, the body that "forms one body" with the whole universe, is the content of his I.

One who represents the Resurrection to himself thoughtlessly will perhaps imagine that Christ thereby recovers the resistant, spiritually impervious body that we are used to. But that thing has been dissolved forever in death; it is the grain sown in the earth. Through the Resurrection, it has become a spiritual motion, that is, a connection that overcomes all outwardness and every opposition, like the flow of consciousness wherein the I sees only its self.[4]

In this way the risen Christ is, in one and the same act, present to himself and to the universe. And his mode of presence far surpasses the presence of our consciousness to itself and its thought-world.

The first manifestation of this immediate presence to himself and the world is his disappearing from the sight of those who, remaining in their mortal condition and sin, are present to themselves only through their hardened opposition to other persons and things in space and time—that is, all those who have not, like Christ, gone through a death to themselves and their sins. The disappearing of the Risen One has its correlate in his appearing to those who, having believed in him before his Passion, have been led by him to Easter faith and acknowledge him as Lord—the disciples.

Christ surrendered himself, came to know death, and conquered it. We cannot use our natural senses to recognize and relate to someone who, having passed through death, no longer belongs to the natural world marked by sin. From now on, only a freedom that has followed him on the path whereby he himself has passed can get in touch with him and recognize him. Encountering the risen Christ is an encounter of the Freedom that conquered death with a freedom that has likewise conquered death. Now, the way to die with Christ and to conquer death, when one does not actually die, is to open oneself up and cleave to him through faith. But the disciples are precisely those who let themselves be brought to this

4 For a fuller development, see our article cited in note 2.

faith. At first they do not recognize Christ manifesting himself to them, because they do not yet believe. But they are stirred by him and strengthened in faith (for example, the disciples on the way to Emmaus), and then they recognize him.

And when Christ finally disappears from their sight, his disciples cleave to him in pure faith, the one wholly true relationship with the Lord of glory for one remaining in the condition of this world.

Application to the Act of Freedom

In every moral act[5] there is a resurrection that likewise necessarily follows the passion brought about by the free determination: "This is my body."

After the carnal man, with his icy senses, has been laid to rest in the tomb, and after the dreams joined to his senses have subsided and entered the realm of unsubstantial shades, there rises an interior, spiritual man. The being for which he sacrificed himself, the community ("you") in whom he chose to become incarnate, is now his true body. It is for him a Self, the Self where there is no more negation for the I: possessing himself and other I's.

In this same body, where non-being shortly before actualized its negations (suffering, weakness, ignorance, selfishness), the free I now unfolds its prerogatives. The objects that enticed the body's sensuous impulses, and whose loss was a cause of sorrow, are now stripped of all charm: "What is raised is imperishable" (1 Cor. 15:42). Thus Ignatius, after his scruples and general confession, received the gift of chastity. Augustine characterized the transformation brought about by his conversion in the same way: "How sweet all at once it was for me to be rid of those fruitless joys which I had once feared to lose and was now glad to reject! You drove them from me,...and took their place, you who are sweeter than all pleasure, though not to flesh and blood."[6]

Where the carnal man saw only obscurity and absurdity, ignominy and dishonor, there now bursts forth a luminous and glorious meaning: "It is raised in glory" (1 Cor. 15:43). Augustine goes on in the same vein: "you who outshine all light yet are hidden deeper than any secret in our hearts, you who surpass all honour though not in the eyes of men who see all honour in themselves. ...But, during all those years, where was my free will? What was

---

5 This entire subsection is taken from *Dialectique*, I, 131-132.
6 *Confessions*, IX, 1, trans. R. S. Pine-Coffin (Baltimore: Penguin, 1961), p. 181.

the hidden secret place from which it was summoned in a moment?..."[7]

What seemed to him a hindrance, a diminution, a weakness, now manifests itself as potential and strength: "It is raised in power" (1 Cor. 15:43).

Finally, instead of being withdrawn into one I, a "living being" (1 Cor. 15:45), but closed to all else and unable to penetrate the being of anyone else, this I now finds itself at home in every other I: "It is raised a spiritual body" (verse 44).

Growth in the Positing of Being

Rising in his individuality, Christ instantaneously posits himself as being, an act of his sovereign Freedom. There is *growth* in the positing of being, but it is in us. For Christ relates himself to us, and everything that occurs in and for him occurs in and for us. This growth constitutes the Church, and it takes place in the Church according to the law of time. It is made up of a sequence of events concerning all of us, in the person of those who were the Church at the time of the Passion and Resurrection—the mother of Jesus and his disciples.

His relationship to us is no longer, as in the First Week, that of representations (the sin of the angel, original sin...) to the consciousness that accepts them, meditates on them, and finds therein the meaning of the history of its sins. Now it is the personal relationship of Christ to people, the Church. The risen Christ establishes his relationship to the Church by first manifesting himself to the woman who never for a moment stopped participating intimately in his life, sufferings, and death. He shares with her the life upon which he has entered, his divine life. Then he manifests himself to his disciples and likewise shares his life with them. Finally, he gradually shares his life with all of us who, since Pentecost, believe in him on the basis of the faith of the apostles.

The Third Week closed with a consideration of "the desolation of our Lady, her great sorrow and weariness" [208]. The Fourth Week opens with the first contemplation, "The apparition of Christ our Lord to our Lady" [218]. The reason for this is that Mary, during the three days in which the body of her son was in the tomb, has been the consciousness, or personification, of humanity in whom the unity of the body and soul of her Son continued to be held together by her sorrowful memories. Towards the end

7 Ibid.

of the last chapter, we said it is in her that "there takes place the transition from sorrowful memories to triumphant hopes." "Consequently, it is in and for this humanity that the new unity of the risen Christ should first manifest itself; the combined elements of body and soul, past and future, having undergone the ordeal of death, now compose being and its presence."[8]

Anyone who does not understand the spiritual life as essentially *historical* existence and experience could be surprised that "the mystery of the Resurrection itself does not constitute the subject matter of this first exercise and that, on the contrary, it is so joined to that of the apparition to the Virgin that the Resurrection seems totally absorbed into the latter."[9] Why not, for example, offer the retreatant some reflections on the Resurrection like those we developed in the opening remarks of this chapter? The answer is that the Spiritual Exercises are an existing and experiencing within history. They view the mysteries not so much according to their notional content (to be appropriated by the understanding and transformed into practical resolutions by the will) as according to their historical reality: events that take place in Christ and for us.

In order for the retreatant to participate with his whole being (understanding, will, affectivity) in what is taking place, he is invited to place himself at the juncture of this historical relationship of Christ to us. Now, at the juncture of this relationship we find, at the time of the Resurrection, not the act of coming back to life that concerns Christ in his individuality (properly speaking, this act is non-historical and absolutely transcendent), but the apparitions. The Resurrection is, of course, the reality that gives the apparitions their foundation, but it is through the apparitions that the reality reaches the witnesses and that they participate therein. This is why the Exercises propose the apparitions to us at the outset.

But why begin with an appearance to our Lady, which the Gospels do not mention, rather than that to Peter, for example, who St. Paul says was the first to witness the manifestation of the Risen One (1 Cor. 15:5)? As though he foresaw our astonishment, St. Ignatius offered an explanation: "Though this is not mentioned explicitly in the Scripture it must be considered as stated when Scripture says that He appeared to many others. For Scripture

---

8 *Dialectique*, I, 132.

9 Ibid. Only the title of the contemplation [299] differentiates the resurrection of Christ from the apparition to Mary; the text [218-225], on the other hand, which is supposed to be the development of the title, mentions only the apparition to our Lady.

supposes that we have understanding, as it is written, 'Are you also still without understanding?' " ([299], and Matt. 15:16). Hence it is not a question of "pious exegesis" as Ignatius says regarding the (hypothetical) apparition to Joseph of Arimathea: "He appeared to Joseph of Arimathea, as may be piously believed" [310]. Rather, it is a matter of an *understanding* belonging to faith, as the passage from St. Matthew that Ignatius recalls here leads us to think.[10] In terms of the viewpoint of Fessard: "Ignatius is actually referring to nothing less than the *understanding belonging to the development* of freedom or faith, as it should exist among the disciples of Jesus from the outset, and even more so now because of the familiarity with his method that they have gained up to the precise moment of development they have reached."[11] And so, by judiciously consulting the structure of the Exercises, we will understand "more profoundly the place granted to the Virgin at the growing edge of the positing of being."[12]

The transition from the First to the Second Week took place in the consciousness of the *solitary* I ("an exile here on earth, cast out to live among brute beasts" [47]) when the comparisons set up between itself and other creatures, itself and God [58-59], had warned it about the nothingness it could be, and "sin grew to the point of making it realize the sense of hell. The contrition that then negated the false existence of sin let consciousness, in its body of sin, perceive the correlative summons of being. In the view of Ignatius, it is also in the *solitude* of Mary, prey to 'great sorrow and weariness' [208] out of compassion for her Son who died and 'descended into hell' [219], that the reversal of the present movement comes about. After three days in the tomb, Jesus appears 'to His Blessed Mother' in 'body and soul' [219] newly joined through the Resurrection, causing her 'to be glad and rejoice intensely because of the great joy and the glory of Christ our Lord' [221]. At both junctures, then, there is a transition from the negative to the positive; from an extreme, somehow infernal sorrow to a no less great, truly heavenly joy."[13]

---

10 In Matt. 15:16 the apostles ask Jesus to explain to them the parable about what defiles a man.

11 *Dialectique*, I, 133.

12 Ibid.

13 *Dialectique*, I, 133. This quotation is the first in a series of extracts from Fessard, pp. 133-140. That section in Fessard should be read and understood in relation to our Note on the Application of the Senses appended to chapter 5 on the Second Week.

We will now consider the setting where this twofold transition comes about and the means Ignatius uses to describe each movement and to involve the soul of his retreatant.

"In the meditation on hell, the growth of sin all the way to the absolute of hell, leaving the field free for the summons of being, takes place entirely within the consciousness of the retreatant, and Ignatius calls upon the imagination to be the instrument of this transition to the limit of sin. As a matter of fact, this exercise is the first example of what he later calls 'applying the five senses... with the aid of the imagination' and /what he prescribes each day as the 'fifth contemplation' [121] for each of the following Weeks."[14] The "imaginative senses" are there purified and become "spiritual senses." The unfolding of the four Weeks has for a goal the gradual awakening and forming of the latter out of the former. The consciousness in which the spiritual senses are formed is thus disposed little by little for the most perfect union with God.

The imaginative senses in Mary are already spiritual senses, and her perception of things of this world is simultaneously communion with the mystery of God. But as she shares in the entire destiny of her Son, she experiences a total night of the senses during the passion; it is a night of death that comes to an end, however, in the dawn of the resurrection. Thus it is in and for Mary that the resurrection of her Son should begin bearing its fruit.

When the body of Christ, after being reduced to the state of a "this," is reassumed by his soul, it rises in glory from the limbo of the most distant past along with the "souls of the just" [219] that it has freed from their non-sense. The triumph of Christ over death, the "wages of sin," is manifested first and foremost for Mary, despite her mortal body, and the relation of her "imaginative senses" and "spiritual senses" is thereby reversed. On emerging from the twofold night in which they have all been buried, the spiritual senses stop being dependent, as heretofore, on the imaginative senses. On the contrary, the spiritual senses, having become directly passive to the divine glory of Christ, govern the imaginative senses, illuminating, sharpening, and strengthening them, just as the soul of her Son (by virtue of the hypostatic union) does for his own body, as soon as his soul has been delivered from the shackles of sinful flesh.[15]

14 Ibid., 134.
15 Ibid., 137.

After positing itself for sinless humanity, the Virgin Mary, Freedom posits itself for those who, while being sinners, have clung to its *image* (Jesus in the world), and who have participated (from afar) in his Passion, and who are to collaborate, from now on, in extending his universal kingdom.

It is for us that there is growth in the positing of being in the Fourth Week. But this relationship of Freedom to us is not accidental or secondary, since the Incarnation is essentially directed to our salvation and transformation into God. The risen Christ therefore manifests himself to men, to his disciples first of all and then, through them, to the whole world (birth and increase of the Church). The growth of the kingdom of Freedom in the world is accomplished through a sequence of events, the first of which are its manifestations to the disciples.

These events are contemplated by the senses of the imagination (seeing, hearing, touching...), but they must be perceived in relation to the Freedom of Christ. Otherwise, we would not get beyond the anecdotal, the picturesque; we would be in the realm of the "wonderful," whereas we must attain the meaning of the signs granted, namely, divine Freedom positing itself in itself and for us in an act of love.

In the Third Week, this relation of the event to Freedom was stated in three points that designated Christ's negating of the negation that is sin. This negating of the negation is the meaning and content of the Third Week. It posited itself in a beginning; the divine Persons positively willed the sufferings of the Passion. It unfolded in a divine non-interference, and it ended in us: "all this for my sins" [197].

But from now on we are beyond this negating of the negation; we are in its outcome. This outcome presents itself according to an objective side, the risen Christ, and a subjective side, the relation that Christ sets up with us. Two special points suffice for indicating these two sides: "*Fourth Point*. This will be to consider the divinity, which seemed to hide itself during the passion, now appearing and manifesting itself so miraculously in the most holy Resurrection in its true and most sacred effects. *Fifth Point*. Consider the office of consoler that Christ our Lord exercises..." [223-224].

The objective side itself has its own subjective inwardness: the Freedom of the Risen One, which expresses itself in the body that it takes up. And the subjective side ("the office of consoler that Christ exercises") likewise has its own objectivity: the Church that comes together, or at least begins to do so, under the influence of Christ who "consoles." To *console*, according to St. Ignatius' definition [316], means to strengthen and to cause an increase in faith, hope, and charity. Through the initiative of Christ on behalf of his disciples, faith is reborn and hope irrupts.

This irruption of hope can and ought to be clarified here, starting from the Choice. The Choice essentially involves a sacrifice. The choice of a state of life, or any other decision, as soon as it is a response to a call from Freedom, entails the renunciation of one-self, of one's own feelings and ideas, in order to take on the feelings and ideas of Freedom. Through this sacrifice I give up actualizing myself by satisfying my own sensuousness, my thirst for possessing, and my own will. I break the circle of self-satisfaction, and I part company with myself; I leave behind me my own substance, and I cleave to Reality. The latter is, nevertheless, still abstract and disembodied for me, since the only body that I have known until now is that of my own senses, affections, and dreams, which I have just left behind. That is why, in this condition of separation or abstraction from myself, I can formulate my Choice in terms which are themselves abstract: I chose virtue, renouncing what had heretofore been happiness for me; I chose moral good, forsaking sensuous goods; I chose what ought to be, forsaking what is; I chose being, forsaking non-being (the false reality of the old man). ...But, as we said, mere virtue (as an ideal) and mere duty could never counterbalance the old "reality" in me and make me choose in favor of a still abstract reality, unless on the level of my choosing I—in Him in whom I believe, Christ, the Son of man—virtue was not already joined to happiness, the ideal to reality, moral good to sensuous good. Christ is an ideal for me, but he is an already existing and present ideal. In him and through him, the I that chooses finds the power to abstract from itself, to sacrifice itself, and to hand itself over to a Reality that is undoubtedly still present merely in the form of relative absence, but towards which the I has been aiming by means of...hope.

This presence amidst absence is, in fact, hope within me. This hope dawns when there appears the One who, by his Resurrection, brings the pledge of the new and definitive union between the ideal and reality. This union is charity. Hope marks the beginning of its reign, even though charity remains a thing of the future, some-thing yet to come. Amidst continuing absence, hope already makes present what was still internal and invisible to faith at the time of the Choice, thus increasing faith. Hope is consequently a mediator between faith and charity.

By calling forth hope, the risen Christ revivifies and strengthens faith, and he ignites charity. *He consoles,* to use the term that Ignatius defines as the increase of these three virtues.

Increase of Faith

It is in the risen Christ that "all things hold together" (Col. 1:17). He is the foundation and bond of the beings of the universe as well as of our act of faith and its internal connections. He manifests himself to his disciples because he is such a bond and in order to lead them to acknowledge him as such. Through his initiative, the disciples whose faith faltered during the Passion take stock of the past. The disciples on the road to Emmaus, for example, reexamine the past in the present moment of the risen Christ, and they thus discover what constituted the internal bond of their faith, Christ in the power of the Resurrection. Actually, it is not a question of merely recalling events left in their contingent and almost disjointed succession; it is a question of reflecting.[16] A reflection is a mental journey back to the first principle of whatever is currently being considered within consciousness; here, the disciples are recalling the events of Jesus' life. The first principle of these events is Christ, from now on in a risen state. Consequently, Christ is not merely the one in whom they believe, but the one through whom they believe.

Christ, in his risen body, is the bond connecting the objects of the faith: the events first lived out by him along with his disciples, then reflected on by the Church elaborating them into dogmatic truths. And he is the bond of the act whereby we are faithful to these objects. This bond is a movement, the process whereby divine Freedom determines and limits itself in an image (incarnation) and whereby it overcomes this limitation (passion and death). This movement is united in the spiritual body of the risen Christ. If this body happens to manifest itself, it simultaneously manifests the whole completed movement, that is, all the events of Jesus' life according to their truth and internal connection. In this way the disciples on the road to Emmaus discover the meaning of all that has happened; their faith is revivified and strengthened; and they adhere to the Master, but they are no longer blind to the truth within the contingent events.

16 I participate very concretely in the disciples' reflection on their past by reflecting on my own past, especially the past events of my current retreat: the first two Weeks, the Choice, and the Third Week.

All the truths of the faith are connected in the reality of the Resurrection. Each of these truths is capable of being represented in an image or account where the content of faith is objectified. The images and ideas are distinct from one another, and they are almost external to the I which knows and adheres to them. But their respective contents are related within the risen Christ, in whom they build themselves into a spiritual and consistent universe that is not external to us. As a matter of fact, in Christ all the events of salvation history and all the I's involved therein are gathered together into a single spiritual body.

Consequently, the dogmas of original sin, the incarnation, the power of Christ over the sins he forgives, his redemptive death, our participation in his death and resurrection through baptism —all these dogmatic affirmations are joined and unified in the reality of the risen Christ; in him they are justified and take on meaning.

The manifestation of the risen Christ has been an increase of faith for the apostles, therefore, and it becomes such for us each time we relive it through unitive contemplation. We pass from a too human and faltering faith to the Easter faith, from that of the apostles before the Resurrection to that of the witnesses of the Resurrection.

Increase of Hope

Hope makes present to us the reality in which we believe. Hope brings us in touch with that reality, while leaving it in the future; we do not yet see it. Or even better, hope turns us towards the future by bringing us in touch with it already in the present. The risen body hands over to the soul the essence of all the things wherein the soul seeks itself.

These things are the realities of Jesus' life, wherein the soul seeks its own good and happiness, the spiritual peace which is the fruit of virtue and the fullness of sensuous satisfaction. Hope hands over to the soul the essence of these realities, that is, the bond that ties them together, the meaning that permeates them. This meaning or bond is the Risen One in person, for he is the Self in whom the moments of salvation history are gathered together and with whom we are all associated.

When this Self manifests itself to and in hopeful faith, all the semblances of being (the entire non-being characteristic of the sinful world) are definitively excluded, and in their place appears the mystical body or the Church, the union of all and fullness for

all, in Jesus Christ. Whence arises the "interior joy" that elevates
the soul above all earthly things which are no longer loved for their
own sake, "but only in the Creator of them all" [316].

Increase of Charity

Objectively, this growing charity is the mystery of the inchoate
assembling of the Church, the society of love since Easter morning.
Subjectively, it is the inflaming of the apostles—and of the I that
is making the retreat. The Ideal, Christ turned towards us in
his being and Freedom, no longer acts merely through the deeds
and words of a man subject to the conditions of life in this world
and affecting others from outside, as before the Passion. The risen
Christ directly and from within affects the senses, understanding,
and will of his disciples. And he does the same with us, to the degree
that we share in his death through faith. Before the Choice, the
exercises of the first two Weeks offered us evangelical representations,
images, and ideas for meditation and contemplation. Whereas after
the Choice, on the level of the unitive life that we reach by our
sharing in his Passion, the mystery of Christ affects us more
directly. It affects us, however, just as it historically affected the
witnesses of the Resurrection: by remaining *future*. Consequently,
we already have a spiritual taste, possession, or enjoyment, and
at the same time our desire is drawn towards the future where, in
relation to us, the mystery of Christ remains.

Now, our desire is both perfect and imperfect. It is perfect in
the sense that it has turned away from all carnal objects; it is
imperfect in the sense that it retains the same basic characteristics
as concupiscence: It is the expression of my own need, and hence
it still brings me back to myself in the very act of drawing me
towards Christ. This is the ambiguity of all desires, even spiritual
ones. The purification of this desire is not within reach of the subject
who experiences it. It is a question of turning what remains "for
me" in these desires into a pure "for God": God desired no longer
for me, but in and for himself. God alone can assume the initiative
for this final purification and lead it to good. He does it objectively
by removing his presence from our intellectual and affective grasp
(the Ascension, which throws the disciples back on pure faith).
And he purifies us subjectively, in our pyschological and reflective
consciousness, by extinguishing every idea (even of God), every
image, every feeling, every felt adherence, even the feeling of faith
(the passive nights of the senses and of the spirit).

From the testimony of all the mystics, this emptying of consciousness is terrible. But every spiritual life provides at least some weak beginning of it—dryness, boredom, darkness, doubts about faith—and it is necessary to know how to discern these events, and then to explain them, as much as they can be explained, to those who undergo them.

It is in this way that charity grows: through a continual stripping away, a renunciation of signs, of securities given at one time, even those that are desirable and good in themselves. Mary Magdalen, who wanted to throw herself at the feet of Jesus when she recognized him, experienced this growth....

The Disappearing of the Positing of Being: Ascension

There is, therefore, an insufficiency intrinsic to hope. Insofar as hope makes us experience his presence, it draws us towards the future by rekindling our "concupiscence," for God certainly, but concupiscence all the same. The three basic drives that constitute man—the desire for love, the instinct for possessing, and the will for autonomy, nay, the will for power—come to life again, and they urge us on to take hold of God in order to enjoy him, as if there were question of a natural being. But these three drives cannot make us reach God as he is in himself, since they invariably bring us back to ourselves. Hence, they must be gradually mortified; and this is why the dialectic ends with a call to love, that is, the aforementioned call to a supreme renunciation. Evangelical renunciation, however, is the hidden life of love.

Hope transcends itself in charity; the ardent desire that hope arouses must be lived out in a renunciation of immediate satisfaction. Here the meaning of the threefold evangelical call is entirely revealed: the call to chastity, that makes desire die and rise; to poverty, opposed to the instinct for appropriation; to obedient humility, that contradicts the exalting of independence and power. This is a threefold surrender, not only regarding the events and beings of the world, but also in relation to God and his most spiritual gifts. It is a threefold renunciation and a threefold resurrection!

Let us see how this transcending of hope by charity unfolds. Hope puts us in touch with its "Object"[17] by a movement that proceeds not merely from consciousness, but also from the

---

17 *Object* is used here deliberately; this Object is, of course, the Subject who does not allow himself to be grasped. But it is precisely this elusiveness that the man of hope must experience more fully.

Object. Consciousness is inflamed in consolation, but it is God who consoles it; the apostles have a rebirth of hope when they recognize the risen Christ, but it is Christ who makes them recognize him. In short, it is the Object that makes itself present.

This presence of the Object is worked out through the antithesis of presence/absence, which characterizes faith and which is sharpened by hope. A sign is given that awakens hope; but the sign is not immediately the Object, which is accordingly manifested as absent. And the clearer the sign, the more lively the hope and the more intense the feeling of absence will be. Whoever has hope spontaneously seeks to fill up this absence by making that aspect whereby hope is a sensuous presence, that is, its sign aspect, increase indefinitely in its own direction. This is the error of Mary Magdalen who, upon recognizing the risen Jesus, seeks to hold onto his feet. Now, the aspect whereby hope is the presence of the Object is relative to its other aspect, that of absence. The Object, in fact, does not make itself present as a sign except to signify itself as still being absent, for it is such that it cannot manifest itself absolutely in this world of signs, our world. It is transcendent.

To become attached to the sign in order to compensate for the absence, and, if possible, to intensify the sign to eliminate absence, is to destroy the mediation that hope gives rise to; it is to rupture the necessary relation of presence/absence and to fall into a contradiction. Instead of living in faith, where presence/absence are combined, each referring to the other, we disconnect them and then fall into the contradiction of an indefinite repetition of the same sterile effort. The more I cling to the sign-aspect of presence, the more incapable I become, because of my very attachment, of really reaching the Object. And the absence of the Object will make itself felt that much more.

Thereby it becomes clear that the Object does not remain indifferent to my attempts; to my effort to seize it, it responds by getting clear of my grip and distancing itself for an increased absence. This is because the Object is transcendent; and through my contradictory and unhappy experience, I begin to recognize this a little better.

It is always possible to let this dialectic drift into the contradiction of an indefinite repetition of my efforts. But if, on the other hand, I let myself learn from experience, the withdrawal of the Object, correlative to my attachment, will rescue me from my attachment itself. I will begin to disengage myself from my vain attempts, and at once the transition to charity will be accomplished; the true mediation of hope will come about. As a matter of fact, to the degree that I detach myself from the sensuous thing (the given sign) that gives birth to my hope and stirs it up, I go beyond the framework of the sign (consolation, apparition of the risen Christ), and I reach the order of transcendence proper to the Object. From then on, the latter becomes for me the sovereignly free Subject in the gift which it makes of itself.

Through this movement, the antithesis of presence/absence proper to faith unfolds, but it unfolds according to the unity, the connection, of its two aspects: Presence returns to absence, and as the latter is experienced more deeply, it prepares for presence. In this way we arrive at the order of charity; the Object is no longer an object for me, but the sovereign gratuity of Love that withdraws from my grip only in order to fill me beyond every desire. In the order of charity, absence unites me to Love as much as presence does, for one passes into the other. Charity forsakes particular signs (signs are always particular), but for it everything becomes a sign, the presence of Love in its very absence: joy and sorrow, good and bad, night and day, sin itself. *Sin* becomes the Savior who suffers and converts what was perverted. *Good* becomes the Lord who works in his members. *Sorrow* becomes Jesus who carries his cross. *Joy* becomes the risen Christ who shines through a human face. Everything is sign; everything is presence, his presence, in absence itself. Charity lives out everything at once, joy and the cross. It accepts all without choosing; and that is to get in touch with the transcendent, the God who is thrice holy. Presence/ absence are especially reconciled in the service of others; it is the Lord whom I see and acknowledge in others. Hence presence, and yet absence, but an absence that I live out from now on as contact with him, in the night of faith.

Regarding this now unfolded mediation of hope, we can make the following observations:

1. It runs the risk of drifting into an indefinite contradiction; this risk is contained within the mediation itself, where the aspect of presence can be willed for itself without that of absence. It is then that hope can beget its contrary, despair, disappointed hope. Not infrequently, it is through some disappointments and even despair that experience succeeds in getting rid of its excessive attachment to sensuous guarantees and raises itself to the order of charity.

2. The negation, not of hope, but of the sensuous sign that stirred up hope, is contained within the very logic of the media-

tion: The negation derives from faith as presence/absence and from the "Object" itself, which is manifesting itself no longer merely in a sign (presence), but through a call to love that comes from above (absence).

3. The call to love is not extrinsic to what has been undergone previously in the dialectical unfolding of experience. It is the very interior of the mystery which has just manifested itself through this dialectic. It is what was already perceived in faith at the beginning (the Call of the Kingdom).

4. Thus ends the dialectic, or rather, thus it explodes in the full freedom of love. Living according to charity, in union with God and other people, is beyond every dialectic, because in such a life oppositions are reconciled and unilateral aspects are corrected. But the order of charity is not lived out absolutely as long as the mediation of hope is not completed—that is, as long as we have not transcended the framework of nature and history, where the sign that stirred up hope manifested itself (the image of the invisible God, the Risen One manifesting himself, consolation in my spiritual life). This transcending of nature and history becomes complete only in death. On this side of death, logic requires that *partial* transcending of hope (and of the dialectic) on behalf of love still keep us within hope and hence within the dialectic. And this is why we make the Exercises over again; we continue to live by making choices, but we try to make our choices conform more and more to this logic.

Note on the Denouement of the Dialectic of the Exercises

(*This exposition adds nothing essential to what we have just said about hope, the disappearance of signs, and admittance to the order of charity. Those who would not be helped by a more formal analysis can omit this long note.*)

"Whatever the growth of the being of Freedom in the course of the Fourth Moment [Week] may be, this being always remains a being posited in the representation; it is an appearance of absolutely trustworthy and transparent Freedom, but it is a mere appearance that makes us long for its substance."[18]

The Object of faith, the risen Christ, manifests itself in nature and history through apparitions, that is, in "representation." Likewise, consolation is the manifestation of God within the

18 *Dialectique*, I, 143.

sensuous realm. This evidence is "absolutely trustworthy": This perceived body is really the Lord of glory; my consolation is a result of the divine presence in me. And it is "transparent": Through it passes a relationship of the Lord to me and of me to him. But at the same time it remains a "mere appearance that makes us long for its substance." It is the presence of an absence, an unveiling that simultaneously veils.

Now here is the difficult point to grasp in this moment of the manifestation of Christ and of the awakening of hope. The manifestation, the evidence, is precisely what reveals to consciousness the extreme distance between the being of Freedom and the sign of its presence that it gives us, even if this sign be the body seen and touched by the witnesses. Likewise in a spiritual life which has realized some progress: Everything that signifies the presence of God signifies still more his transcendence, his radical absence.

The distance is infinite. ... The fullness of presence withdraws into the future to the very degree that this presence, in its relative manifestation, has been perceived. The apostles experienced this. At first they thought that the apparitions of Christ were the very coming of his kingdom. Then the idea of the Parousia was postponed to the near future, as the epistles of St. Paul to the Thessalonians seem to testify. Finally, insofar as the Resurrection was understood, hope realized that its "Object" was eschatological; the Parousia could only occur at the end point of the "time of the nations," in the far distance.

Nevertheless, hope is dedicated to crossing this distance, somehow. And hope can do so, because this distance is not the result of an internal contradiction within the relationship of consciousnesses to the Object. The presence/absence antithesis can be dismembered and lead to an indefinite and contradictory pursuit of the Object, but this is not consonant with its essence. Presence/absence certainly develops one aspect of reciprocal opposition, but this opposition must be understood and experienced amidst a union that is more essential. In any case, the crossing of this distance is extremely difficult because the efforts expended to cross it run the very risk of upholding and even increasing it. These efforts come from hope, and thus they rest on the sensuous evidence that stirred up hope; they actualize an advance, but do so in the direction of that evidence, and this is precisely what should not happen. If this does happen, the attachment to the evidence, the sign, deviates from what is signified, and the Object slips away into infinity—this is what occurs through my fault and...through the kindness of the

Object itself which, through the feeling of increased absence, tries to engender a detachment in me.

In summary, the only possible way to negotiate the distance is to accept the antithetical conditions that engender it; to rely on the evidence received, without clinging to it or seeking to increase it or even merely to retain it; but to turn resolutely towards the service of Love within the Church and the world. It is thus that the risen Christ manifests himself to his own only in order to awaken their faith and to entrust them with a mission: "Go tell my brothers. ..." "Go teach all nations. ..." The gap between sign and signified is then transcended in truth; God draws near while the conditions of life in this world, hope and its play of antitheses at once posited and transcended, opposed and reconciled, are upheld without becoming hardened.

We do not overcome the presence/absence opposition except by passing through it. The time of this opposition is, in the framework of life, the hope that engenders a certain hopelessness. Reflection formulates this opposition by stating the following dilemma:

If the future (that is, the Object felt as absent during the very time in which it becomes present in a sign) becomes really and totally present within nature and history, it negates itself as future. As a matter of fact, this real and total presence would take place within the framework of the sign received (consolation, apparitions of Christ). But then the future, that is, the transcendence of the kingdom of God, would be actualized within a framework that is not his, that of nature and history. This is as much as to say that it would not be actualized; there it could only decay, degenerate into illusion, and thus negate itself. Hence it is important to maintain the dimension of the future.

But if the future remains definitively future—that is, if we harden the presence/absence opposition by ceasing to understand that it is entirely relative both to our natural-historical existence and to the necessity of preparing ourselves to transcend this framework of existence—the presence that it provides itself through the apparitions (or the consolation) remains deceptive. Instead of signifying for us the reality of the risen Christ among us, it deceives —deluding the senses and faith!—and the truth of this deceptive presence is total and definitive absence.

The dilemma is perfect. It is not a witticism; it is the path that leads hope to charity. One must go as far as the absence which, in immense anguish, is experienced as definitive in order to have access to absolute presence.

Hope contains a promise. If hope claims to fulfill it here and now, that is, within the framework of the sign, it makes the future present. But suddenly this future that is present in nature and history is only a pseudo-reality, a human project that believes it "has arrived": a spiritual high, getting drunk on activity. . . . Such an aberration perverts the experience of faith and of hope.

But if, on the contrary, hope leaves the future in a background that withdraws in proportion as we advance (for example, the myth of indefinite progress for man), it ends by negating the truth of the promise that it contains. For the presence/absence relationship in hope signifies the reality of the coming kingdom as absolute, but not as inaccessible.

How can we resolve this dilemma? How can we exclude non-being, the natural and historical element necessary for the sign, without negating the reality of the sign —that is, without destroying the very structures of the manifestation through signs? How can we affirm the reality of this world (and we must affirm it, since the sensuous evidence that arouses hope is given in the world), and how can we have Being, the glorified Christ and his kingdom, appear in the world without thereby belittling them? These questions arise from the dilemma understood according to its presence/absence antithesis, which is not its ultimate truth. But we can only arrive at its ultimate truth by passing through that antithesis. We must arrive at the point where all paths are cut off, where the two horns of the dilemma are experienced as equally disastrous and equally false to both faith and hope, even though their opposition, to all appearances, is generated by faith and hope.

To decide in favor of the *present* is to abandon the future as a mirage, and in this case the present would be the natural and human world, recognized today as the sign and content of the final reality. This is the temptation of the Marxists, for example, who ascribe to themselves the kind of a world whose possibilities Christianity has manifested, and who reject Christianity and its eschatology as a mirage.

To decide in favor of the *future* is to negate the truth of the present, and in this case the future is nothing but the imaginary world constructed by the believer who would postpone and project his hopes into a future unconnected to the present, although the present caused him to conceive these hopes. The correlative of this projection would then be a disinterest towards the present world.

The two terms of this alternative, however, are mutually repellent by reason of their corrupting one-sidedness. What follows then?

If both of these contrary options are really rejected outright, this can happen only by virtue of a profound understanding of the dialectic that has brought us to this point. In addition, it demands a heroic fidelity to faith and hope despite the anguish felt at finding oneself at an impasse. This anguish, the negative aspect of the salvation to come, must first be borne courageously. For in rejecting the two contrary options, we do not automatically go beyond the dilemma. Such a repudiation, if I really will it, merely leads to a testing of my patience. I then hope that Freedom will deign to posit itself in the midst of the antitheses, which serve as its cradle, and that Freedom itself will bring about the conversion of the present to the future and of the future to the present.

Here it becomes entirely clear what has been going on from the beginning, through the oppositions of being and non-being, of Freedom and the sinful I, and so on, which have filled the four Moments [Weeks] of the experience. What was present at the very outset, the Freedom of being and the freedom of sinful man, meet again at the end, face to face. But now there is, in addition, the clarity of vision gained from the conversion and the choice; one can no longer act unawares. In a sense, the choice is called into question again by this conclusion, but it cannot be otherwise. Every deepening of a choice once made summons one to choose anew on a more profound level. Here there can be no more hedging; in order to resolve this final opposition (present/future) in which everything culminates, one must choose between oneself (by throwing oneself into a one-sided choice that feigns salvation, or else by becoming the prey of despair) and divine Freedom, which is simultaneously present and absent. Divine Freedom is intensely *present* through the very urgency of the oppositions that it has engendered by manifesting itself in the sensuous present; and it is sorrowfully *absent* by the very fact of its transcendence, which is now very acutely felt. Here representations can no longer serve as substitutes. The episodes of the life of Jesus, experienced by the apostles and contemplated by us, provided the feeling and reality of a certain presence. But this form is now transcended, for it is Christ in glory who has manifested himself, and this manifestation has outshone all figures. There remains a bottomless void or total presence.[19] Upholding the two horns of the dilemma opens up a bottomless void in the soul. Or there is total presence. . . .

---

19 Such at least are the extremes of this experience, though each person need not have arrived here and now at these extremes. But we will not enter into the contingencies of particular experiences.

As we have said, however, the dialectic of itself will not sublimate the dilemma that lies there gaping in thought and especially in existence. The dialectic "does not posit being, but it disposes the elements of becoming and necessity in such a way as to allow Freedom room to posit itself."[20] The dilemma is the necessary result of the entire dialectic; everything culminates in this necessity. But at the climactic point, in the very act in which consciousness realizes that the dilemma is only the underside of total presence and Freedom—an act that is already freedom in consciousness and a result of Freedom—the situation resolves itself...or is about to resolve itself. The situation will resolve itself more or less rapidly, for there can be a divergence between the *thought* that understands the dilemma as the underside of presence and the *experience* of this presence. This divergence tells us quite simply that the thought that reflects and understands is not identical with the Freedom that posits itself by allowing itself to be posited. Freedom—my freedom in relationship to the Freedom of God—is the soul of the entire dialectic, and it may not be confused with any of the necessary moments in the dialectic or even with their summation.

The experience of total presence, the final and total reflection that gives way to this presence, ultimately coincides with death, whereby present and future are joined together from their most extreme opposition. Death comes at an hour that no one knows. But death is present even now in this sorrowful awareness that all exits are blocked, that there is no way at all to advance the dialectic. That is, there is no way to think and act, for everything has been said and done. At that moment, the hour of God strikes. It is the hour of death...or the hour for living again, but from now on it is a living from and through God, for whom everything has not yet been said or done.

In life, the dilemma is experienced in a relative or alleviated form; and hence the presence that resolves it stays just as relative. God becomes present little by little. We have just presented the logic of some "critical hours" of existence. But within existence, no critical hour fully actualizes logic. This is why there ensues only a partial resurrection and presence of Freedom. It is death, death in abandonment, that actualizes this logic absolutely; and this is why only death is followed by total presence. It is possible that a great many are spared the extreme throes of such abandonment.

20 *Dialectique*, I, 144.

Jesus on the cross was not spared them, and they are undoubtedly the lot of many who do their utmost to follow him most closely.

Gaston Fessard writes of the dilemma we have presented: "Let us see how the dialectic resolves this problem. Actually, the dialectic does not resolve it."[21]

This is an important statement, the most important one in the whole book. For it determines the meaning of everything. We will comment on it for the sake of a deeper grasp of what we have already said. The dialectic does not resolve the problem: true, in the sense that, as the connection of necessary moments, it can never substitute its mechanism for the freedom that animates it. Shot through and through with freedom, the dialectic is simultaneously the connection of moments which are necessary in relation to each other. But here the dialectic has arrived at the instant of its final summing up. There is no longer anything for the present moment to pass into; there is no more transition beyond this instant. And so freedom itself appears, unveiled, but not in arbitrariness. Quite the contrary, its different possibilities are perfectly defined. But nothing can force freedom to choose one rather than another, not even the fact that a single outcome may be logical and shown to be such. For the choice we make conditions our reading of the total situation at the same time as our reading of it conditions our choice. Thus if I commit myself to a one-sided option, I could find, in the "special logic" created by this option, reasons that "justify" me. The more I fall into a contradiction with reason by a one-sided option, the more justification I find for what I am doing, although this justification is nothing more than a reiteration of my contradiction.

The dialectic "disposes the elements of becoming and necessity."[22] This disposing is inevitably negative, since its positive side is the total presence of Freedom. It consists in strengthening the two horns of the dilemma by understanding that it is (logically) impossible to choose one term rather than another. This strengthening of the two terms in their opposition amounts to understanding that the dilemma is engendered only because the presence/absence antithesis is considered from the viewpoint of the opposition of one term against another, that this opposition must be transcended, but that it cannot be transcended by any further dialectical development. The dialectic is at its end point. We must therefore stay there, in

21 Ibid.
22 See above, note 20.

patience and suffering, if need be. In other words, we must be willing to live out this very *real* conflict of presence and absence, wherein presence becomes more and more feebly felt as presence, but more and more strongly felt as the urgency of what is still absent.

The dilemma itself is only the episode of a moment, and therefore it is temporary and to be transcended. But since no new initiative of human freedom can bring about this transition, we must be on our guard against an exclusively intellectual attitude that would consist in saying, on the basis of a supposed insight: The dilemma as dilemma must be rejected and transcended. Consciousness cannot reject the dilemma, for consciousness is presently defined by it. It is therefore necessary to endure it up to the very end, and the end, we have said, is...the end of life. The dilemma has the merit of thoroughly exploiting the present as opposed to the future, and the future as opposed to the present. We are in an existence defined by this opposition, even if faith knows, understands, and says that this opposition rests on a connection with, and unity in, Jesus Christ. To suffer this situation, to wait in a mixture of anguish and hope, to work humbly in charity (we have already defined this word, and we will do so again)—are all one. For this is to be simultaneously in the dilemma and beyond it; this is already the final and total reflection that is to unite its two terms.

Concupiscence is, in the midst of the dilemma, the effort to go beyond it: "to pounce directly on its object, as on its prey, convinced that if it seizes it, it will be satisfied."[23] The concupiscence that persists in this "moment" of the Resurrection is the concupiscence of the new man for the good. This concupiscence is not enlivened merely by the natural dynamism of passionate desire, the instinct to possess, and the will to power. It is additionally strengthened by the supernatural gift of himself that God in his Christ made by handing himself over in the form of a guarantee (the Son of man now dead and risen, or consolation in the spiritual life of anyone). In a sense, therefore, the new concupiscence that rushes toward this sensuous guarantee is aligned with the gift of God. This is the source of its force and also the source of the intense anguish that is engendered when the total logic of this gift causes it to escape the grip of concupiscence and flee to infinity.

This intense anguish was undoubtedly spared the apostles because they were raised to the level of the trial by a grace incarnate in the Virgin Mary present among them. But anguish waylays

23 *Dialectique*, I, 144.

the believer who is less attentive to all the aspects of the mystery of the Fourth Week; it is not enough to rejoice with Christ when he is present; in addition, we must pray fervently with Mary at every hour of the day. It is thus that the apostles prepared themselves for the trial of the Ascension and were able to pass through this new "time of death" that lasted until Pentecost. This fervent prayer is always possible for one who remains in the Church, even if he does not attain that full union with the mystery that the mother of Jesus lived out and embodied among the disciples.

Let us stress this point: The new concupiscence is enlivened by a fidelity to the gift of God, but by a fidelity which is not complete and hence which shifts to infidelity, if it continues indefinitely in the same direction. The gift of God, Christ, permeates nature and history. At the same time, he is greater than nature and history, and this is why he achieves his identity by dying to both of them. He thereby signifies the transcendence of that very reality he embodied in the world. But here he signifies it negatively and in direct contradiction to his act of becoming embodied in the world; passing from life is diametrically opposed to entering into it. Through death, therefore, the transcendence of the gift of God is signified ambiguously. For death does not exclude the possibility of transcendence being the opposite of presence in the world. Of course, death is not the end point of the movement of the Incarnation and the manifestation of the gift of God as wholly transcendent. Christ rises, and thus signifies his transcendence positively; transcendence is simultaneously presence in the world, beyond the opposition of life and death, of presence and absence. The Lord of glory himself takes up again the body placed in the tomb and inserts himself back into history. But the guarantee that he gives to his disciples by manifesting himself to them as Lord of glory is not absolutely identical with the Lord of glory as he is in himself and in the depths of the Blessed Trinity. Even in the apparitions there remains a gap between the sign and the signified, and this is why the new concupiscence of the disciple who believes with the aid of the apparitions ought not to "pounce on this guarantee" as if the latter by itself could lead him into absolute presence. Fidelity recovered with the aid of the guarantee becomes infidelity if it becomes attached to it.

The Son of man, in his mortal life, fully reveals the Son of God in his humiliations, but the apparitions of the risen Christ do not fully reveal the Lord in his glory; to become attached to the apparitions is to begin to turn away from him whom they manifest.

For they are only a sign. Therefore, by the mere fact that they take place, they open up an infinite distance between sign and signified, between the immediate presence of glory in a sign and the fullness of this same glory. Now we can see where the new concupiscence remains imperfect: it is aligned with salvation history, but at the same time it does not fully comprehend it. It is "aligned with salvation history," and of course it goes quite far in comprehending this history; it goes to the point of understanding the Resurrection and the apparitions as a manifestation of the glory of Christ. Purified by some participation in the death of Christ, concupiscence from now on flows not from nature alone but also from faith, which reinforces and justifies it. Not to strive, through the dynamics of a nature renewed by faith, to reach Christ, who manifests himself in nature and history, would be contempt or disaffection. And yet such a concupiscence is imperfect, for it is basically the sign alone which it is aiming at and...which it would attain, if the signified did not protect the sign from its grip by withdrawing.

The distance which is opened up between the immediate presence in a sign and the fullness of presence that can only be future (the end of time) does not affect Christ in himself. It intervenes between Christ and us, between his individual person and men in the world. This relationship of present/future is at once incommensurable and commensurable. It is incommensurable because it expresses the difference between the divine transcendence in itself and the sign that manifests it in nature and history. It is commensurable as the distance from today, from the hope raised by the sign, to the end of time, when the signified will shine in the full splendor of his glory. The illusion for hope here would be to imagine that this end of time will come about through continuous growth on the temporal plane; such growth would merely be a relapse into the indeterminate, with the Object of hope forever receding ahead. This illusion —and this is its extreme subtlety—arises, in a sense, from the very logic of what has taken place up to now, and especially from the apparitions of the risen Christ. To hope in a kingdom of God on earth and to work to establish it—isn't this simply to prolong what Christ does in appearing to his disciples? No. Because the prolongation, within duration, of this visible reinsertion of Christ into the world is surely unfaithful to the very essence of this reinsertion. For, although Christ does manifest himself, he does so without revealing his glory, and even without being able to. Between this present manifestation and the full splendor of his glory there is an incommensurable difference. Christ has personally leaped across this difference, but neither the world nor men, even believers in the Resurrection, have yet crossed it.

For us, therefore, the truth of the appearances of Christ to the apostles is his disappearance. His disappearance signifies to the apostles the distance which, in his very manifestation, separates sign from signified. It would be insufficient to say that the disappearance of Christ (the Ascension) is a divine pedagogy that allows the apostles to purify their new concupiscence; his disappearance is inscribed within the very mystery of the appearances; it is their truth.

Through the disappearance of the Object that engendered hope, hope is suppressed as concupiscence and is fulfilled as charity. Charity is the paradoxical union of all the elements which, on the level of hope, present themselves within a dilemma. Charity believes all and hopes for all; the least trace is a sign to charity of the Risen One, who revivifies its hope. Since charity is free regarding any particular sign, it sees signs galore, and this freedom puts charity, in the midst of absence, in touch with the future, the Parousia. Absence as well as signs of presence (successes and failures, human virtues and vices, consolation and desolation, night and day) unite charity with God and make it contemporary with the end of time. Such is the charity that wends its way in the world; it is ready to persevere in this fashion as long as God wants it to, even forever. It is united with God, and heaven itself could not provide it with greater union. In this way, in service and labor, is accomplished the "final and total reflection"[24] that is cut off from absolute presence by an ever finer veil. At this point a saint would be ready to agree to the supreme folly of being cut off from God forever, whether by staying on earth or even by going to hell, provided that he have charity. "For I could wish that I myself were accursed and cut off from Christ for the sake of my brethren" (Rom. 9:3). But God is keeping watch. . . .

We can now cite a long passage from Gaston Fessard: "The movement of concupiscence, the new as well as the old, is to pounce directly on its object, as on its prey, convinced that if it seizes it, it will be satisfied. The movement is, for example, the spontaneous gesture of Mary Magdalen, who stretches out her hands towards her Master. . . . It is the more reflective thought of the apostles who, discovering their leader more glorious and powerful than ever,

24 Ibid.

see their dreams revive.... It is the inevitable tendency of the soul enticed by sensuous consolation. Having tasted true Freedom for an instant, the soul hopes for nothing more than the continuance and extension of this consolation to the limited world for which it has sacrificed itself.

"At first sight there is nothing impossible with this desire. The sacrifice which the soul made at the end of the second Moment did not appear at all to be a choice between good and evil, but between the better and the less good. Between the carnal and spiritual aspects of the kingdom of Israel, it chose the spiritual aspect. But what is there to prevent everything which is good in the carnal aspect from coming to join the spiritual aspect? There is no indomitable opposition between less good and better, but simply a finite, momentary void to fill in. Since the King has clearly manifested himself first, the only thing to do is to have him acknowedged by the various members of the community. Since the apparition of Freedom is real and sensuous, and since it unfolds and grows in time, it is hence a question of more or less, a question of time.... 'Lord, will you at this time restore the kingdom to Israel?' (Acts 1:6). By acting in this way concupiscence only goes along with a dynamic which is not its own. Is not the being which it now enjoys the guarantee and promise of what it longs for? Is it not He who speaks of the proximate fulfillment of the promise? 'While staying with them, he charged them not to depart from Jerusalem, but to wait for the promise of the Father' (Acts 1:4-5). Concupiscence is not acting on its own when it imagines the fullness which will leave nothing more to desire.

"Thus hope at first inevitably stirs up this dream of a messianic kingdom for Israel, a 'heaven on earth,' a future which would be present like the actual, sensuous presence of things. But this happens in order that concupiscence may reexperience here, in the state of grace, what it formerly experienced in the state of sin. Insofar as concupiscence is united with its object, concupiscence destroys it, and in destroying it, concupiscence feels more poignantly the void hollowed out amid its desire. The scholar, insofar as his intelligence pursues being, sees it disappear in order that the consciousness of his essential ignorance may become concrete wisdom. The same is true here of the soul. The soul does not at all destroy its object because the object is indestructible, but the more the soul stretches toward it, the more the object withdraws. And since it is a matter of the human soul and a divine object, at the first try the object flees to infinity....

"The gesture of Mary Magdalen, the question of the apostles, and the concupiscence of the soul are so many attacks of non-being on being which call forth their negation.

" 'Do not hold me, for I have not yet ascended to the Father...' (John 20:17). This is as if he had said: You could not be expected to understand this—it is when you have lost hope of touching me that you will embrace me!

" 'It is not for you to know times or seasons which the Father has fixed by his own authority...' (Acts 1:17). In other words: You could not be expected to know that time has nothing to do with the matter and that the kingdom of your dreams will be set up when you no longer dream about it!

"And the concupiscence of the soul sees itself sent back to the concrete, to the present that continues to flow despite desires to stop it. 'Why do you stand looking into heaven?..' (Acts 1:11).

"At the very moment when the sensuous effects of consolation tare in danger of deceiving one about the true nature of Freedom, the dialectic makes them disappear."[25]

Christ ascends again, therefore, to his Father. He rises by his own motion, for his disappearance is intrinsically demanded. At the same time, he is dispelled or blown away by the impulse, the contradictory quest, of concupiscence. "The guarantee of hope, at the moment of actualizing the 'kingdom of Israel,' escapes from the confines of space and time."[26]

Objectively, this flight is primarily the return of Christ to the vertical transcendence of God, who is always present. But this ascension is simultaneously the fulfillment and recapitulation of the whole of time. It therefore presents itself to us, who are within time, as a transfer of the glorious Christ to an end of time which we should be heading for in hope and charity, inasmuch as Christ takes time upon himself and recapitulates it. Within our representation, that is, our natural and historical way of recording and living out the ascension, the delay of the end of time inevitably takes on the appearance of a transfer to an indefinite future—which is in itself, however, perfectly determinate.

For Christ at that limit of time—which has come for him—rejoins his Origin, the Father. Even if the end is portrayed to us as indefinitely removed from the beginning, the two are joined in Jesus Christ. We must therefore break through the alienation produced

25 Ibid., 144-145.
26 Ibid., 146.

192

by the new concupiscence that projects its Object along an indefinite line, for the Object is implicitly present and hence the most distant future coincides perfectly, here and now, with the most remote past. Insofar as beginning and end coincide for us, we are transcending the representation of the straight line and the entire portrayal of the four Moments of the dialectic as a linear progression.

"In that way, far from losing its value, hope gains it."[27] It is precisely insofar as the guarantee of hope disappears that what it designated and made tangible becomes more perfectly present—for faith permeated by charity. Hope bridged the gap between the less good, the sensuous being that I renounced by the Choice (human joys, projects, dreams...), and the better, the spiritual (becoming attached to Christ in an inevitable sacrifice). Transformed into charity, it now bridges the gap between the better and the perfect. As a matter of fact, the better from now on tends to become the perfect, in the sense that it is no longer defined in opposition to the less good; *consoled* hope unites the sensuous (less good) and the spiritual (better).

But this unity remains partial; it is not total presence, but merely presence in the "limited world" of my consolation. It is charity which causes me to pass from this partial and transitory unity to a more perfect unity, such that the union of the sensuous and the spiritual is permanent and universal. In fact, as we have already said, charity transcends the opposition between consolation and desolation, success and failure, night and day. For charity, everything is a mark of God's presence and affords union with him. Everything sensuous, consoling or not, is—for charity—linked to the spiritual. There is, therefore, a permanent union of the two. Moreover, this union does not remain limited to the "limited world" of its first choice. It extends to the totality of the sensuous world, to every action in this world, without being attached to one project rather than another; the life of charity is coextensive with the kingdom of God, which transcends any measurement. Such is the charity that believes all things, hopes all things, endures all things....

On the day of the Ascension it was to this nascent charity that the promise was made: "This Jesus, who was taken up from you into heaven, will come in the same way as you saw him go into heaven" (Acts 1:11).

27 Ibid.

"The future, the time to come, though extended to infinity, always remains a real hereafter; He will come. Our hope is therefore quite a different thing from a mirage that makes possible an indefinite progression. And, on the other hand, this time to come will no longer be this or that future, this or that kingdom for Israel, but the One who is to come, identical with the Origin, seated at the right hand of the Father, and who, after having destroyed all non-being and having recapitulated all being in himself, will then offer himself in an eternal present in order that God may be all in all.

"Just as at the end of the second Moment faith was reflected and redoubled in order to let hope appear, the latter, in its turn, sees its two component elements objectified and distinguished. The presence of the future was asserted first of all as *presence*, through the confidence hope kept in its essential union with Christ and through the anticipated return of what it had lost; and secondly, as presence of the *future* by allowing the sensuous element that hope contained to disappear forever.

"The Ascension dismembers hope in order to open it up to the degree of presence that precisely is supposed to be revealed in it."[28]

28 Ibid.

Chapter 9

THE CONTEMPLATION TO ATTAIN
THE LOVE OF GOD

The four Weeks of the Exercises come to an end in a contemplation which explodes their temporal and historical framework, and which places the I, converted to the point of consenting to the stripping away that the Ascension imposes on him, in the presence of God, who is present to everyone in the universe. The bursting of the historical framework and of all representations should not surprise us; it is the fruit of the Fourth Week as lived out to the Ascension. Hope is there transformed into incipient charity; it is this charity which we ask and hope for in this final contemplation.

This "final" contemplation is no more last than first or intermediate. Since the temporal framework explodes here, the Contemplation to Attain the Love of God ends by revealing that it is rather the very core of the experience of the Exercises, its foundation and summit, beginning and end. It is as such that it here sets an end point, a final point which, along with the starting point of the Principle and Foundation, frames and defines the Exercises.

The representation explodes, but we are not hurled into the indeterminate. The starting point of the process was rather vague and commonplace; there is no privileged point for entering into the experience of reality. As the geometer says, "Let the point be zero," and everyone agrees. Likewise, entry into this experience requires only the general goodwill of the believer, and the Principle and Foundation was only a simple exposition of the most general conditions of the free act. But as the starting point should be tame, neutral, and indifferent, so the final point should be unique, full, somehow absolute, and perfectly determinate.[1] Every representation bursts here, but the explosion occurs *at the end point* of the four

1 See *Dialectique*, I, 147.

Weeks, along the lines of force and rationality that they have marked out. We wittingly allow ourselves to be carried beyond what can be said in words. And the schema of the four Weeks will be met again in the four points of this exercise.[2]

The exercise begins with two remarks. "They both aim at specifying the special nuance which love assumes for anyone who has posed the problem, how can I join my freedom to that of God?"[3] Ignatius writes: "The first is that love ought to manifest itself in deeds rather than in words" [230]. This calls to mind St. John: "Little children, let us not love in word or speech but in deed and in truth" (1 John 3:18). The accent is thereby placed on love as an active straining towards the future with an eye to service. The deeds are essentially letting oneself be taken hold of by God by being open to whatever happens. Secondly, deeds involve the service of others. It is in others that God needs to be served. In himself, God has one single need: that we allow him to love us, to do in us what he wishes and thus fill us.

The second remark defines love as an existential relationship of reciprocity, the sharing of what one has and of what one can do: "The lover gives and shares with the beloved what he possesses, or something of that which he has or is able to give; and vice versa, the beloved shares with the lover" [231]. The exchange consequently bears not only on having, but also on the ability of two freedoms to give. And what they exchange are ' knowledge," "honors," and "riches." This enumeration takes up again, in reverse order, the gradation of the "snares" and "chains" which the meditation on Two Standards warned us against [142]. "Knowledge" replaces "pride," and this knowledge is, above all, "eternal life, that they know thee the only true God" (John 17:3), the specific remedy for the radical pride which is the fruit of "the tree of knowledge." "Honors" appropriate to the Divine Majesty replace the "empty honors of this world" which the rich feed on.

Finally, the "riches" of God replace the temptation of Satan "to covet riches." If one has wealth, "he shares it with the one who does not possess it" [231]. God has a need to fill us. Therefore, it is our poverty which we must offer him. God suffers if he cannot be God generously enough with us!

2 At least according to the interpretation of Fessard, who "would not be sorry for having suggested it, even if it is challenged and ultimately rejected, as it appears to offer so much material for reflection" (ibid., 149).

3 Ibid., 147.

For this contemplation, the composition of place is nothing less than the entire Mystical Body. Historical time, as we said, explodes. This contemplation is in the heavens and "on earth as it is in heaven," for in and through it the petition of the Our Father is fully realized: Thy will be done on earth as it is in heaven!

The exercise includes four points, with no mention of Christ. This is because Christ ascended into heaven is invisible to our gaze. The entire representational framework of the evangelical mysteries, which had hitherto served to lift us up to this summit, is now empty.[4] From now on Christ is the Self who is All: Christ is at home everywhere, and the Self of Christ has become my own I.

First Point

I am to call to mind the gifts which concern universal history, creation, redemption,...and those which concern my particular history. The latter tend to introduce me to the fullness of the former: Everything is mine.

After the "quantitative" remembrance, there is a "qualitative" evaluation: "I will ponder with great affection how much God our Lord has done for me" [234]. This is the same process as in the First Week when I was invited to "call to mind all the sins of my life," and then to "weigh the gravity of my sins" [56, 57].

"Once this global and objective 'knowledge' has been acquired, I must subjectively 'acknowledge' it by opening myself up to the same degree, in order to establish between God and myself the 'mutual sharing' that constitutes love."[5]

The beloved then responds to the lover: *Take*, Lord (the fervent decisiveness of giving!), and *receive*.[6] This second verb tempers the ardent imperative of the first with a humble reserve. It is never enough for me to say to God, "Take," with heartfelt enthusiasm; because he is the Lord, it is still necessary for him to wish to receive.[7]

---

4 See ibid., 155.
5 Ibid., 151.
6 These are the first words of the famous prayer of Ignatius in the *Exercises* [234], and it is rightly known by its opening words: Take and receive...*Sume et suscipe*.
7 See *Dialectique*, I, 162. We are thus continuing to borrow some passages word for word from Fessard's book. Our presentation should not dispense one from reading these same thought-provoking pages of Fessard on the Contemplation to Attain the Love of God, pp. 147-164; not to mention the following section, pp. 164-177, which compares the circularity of the Exercises with the "absolute knowing" of Hegel.

Second Point

The understanding contemplates the being of God in beings. Every being is a gift which the divine generosity offers me,... and the chain of beings culminates in the "indwelling" of grace in me.[8] "God dwells in creatures," Ignatius writes [235], in order to come to dwell in me.

By constituting me a creature in his image through the gift of being, the divine Freedom simultaneously gave himself the possibility of an action which would transform my freedom into the likeness of his own and make me his temple. This is a total reversal of perspective from the Principle and Foundation; from being a creature wholly directed to God, I become a creature to whom God wholly directs himself. But this reversal is more effective in fostering my understanding of the divine generosity, in arousing my own generosity, and consequently in getting me to actualize love as a mutual sharing through knowledge and gratitude.[9]

Third Point

The understanding again contemplates the divine activity proceeding from his being in creatures: "God works and labors" [236].

"Works" (Spanish, *trabaja*) has a nuance of pain, the *travail* of suffering. Ignatius is thinking of the Passion. The word *trabajar* occurred five times in the Kingdom meditation.[10] At the same time this divine activity is a sovereign operation of unruffled divinity: God *acts*.

In the Principle and Foundation Ignatius wrote, "The other things on the face of the earth are created for man" [23], with the intention of pointing out that, since man has no more right over anything else than he does over himself, he ought to make use of everything solely according to the divine pleasure. And while waiting to come to know the divine pleasure, man ought to make himself "indifferent to all created things" [23].

Now, on the other hand, Ignatius writes: "God works and labors for me in all creatures...." It is God's turn, as if he had been stripped of any right to benefit from the object of his Choice (that

8 Ibid., 154.

9 Ibid., 157.

10 [Translator's Note. Pousset says "three times," but the verb and noun forms of *trabajar* occur five times in the Spanish text, which Puhl translates as *work, toil,* and *labor*.]

is, me), to use all creatures in order to "work" for the gratification of man. And since He is not unacquainted with what pleases him, God must show himself, through everything, passionately eager to make man deeply joyful. God subordinates himself to man's "good pleasure."[11]

God is now in the service of his creature! "Whatever you ask in my name I will do it" (John 14:13).

Fourth Point

At the culmination of his endeavor, Ignatius falls back on some comparisons and images drawn from Scripture, the best ones being the poorest and simplest. He highlights the relationship of the being of creatures to the uncreated God. The elemental simplicity of such a relationship appears in the expressions which serve to specify it:

"Consider all blessings and gifts as descending from above.... justice, goodness, mercy, etc., descend from above as the rays of light descend from the sun, and as the waters flow from their fountains" [237]. These are the fruits of the unitive life—loving God in all creatures and all creatures in him.

11 *Dialectique*, I, 159-160.

Chapter 10

THE RULES FOR THE DISCERNMENT OF SPIRITS

The Terrain of the Spiritual Life

We are going to study the rules for spiritual discernment. If there is material for discernment, it is because the spiritual life is *experience for me*. The spiritual life is not "something" in the depths of the soul (or at the fine point of the soul —the two images coalesce) which may be talked about, but which would not be my own lived experience. On the other hand, the spiritual life is not to be confused with the life of consciousness (sensory perceptions, feelings, fantasies, ideas), although it manifests itself in and through consciousness. Besides, the life of consciousness as we have described it is not the whole of our existence as conscious human beings.

Between the "depths" of the soul where God dwells, but which are not within the immediate field of our experience, and the very conscious zone of our perceptions, our most sensitive feelings, our fantasies, and our formed ideas, there is situated the activity of the subject who thinks, reflects, deliberates, and judges in conformity with the true, the good, and the beautiful, and who decides and governs his actions. This activity, well on this side of our conscious life, is nourished by a sap that rises from the roots of the subject's being and freedom, and it emerges in the surface zone. But it takes place within an intermediate chiaroscuro where it is frequently struggling mightily to reflect, to see clearly, to judge, and to decide with full awareness. It is within this middle zone that our responsible deeds take shape. We first have to learn to distinguish our responsible deeds from what is happening on the "forestage" where there cross a thousand influences from without and from within which are out of our control and which give birth to impressions, fantasies, even obsessions that do not directly implicate our responsibility.

In an initial period of spiritual education, it is frequently advisable to help someone free himself a bit from a sense of guilt he harbors as a result of everything which he thus experiences outside his authentic willing, and to help him discover the true terrain of his freedom. We begin by identifying this terrain with the middle zone of his activity, while admitting the possibility of freedom later gaining ground from both the "depth" and the "surface" sides. This terrain of freedom is identical with that of the spiritual life.

With this identification, an initial question arises. Since a human freedom cannot posit itself and develop except in relation to another freedom, must we say that in the spiritual life my relationship with God is my relationship with other people, and that the latter is the only thing that counts because it is the sole verification given to me about my relationship to the Father? Some think so, and they appeal to the passage of St. John which is always cited in this type of discussion: "If any one says, 'I love God,' and hates his brother, he is a liar; for he who does not love his brother whom he has seen, cannot love God whom he has not seen" (1 John 4:20).

In our opinion, this is a misuse of the passage from St. John. The perfect unity of a really simple attitude (that of Christ himself), which loves God in all creatures and all creatures in him, is a fruit of the Holy Spirit, the crowning of a courageous and patient ascent, not an initial given. The second commandment, "Thou shalt love thy neighbor,.." is like the first, and by observing the second we prove that we are also keeping the first. But the first commandment is the foundation of the second, and they do not become identical with each other as long as we are not perfected in unity. In our ordinary condition, we in fact experience a certain duality in our relationship with God and in our relationships with other people, and this is, moreover, not the only duality that characterizes our existence.

As finite beings we exist in accordance with contrary poles which we unify through a dialectic, and not by quelling all opposition: day/night, high/low, man/woman, spirit/flesh. ... And if one day our human and spiritual life comes to be experienced as some kind of identity of contraries, this will not have been without labor and especially not without patience. Ultimately, it is through a gift of the Spirit that we become, in God's image, gentle as a snow that refreshes without piercing, aglow like a fire that burns and causes no pain. We can and ought to long for this unification which is the secret of the children of the Kingdom. But it is important to accept ourselves where we are today: in the condition of finite beings who, in addition, have sinned. Sin hardens all our dualities, and we must suffer on the paths of patience before rediscovering these dualities as the Creator willed them: a harmony that goes on renewing and modifying itself to infinity—day/night, man/woman, flesh/spirit.

The Christ who assumed our condition presented himself to us as one who was part of an ensemble of dualities and whom we must prefer. He is, however, the Son of God, who is not numbered among creatures; who is not a competitor of anything or anyone; and hence who ultimately does not have to be preferred to them, since he transcends them all as the being of their being. Yes, we are to love God in creatures and creatures in him, *ultimately.*

This is indeed where we are going. But only one who has absolutely preferred the Lord knows what it means not to prefer him any longer because he is all in all.

Therefore, we accept as true the initial qualification that, here and now, our relationship with God is not yet the same as our relationship with other people. We accept this even if we are thereby admitting that, in such an imperfect condition, the God of our faith is not yet absolutely the Father as Jesus knows him, nor are other people yet our brothers in Jesus Christ, as they ought to be. We are on the way, and while we are on the road, what is not yet full truth is not necessarily fatal error. To believe it is would be just as harmful a mistake as accepting a merely thought truth for the reality of my life.

We are accepting as a good starting point the acknowledgment of both a special grace and a limitation: "On one hand, I had a sense for God, but on the other hand, I also had a sense for my neighbor, without being able to arrive at a unification of the two. I was really wavering...."

What will indicate that the life of my freedom, beginning from this sense for God and this sense for my neighbor, is a spiritual life? An uprooting will do so, a clear and precise call from the Lord who invites me to make a break. Whether it is a matter of breaking with a life-style, past habits, or some intellectual certainties, in one way or another the first word of the Israelites' history reechoes for me: "Go from your country and your kindred and your father's house to the land that I will show you" (Gen. 12:1). But at the same time there appear the first signs of a simplifying and a unifying. An uprooting which would merely separate, harden, and divide would have all the marks of psychological complications that come from us and not from God.

The spiritual life is always paradoxical. And the more it is God's life in us, the more definite the paradox becomes, to our own astonishment and that of others besides. Thus the stripping away, which "usually" is the result of deliberate effort, will become, in the spiritual life, a sincere attitude which intrudes itself without my seeking it; which becomes so indispensable that I scarcely need to will it anymore; and which ultimately I am not even very aware of. Spontaneity and abnegation "usually" do not go together. One is spontaneous, but without sacrifice; or one denies himself, but not easily. To the degree that one's spiritual life takes root, abnegation becomes easy. This is not an initial given, but it does define an orientation.

We could underline the same paradox in connection with recollection, the interior vigilance which is quite rightly recommended by all ascetical schools. The more one advances in recollection, the more he does what he is doing without thinking about it, and the more he is what he is without noticing himself. This is the simplicity towards which God leads us.

We have been trying to survey the terrain of the spiritual life; it is the terrain of the freedom that allows itself to be drawn toward these paradoxes. To the degree that we live them out, unity is brought about, and this life reaches into all the layers of our being; all the way to the "depths" of the soul where the indwelling God conducts us "into the chamber of the king"; to our feelings and our most external impressions; and to the extremity of our bodily senses through which our peace will radiate to others.

The next several paragraphs are a personal testimony, and they indicate a direction. For, in order to comprehend what the spiritual life is, we do not need a definition so much as a direction offered to our freedom.

"At the outset and for evermore, constant union with God in faith. Correction at the least slip, without getting upset or excited. Before all else, remaining peaceful in order to communicate peace. Gently and simply admitting that I am a sinner and not being 'overwhelmed' by it.

"They say that I am successful with other people, that I bring God to them, and that I also bring them something at the human level. It is possible, but most of the time I only believe it because they say so; I myself am unaware of it. In their presence, I feel poorer and more diminished at every moment, amidst a stripping and denuding that becomes more and more intense in my life. Of course, it will sometimes happen that I have no solution for the problem some brother in trouble may unexpectedly raise, that I do not know what 'character' I am going to run across and what I will be able to do, humanly speaking. But even everyday life finds me bereft and empty....

"I have learned and I am still learning to 'take my lumps,' to be where I should, to go where there is need, and to live in Him by abandoning everything to Him and counting on Him for everything, accepting in advance the feeling of panic that seizes me as soon as I think about what needs to be said, done, or made when I do not know how. It is a stripping that does not paralyze and that makes me go beyond my own impressions very quickly, beyond what 'I' have or what 'I' still am, in the bad sense of 'I.' This perpetual stripping digs deeply, sometimes into live flesh. But it is very good, for it is not willed or sought after for itself, for the sake of spiritual progress. Oh, I do not know how to say it, but what a liberation this way of living has brought me—living only in Him and in His presence, without looking for what to say or do!... It is a liberating, simplifying, and unifying of my whole life....

"As for the reflection of another that you quote, 'She has found true life,' yes, Father, of course, but not in order to possess it. I am possessed by it, yes, but I myself have nothing and possess nothing. ...They call me a light-bearer, but I am in the dark myself. That matters little, of course, and it is very good this way. I do not want anything else; I am really happy."[1]

Another text can help us go into details about the terrain and the expression of a spiritual life. It is a letter of St. Ignatius to Francis Borgia, written June 5, 1552.[2] This letter reminds us that the spiritual life is situated on the level of our decisions; that we there experience the shift from doubt to certitude (a sign of the Spirit of God); and that we there live out the unity of opposites in a completely paradoxical fashion.

The issue is the choice Ignatius made concerning the offer of the cardinalate to Borgia, regarding which Ignatius successfully resisted the pope and the emperor.

The *object* of the choice: "It was as though I had been informed that the emperor had as a matter of fact nominated you and that

---

1 Selections from a contemporary woman's personal testimony, published anonymously as "La Glorie de Dieu dans la vie quotidienne," in *Christus*, no. 11 (1956), pp. 373-380; emphasis added.

2 See William J. Young, S.J., trans., *Letters of St. Ignatius of Loyola* (Chicago: Loyola University Press, 1959), pp. 257-258.

the pope was willing to create you cardinal. At once I felt impelled to do all I could to prevent it. And yet, not being certain of God's will, as I saw many reasons for both sides, I gave orders in the community that all the priests should say Mass and those not priests offer their prayers for three days for divine guidance, to God's greater glory."

The *deliberation:* "During this space of three days I reflected and talked with others about it, and experienced certain fears, or at least not that liberty of spirit to speak against and prevent the project....At other times...I felt that these fears had taken themselves off...now with the fears now without them...."

Light and *decision*: "...finally, on the third day, I made my usual prayer with a determination so final, so peaceful and free, to do all I could with the pope and the cardinals to prevent it. I felt sure at the time, and still feel so, that, if I did not act thus, I should not be able to give a good account of myself to God our Lord —indeed, that I should give quite a bad one."

This certainty unites opposites: a judgment "so final" and a will "so peaceful and free." Decisiveness without freedom of spirit is opinionatedness or obstinacy. Freedom of spirit without decisiveness is instead inconsistency and fickleness. Neither extreme is a sign of the Spirit of God or of a spiritual attitude.

But, in Ignatius' case, the judgment "so final" and the will "so peaceful and free" are united in readiness of spirit; he is ready to admit that others can think otherwise and still be likewise moved by the Spirit of God. His firm judgment here knows that it is not being put forward absolutely —that is, having accounted for *all* the elements that enter into the situation. God alone thinks of everything and accounts for everything; and the thought which he grants me is of necessity not his entire thought. God acts through one person according to one perspective, and through another according to another perspective, but without the two appearing compatible to me, even though this diversity is not contradictory in and for God. Combining firmness with adaptability, certitude with a ready openness for the unexpected, I am free for a higher appeal to stand out clearly. This is the sign of spiritual certitude.

Ignatius concludes: "Therefore, I have felt, and now feel, that it is God's will that I oppose this move. Even though others might think otherwise, and bestow this dignity on you, I do not see that there would be any contradiction, since the same Divine Spirit could move me to this action for certain reasons and others to the contrary for other reasons, and thus bring about the result desired by the emperor. May God our Lord always do what will be to His greater praise and glory."

The Rules for Spiritual Discernment
General Characteristics

The preceding quoted passages provide the cue for distinguishing a spiritual life from one that is not spiritual or is too mingled with elements coming from our psychology. We will now take up the rules for discernment.

In the history of the composition of the *Exercises*, these rules formed the original center from which emerged the analysis that unfolds in the four Weeks. Closely bound up with the structure of the Exercises, these rules answer the same question as the Exercises: How can I make a decision in conformity with God's will? Insofar as this question arises concerning the root of my life—for example, about marriage, a religious vocation, and so on—the search for God's will often takes place in an atmosphere of spiritual struggle. For wherever God acts intensely, the enemy likewise manifests himself actively, nay violently, as St. Paul warns us in the letter to the Ephesians (6:10-17), where he describes for us, without exaggerating, the spiritual context of an important choice: "For we are not contending against flesh and blood, but against the principalities, against the powers, against the world rulers of this present darkness...."

Consequently, we have to remind ourselves that it is a question of making a decision; it is about a spiritual battle. At least it is within this context that we must understand the literal meaning of these rules. It is quite obvious, however, that discernment can be carried out according to these same rules in daily, run-of-the-mill situations, and in the micro-decisions of each moment, without any intense struggle.

One last point will help in appropriating these rules correctly: They are meant for someone who is alone with God, as throughout the Exercises. The Church is present in a very attentive, but very discreet, way in the person of the director, who assists in comprehending and using the text and in discerning what is taking place.

Let us stress this relationship with God alone. In a person's life, there are some important times, such as that of a major decision or one's own death, which can only be lived out with God alone. Moreover, even if my entire fraternal community serves as my director, at a critical hour for me it can ultimately only help me by its presence and its prayer to live out my solitude before God. Think of Christ in his agony: How little was asked of the disciples and yet they failed to do even that! Think of Christ on the cross (despite the presence of his mother), or even of Christ being tempted in the desert, at that hour when he opted for those fundamental attitudes that entailed certain apostolic "methods" and ultimately his own death.

A reflection on our creaturely being, defined as an intrinsic relationship to God, could find its place here.

The Historical Context

In order to clarify the historical context of these rules, one could read or reread St. Ignatius' autobiography, a document dictated by him towards the end of his life, concerning his principal spiritual experiences.[3] One sees by Ignatius' very history that he owes these rules not so much to a cultural heritage he received in the schools as to his own personal experience. In fact, Ignatius did not have much literary and theological training. Even after his studies, when he was in Rome as general of the Society and author of its *Constitutions*, he entrusted the care of documentation to his colleagues who were better versed than he in the humanities and theology. His sense of the Church and tradition shows in his concern for this documentation, but he was not able to see to it himself. The *Exercises* were already written by the time Ignatius was in Rome. And while Ignatius had rediscovered a very traditional spiritual vein in the Exercises, they had nonetheless come essentially from his own experience, as he says in his autobiography.[4]

What had been of major importance from the beginning of his experience was feeling the action of two contrary spirits drawing the soul, the Spirit of God and the spirit of the evil one, which Ignatius also called the good and the bad angel. Below is one of the first passages in his autobiography that makes mention of these different spirits.[5] After having recounted some "vain and worldly

---

3 See *The Autobiography of St. Ignatius Loyola with Related Documents*, ed. John C. Olin, trans. Joseph F. O'Callaghan (New York: Harper & Row, 1974), or for an edition with the standard paragraph numbers, *St. Ignatius' Own Story as Told to Luis González de Cámara*, trans. William J. Young (Chicago: Loyola University Press, 1968). The Spanish and Latin texts are in *Fontes narrativi de S. Ignatio*, I, 354-507 (Rome: The Historical Institute of the Society of Jesus, 1943).

4 *Autobiography*, no. 100; in O'Callaghan's *Autobiography*, pp. 92-93.

5 *Autobiography*, nos. 7, 8; in O'Callaghan's *Autobiography*, pp. 23-24.

ideas" that came to him and some thoughts of imitating the saints, Ignatius goes on:

These thoughts also lasted a good while, but when other matters intervened, the worldly thoughts mentioned above returned, and he also spent much time on them. This succession of such diverse thoughts, either of the worldly deeds he wished to achieve or of the deeds of God that came to his imagination, lasted for a long time, and he always dwelt at length on the thought before him, until he tired of it and put it aside and turned to other matters.

Yet there was this difference. When he was thinking about the things of the world, he took much delight in them, but afterwards, when he was tired and put them aside, he found that he was dry and discontented. But when he thought of going to Jerusalem, barefoot and eating nothing but herbs and undergoing all the other rigors that he saw the saints had endured, not only was he consoled when he had these thoughts, but even after putting them aside, he remained content and happy. He did not wonder, however, at this; nor did he stop to ponder the difference until one time his eyes were opened a little, and he began to marvel at the difference and to reflect upon it, realizing from experience that some thoughts left him sad and others happy. Little by little he came to recognize the difference between the spirits that agitated him, one from the demon, the other from God.[6]

One other important observation will allow him to establish an essential rule of discernment: The evil spirit troubles the soul which is purifying itself, and the good spirit soothes it. It is characteristic of God to drive away trouble and sadness.

Role of the Rules for Discernment in the Exercises

It is advisable now to consider the text of the *Exercises* in their entirety for some indications which will introduce us directly to the study of these rules. At the center of the Exercises, in the Choice, each person is supposed to make a decision objectively, that is, in conformity with the genesis of true Freedom that the four Weeks develop. The schema of this genesis, however, remains quite formal

---

6 [Translator's Note. Pousset adds a marginal note of Father Luis Gonçalves da Câmara, to whom Ignatius related his life, which is not included in the English versions: "These were the first reflections he made about divine things, and later when he made the Exercises he began to get some light on the different spirits."]

with respect to the individual freedom that seeks to determine itself concretely.

"Consequently, the question arises: How can we apply this universal framework to the particular situation of each I? With respect to the fundamental choice envisaged by the Exercises, that of a state of life, a general answer is given at the end of the Second Week by the considerations directly concerning the Choice, the different times and ways of making a good choice.... But this macro-decision is not brought forth all of a sudden. A certain amount of time elapses before it is definitively fashioned, and afterwards some time is also necessary for the choice to mature and be capable of being carried through. During this twofold interval, the meditations and contemplations should inevitably provoke different motions, inclinations, and projects in the I, leading to a multitude of micro-decisions in which the outline of the concrete choice is first sketched and then the definitive design is filled in. Obviously, it is important that these anticipations or consequences of the Choice be themselves guided and oriented from the outset in the direction defined by the entirety of the method.

"The goal of the Rules for the Discernment of Spirits is to assure this guidance and orientation, and by that very fact to allow the general schema of freedom to be applied to each free act, at every moment. In these rules one meets again the elements which the four Weeks spread out over a time span and display in their general import. But the rules for discernment present these elements in such a way as to make them converge on the concrete I and thereby illuminate its particular becoming."[7]

Although these rules aim at assuring the application of the method after the Choice as well as before, Ignatius has provided rules only for the First and Second Weeks. This is because, from the viewpoint which absorbs him, that of our free decision in the direction of God's will, we can only be in two basic types of situation: that of being converted, where we are still drawn "downwards," and that of progress "upwards," once we have passed the first stage of upward movement. Between "up" and "down" there is no third term.

In the situation of the First Week, the I is struggling to follow the call to conversion. At the start, the I is especially liable to discouragement, whether it comes from its own natural weakness

7 *Dialectique*, I, 236-237.

or from the intrigues of the enemy. Ignatius will therefore concentrate primarily on spiritual desolation.

In the situation of the Second Week, the I has been encouraged by its initial progress, and having passed completely under the influence of grace and divine light, it is less vulnerable to gross temptations, but more liable to subtle temptations "under the appearance of the good" it is pursuing. Accordingly, the rules for the Second Week essentially constitute a little treatise on spiritual consolation (true and false).

In commenting on these two series of rules, we will be trying to highlight the dialectic of freedom which inspires them and connects them to our analysis of the four Weeks. In this way we will extricate the Ignatian method from a vocabulary and expressions which are sometimes out of date and which run the risk of hiding from us its value for our age. Within these perspectives of promoting freedom in conformity with the divine will, we hope these rules will appear useful for discerning the Spirit of God and its opposite —not merely in the interior happenings of a private spiritual life, but even in the external events of social existence and of the history being made in the world every day.

Consolation, Desolation

We have just introduced two essential and precise terms in the Ignatian vocabulary, consolation and desolation. Despite their old-fashioned sound, they conceal a highly significant content for a freedom which must make itself and which is always in danger of unmaking itself. Let us examine this content now.

True consolation is the action of God who helps the creature consolidate itself, secure its firmness, and fortify its personality and identity. To console is to place man on his own two feet, to promote his personhood as a man and a son of God. He then enjoys a greater moral and even physical health, and he feels it as a lasting peace and joy. The latter are very sure signs of the Spirit of God, and they are even the substance of the Spirit's gift. The *false consolation* which comes from the enemy mimics this action of God in order to hide his perverse intention. False consolation is quick to dissolve firmness of spirit, which dissipates in mists of illusion and pride. It crumbles the foundations of the person, as seeping water disintegrates a laminated rock by separating its layers. It looks solid, but it crumbles away at the slightest pressure.

Desolation is the opposite of consolation. Desolation can come from ourselves or from circumstances to which we respond badly.

210

But in its acute form desolation comes from the enemy who directly assaults the energies of the person, his clarity of understanding and his power of decision. It renders us vulnerable to the hazards of existence. It tends to weaken the core of our personality and, if possible, to depersonalize us.

Thus, great human and spiritual stakes are at issue whenever St. Ignatius expresses himself in terms of consolation and desolation.

Rules for the First Week

"Fourteen in number, they are grouped according to a plan which is as simple as it is logical. The first two rules describe the two existential situations of freedom and the tactics of the good and of the evil spirit in each of them. The following two rules, with their terms *consolation* and *desolation*, define the states of souls which find themselves in these two situations. In the fifth through the eighth rules, Ignatius recommends the behavior we should stick to in time of desolation, and in the ninth rule he enumerates three causes of desolation. The next two rules suffice for him to indicate how we should act in time of consolation. Finally, the last three rules disclose the general tactics of the enemy."[8]

St. Ignatius is not aiming so much at describing states of the soul as at delineating the directional forces which draw the I "upwards" (toward God) or "downwards." We could indicate these forces by means of two axes intersecting at right angles to each other. The horizontal axis represents the temporal dimension in which freedom goes from the before to the after, and the vertical axis represents the two opposite poles of "up" and "down." Within these coordinates would be inscribed the two possible movements "upwards" or "downwards": progress according to God's call, or decline towards the less good and then the bad. The point of intersection would represent the present moment in which the I stands and in which it is drawn in one direction or the other by the various movements of consolation and desolation.

All the rules for discernment, those for the Second Week as well as those for the First Week, will be described, arranged, and unified in relation to this basic diagram. The affective state of the I and the motions which it undergoes or ought to carry out will be expressed in terms of tensions or oppositions.

8 Ibid., 239.

Rules 1 and 2: the Twofold Existential Situation of the I

The end which the Exercises hold out for us is to enter into the true Freedom of the risen Christ. In relation to this end, the I can find itself in either of two diametrically opposed postures: either turning away from the end and going "from one mortal sin to another" [314], or else turning towards the end by renouncing sin and vice and courageously seeking "to rise in the service of God our Lord to greater perfection" [315].

The I which turns away from this end becomes more and more distant from it, but the enemy will typically conceal this growing absence by filling the person's "imagination with sensual delights and gratifications" [314]. The Spirit of God, on the other hand, will prod the guilty person by rousing his conscience through the voice of reason.

This twofold way of acting is reversed in the case of "those who go on earnestly striving to cleanse their souls from sin and who seek to rise in the service of God our Lord to greater perfection" [315]. The enemy seeks to obscure the presence of the approaching end, "to harass with anxiety, to afflict with sadness, to raise obstacles backed by fallacious reasonings that disturb the soul. Thus he seeks to prevent the soul from advancing" [315]. Whereas the Spirit of God promotes the movement of the I moving towards its end by giving "courage and strength, consolations,...by making all easy, by removing all obstacles so that the soul goes forward in doing good" [315].

The respective actions of the two spirits are easily recognized; it is enough simply to compare the direction in which they are heading with the essential end. In the first situation, the I is turning away from its end. The enemy encourages this distancing; the Spirit of God hinders it. In the second case, the I is approaching its end. The enemy opposes this progress; the Spirit of God supports it.

Rules 3 and 4: Definition of Consolation and Desolation

Once this framework has been set up and the twofold intersecting opposition which constitutes its internal structure has been defined, Ignatius will more carefully characterize the end, the Freedom that manifests itself through equally diverse effects. By describing consolation and desolation in relation to his central schema,

Ignatius is going to define them as fluid realities capable of flowing into one another—in short, as forces in dialectical tension.[9]

These two rules present the same movement of thought. Ignatius begins by mentioning some of the signs by which consolation and desolation can be perceived in consciousness: "interior movements" by which the soul is inflamed with love; "tears" and all forms of interior impulses which lead to love "of Christ our Lord," to his service, to his praise [316]. Or, in the case of desolation, some signs are: "darkness of soul, turmoil of spirit, inclination to what is low,...restlessness" [317].

But he at once indicates the meaning of all these affective phenomena in relation to the end sought by the Exercises, Freedom identified with Love. The signs refer to what is going on in the depths of the soul. In the case of consolation, it is an increase of faith, hope, and charity by the agency of Love; and in the case of desolation, it is the opposite ("want of faith, want of hope, want of love" [317]). Thus defined in function of the essential element, which is the theological life in us, consolation and desolation appear as opposing tensions: either an increase of the theological virtues by which personal freedom is united to divine Freedom, or the danger of seeing these same virtues decrease.

"Thereby peace and joy, or restlessness and darkness, as well as all the sensuous phenomena which may accompany these basic feelings, are rigorously characterized by reference to their opposite directions on the vertical axis, for which the relevant phrasing is: 'Consolation...invites and attracts to what is heavenly. ...I call desolation what is entirely the opposite,...inclination to what is low and earthly' [316, 317]."[10]

Ignatius thus moves from the surface, where these sensuous motions are experienced, to the fundamentals (faith, hope, and charity, or danger of falling into their opposites), and he moves back up from there by indicating the outward radiation: "all interior joy that invites and attracts" [316], or despondency in which "the soul is wholly slothful, tepid, sad, and separated, as it were, from its Creator and Lord" [317].

Rules 5 to 9 : Tactic to Follow in Desolation

After having defined the axis on which the I can be moved in opposite directions, Ignatius sets about to deduce the tactic to

9 Ibid., 241.
10 Ibid.

follow when one is exposed to the action of the enemy. This tactic consists in *running counter* to the tension whereby the enemy and the sin in me are opposing my progress towards Freedom. We would like to point out that this tactic—that of the famous *agendo contra*—is dialectical and not systematic. Ignatius is not proposing the *agendo contra* as a general rule for spiritual conduct in all circumstances; he is suggesting it as the direction to follow in order to check the action of the enemy and of sin in us. The intensity of the *agendo contra* should therefore wax or wane according to the violence or the slackening of this baneful action. And what Ignatius is ultimately aiming at is the peace in which the I follows the direction of the middle course, without excess. We can easily recognize this evolution in the very life of Ignatius.

Here is the tactic: (1) Remain firm in established positions (rule 5, [318]); (2) proceed to counterattack and strive to turn the tide by raising oneself upwards through persevering prayer, while keeping a watchful gaze on what is taking place (survey through the examination of consciousness) and while directing a vigorous and reasonable attack downwards (penance) (rule 6, [319]).

Fidelity in following the first suggestion is crucial: We must not make an important decision in a period of crisis or intense trial. For then we are not master of all our faculties, not of our intellect which must make a judgment, and still less of our will and affectivity. To change our direction is then the temptation that will almost always be present, sometimes obsessively. We then posit acts which are more ascribable to fate than to freedom; we enslave ourselves, sometimes for a long time.

If, on the other hand, the I holds onto these two rules, it ends by acquiring a reversal of the situation. Not that the desolation changes into consolation (though this can happen), but instead of being an obstacle, desolation becomes a means whereby one can progress with great strides and still attain the objectives of each of the four Weeks. In fact, desolation offers the I an opportunity to become aware of its radical weakness in the face of sin and the enemy (First Week): "When one is in desolation, he should be mindful that God has left him to his natural powers to resist the different agitations and temptations of the enemy in order to try him" (rule 7, [320]). Next, desolation calls for the act of faith which conquers sin and the enemy (Second Week): "He can resist with the help of God, which always remains, though he may not clearly perceive it" (rule 7, [320]). It demands patience and perseverance as in disagreeable labor (Third Week): "When one is in desolation, he should strive to persevere in patience. This reacts against the vexations that have overtaken him" (rule 8, [321]). Finally, desolation calls forth an act of hope in the presence of Him who is our true end and who will come shortly (Fourth Week): "Let him consider, too, that consolation will soon return" (rule 8, [321]).

Founded on faith and strengthened by hope, the I becomes aware of this overturning of the situation, and now that it is the victor, the I discovers the three principal causes of desolation (rule 9, [322]).

In the first place, the concrete origin of desolation is the reality of my own sins. The second reason for it is to make me experience the slight worth of my subjective freedom: "God wishes to try us, to see how much we are worth, and how much we will advance in His service and praise when left without the generous reward of consolations and signal favors" [322].

Thirdly, we are radically impotent, as incapable of freeing ourselves from our sins as of acquiring and preserving "great devotion, intense love, tears, or any other spiritual consolation" [322], that is, a little incipient freedom. Intimate knowledge of this radical impotence is absolutely necessary for anyone who wants to cross the threshold of the spiritual life; such knowledge precisely *is* this threshold. There is nothing in the spiritual life which is as decisive as this intimate and felt knowledge. To the astonished question of the disciples, "But then who can be saved?" the Lord replies very clearly, "For men, it is impossible." We read this text a hundred times without hearing it. Often enough in our youth we are converted from negligence to generosity, and we go on, careful to do our best. But basically nothing changes; we keep our faults, continually falling back into the same ruts. We end by noticing our faults, and then there is great danger of becoming discouraged or of rationalizing them. This is the hour when a decisive threshold could be crossed, when God could convert us from good will to the love which, confirmed in faith and hope, relies only on him. The condition for this second conversion, the decisive threshold, is this intimate and felt (but not discouraged or discouraging) knowledge of our own impotence. In relation to this threshold (which not everyone crosses), spiritual desolation should undoubtedly be considered one of the most important graces in our life—if it is borne as St. Ignatius recommends.

Life in Faith and Freedom

Rules 10 and 11: Conduct to Follow in Consolation

Two quite brief rules suffice for treating this topic, for in consolation, when the I is drawn upwards by divine Freedom (the possibility of false consolation in the First Week is scarcely envisaged), it needs only to allow itself to be carried aloft. No dialectical action is desirable or even possible at this moment, since it is God himself who is acting.[11] In this case, therefore, we can say that the method of the Exercises is suppressed. There is no more dialectic, but merely the simple yes of welcome and adherence. This is, however, the very goal that Ignatius' method sets forth: "To actualize the unity of human freedom and divine Freedom. Sought through the unfolding of the four Weeks, this unity is called the Choice. When, on the other hand, this unity is granted at any instant in this unfolding, it is consolation. To the degree that this unity is actually attained in one form or another, it is quite true that Ignatius' method is suppressed. Like every authentic dialectic, its end is not to perpetuate itself, but to make itself useless by going beyond the contradictions that made it necessary."[12] This is exactly what happens temporarily with the consolation that actualizes an almost purely vertical upward movement, like a Choice according to the "first time." As a matter of fact, Ignatius is not yet considering this kind of consolation in these two rules. Consolation here is rather the most frequent variety, an enduring state that is wedded to the fluctuations of consciousness and is liable to the hazards of consciousness. A dialectical action is then possible which aims "not at restraining the ascending movement of the I but, on the contrary, at freeing the I by exerting itself against the opposite force (which could merely be our natural inertia) that keeps the I from allowing itself to be transported vertically and even threatens to reverse its direction."[13]

In the time that elapses, we can foresee that desolation, for one reason or another, will not take long to return; or it can even happen that the consoled I ends by entertaining some kind of illusion about its real strength. Because of these two possibilities, Ignatius recommends a twofold action, one looking to the future, the other to the past: (1) "Let him consider how he will conduct himself during the time of ensuing desolation" (rule 10, [323]); (2) "Let

11 Ibid., 243-244.
12 Ibid., 244.
13 Ibid., 245.

216

him recall how little he is able to do in time of desolation, when he is left without such grace or consolation" (rule 11, [324]).

"The conjunction of this twofold action in relation to the past and the future will reinforce the movement of consolation and prolong its benefit. In fact, it tends to humble the I and to lower its trust in itself ('to humble himself and lower himself' [324]), and it thereby disposes the I to receive from divine Freedom all the strength it needs in order to resist the assaults of the enemy ('by making use of the sufficient grace offered him, he can do much to withstand all his enemies' [324]).... To compensate for the downward inclination of desolation by recalling the upward lift of consolation, and conversely, to moderate and reinforce consolation by remembering desolation, are two different ways of pursuing the same goal: preparing human freedom to recognize that divine Freedom comes from above and draws the person up towards itself. This recognition can occur either through the very meanderings of the fluctuations of consciousness, as the 'second time' for making the Choice supposes, or beginning with a 'time of tranquillity' and by means of the 'two ways' of making a Choice in the 'third time.' At every time as in every case, the sole issue is for the I to dispose itself to welcome the divine Instant in order to simply coincide (if we can say this) with its vertical direction."[14]

Rules 12 to 14 : The Tactics of the Devil

These three rules explain the tactics of the devil and show how to counterattack. They use three symbols of vital importance: man, woman, and a warring commander. Man and woman are the two terms of a basic human relationship, that of love, which is at the source of every agreement. The military leader is the dominative agent of another basic human relationship, that of power or struggle, and his correlative is the "slave." In fact, the enemy conducts himself like a military commander who is trying to conquer us and reduce us to slavery. "The relation of man and woman, on one hand, and war or a struggle to the death on the other, are two basic situations which directly relate to the genesis of freedom and which allow us to analyze its various moments."[15]

---

14 Ibid., 245-246.
15 Ibid., 247. These two situations are analyzed at length in G. Fessard, "Le mystère de la société, *Recherches de science religieuse*, 35 (1948), 5-54; 161-225. This article has been reprinted in Fessard, *De l'actualité historique*, Vol. 1 (Paris: Desclée de Brouwer, 1960). See a shorter analysis of these same basic relationships in our contribution to the article "Homme" in the *Dictionnaire de spiritualité* (Paris: Beauchesne, 1969),

We can notice that rules 12 and 13 consider man and woman alternately according to their "good" and "bad" aspects. In rule 12 [325], the enemy is in the position of a weak but vindictive and fierce woman, and "one leading a spiritual life" is invited to behave like a courageous man who "faces his temptations boldly." In rule 13 [326], the enemy is in the position of a false lover who is secretive and malicious, and "one leading a spiritual life" is invited to behave like a woman who finds her strength in her very weakness, by being open and confiding in a strong person of sound advice. In order to comprehend this symbolism, we can refer to the analyses in footnote 15 above, and we must especially avoid confusing the symbolic "man" and "woman" with existing individuals who are male or female. Each person contains in him or herself masculine and feminine polarities. Women, who are symbolically portrayed here as weak, have their own way of being strong, and, besides, they too are advised to "face temptations boldly," like a brave man against a beast. As for men, who are symbolized here as strong, they are subject, like women, to the intrinsic weakness of every creature.

Ignatius is not trying to portray the devil's character for us. He is revealing a threefold aspect of human freedom during its genesis, a development which is simultaneously a struggle against the nothingness of creaturehood and the malice of sin.[16] At the outset, rule 12 is concerned with the freedom which is beginning to posit itself by entering on the path of conversion. The enemy, who redoubles his creaturely nothingness by the worst malice, behaves like a weak and feckless woman, whose strength lies in the obstinacy of her negative will. As a matter of fact, freedom is not attained except by passing through a period during which the enemy never stops opposing freedom's progress, and the enemy can end by getting the upper hand through the steadfastness of his opposition. If human freedom, after having shown the fearless face of reason, begins to let itself be mastered by the senses, it will experience the unleashing of a wild animal whose rage and malice "surge up and know no bounds."

Through the stubborn force of his negative will, the enemy can thus find himself in a position of power "like a man confronting

Vol. 7, or in Part I of *Un chemin de la foi et de la liberté*. [The articles "Homme" and "Homme intérieur" from the *Dictionnaire de spiritualité* are available in English as *A Christian Anthropology*, by Joseph Goetz, S.J., et al., trans. Sister Mary Innocentia Richards, S.N.J.M. (St. Meinrad, Indiana: Abbey Press, 1974).]

16 *Dialectique*, I, 248.

an I whose fickleness is now equivalent to the woman's."[17] But since the enemy still remains basically ineffective, "he must seek an ally in the I itself that can supplement his radical weakness."[18] He will find his ally in the *inconsistency* proper to the creature, which, according to the etymology of the word, is incapable of "*staying with* itself in existence"[19] if it ever loosens the bond joining it to the Creator, the source of its being and strength. We will be more explicit.

We have only too much experience of our fickleness. In our temporal existence, our own effort by itself does not last. It soon flags, and we are, as it were, drawn towards a congenital indolence. But we hardly perceive that this inconstancy stems from a more radical inconsistency; we are not the source of our existence—we owe that to God. Of course, in creating us God entrusts us to ourselves, that is, he lets us subsist in and by ourselves. But sin tends to cut us off from God and thus to separate us from our origin. Sin makes us fall into an inconsistency that is proper to us, as soon as we are no longer joined to our beginning. It is from this latter inconsistency that the enemy is going to try to make an ally for himself, thus drawing his strength from our weakness.

By what trick will the enemy attempt this? Rule 13 answers: by the flattering lie which gives a semblance of being to what has no being and which conceals from each person his own weakness and that of his enemy. "Hence the necessary and sufficient condition for the enemy to abort the growth of human freedom is that the twofold impotence characterizing the enemy and human freedom 'remain hidden and...not...be discovered' [326]."[20]

Consequently, far from assuming a terrifying appearance as in the preceding rule, the enemy will now act like a seducer by worming himself into the good graces and intimacy of human freedom. Hiding his evil intention with charming words, he coaxes like a Don Juan approaching the daughter of a good father or the wife of a good husband. And, in fact, is it not by means of this twofold relation (to *the* Father and to *the* Spouse) that Christ, beginning with the Second Week, will disclose to the I both the ontological relationship that grounds its being in the divine Paternity and

17 Ibid., 249.
18 Ibid.
19 Ibid.
20 Ibid. The remaining paragraphs in this section rely heavily on ibid., 249-253.

the historical event (the nuptials of the Word and humanity) that frees the I from non-being in order to raise it up to Freedom identical with Love? With this twofold image of the father and husband, Ignatius designates the two basic truths which the enemy's lie must deny; the first involves the exposure of the nothingness proper to the creature, and the second involves the rejection of sinful malice and the announcement of total victory and the reign of Freedom. To prevent this exposure and give the lie to this announcement, the enemy only needs to do one thing, namely, persuade the freedom seduced by his promises to keep his words and suggestions secret.

If freedom agrees to resort to trickery and deceit, feminine weapons par excellence, in order to maintain silence and keep these false promises secret, it thereby compromises itself and immediately becomes a prey destined for the same perversion as its seducer. If, on the contrary, freedom discloses these false promises to its father or husband, the tempter readily foresees he will not be able to bring the affair to its conclusion.

By having recourse to another person, an astute confessor or spiritual director, created freedom acquiesces in its true condition in relation to absolute Freedom. It (1) becomes aware of its ontological inconsistency, and (2) on the foundation of this radical humility, it simultaneously posits the most appropriate act for protecting itself from its temporal inconstancy. This is the basic twofold truth which the enemy's lie aimed at keeping veiled from freedom.

Freedom exhibits masculinity through its fearless confidence at its beginning stage and then femininity through its distrust of itself and its openness to another as long as its genesis lasts. But freedom must ultimately combine these two attitudes at every instant in order to assure its not falling back into the slavery of sin and its being able to advance towards its end. Rule 14 [327] points out that the enemy has his own tactics which combine fearless confidence and distrust of himself. He is the military commander who is sure of himself, but who prudently tries to attack at the weakest point: "Your adversary the devil prowls around like a roaring lion, seeking some one to devour" (1 Pet. 5:8). Ignatius therefore warns us that we ought to consider ourselves like a fortified stronghold which the enemy investigates from every side in order to attack at the weakest point. In other words, we ought to employ the same prudent and vigorous tactics, conducting ourselves inwardly, like the military leader who is attacking us outwardly, with constant vigilance.

The three attitudes fostering the development of true freedom have now been treated: fearless faith, radical humility, and constant vigilance, symbolized by man, woman, and military commander.

"By using the man-woman relationship to characterize two strengths and two radically opposed weaknesses, was not Ignatius led by the very exemplars of man and woman (Christ and the Virgin) who, in the rest of the Exercises, are going to become the images of these two complementary aspects of freedom and authentic existence? And is it not evident that, by presenting authentic existence in the form of a death struggle between two military leaders, he is preparing his retreatant to hear the call of the Kingdom as well as the instruction of the Two Standards?"[21]

Note on the Weak Point

The language of war fits certain phases of the spiritual life, notably when one is making the Exercises. But such language should not be extended thoughtlessly to the whole of our existence, which includes periods of calm and of long peaceful journeying. Nevertheless, each day we carry about our *weak point*, a veritable crack in our personality. In that respect, this fourteenth rule is always useful in terms of vigilance, or at least foresight.

We excel in hiding our frailties or deep-seated deceptions from ourselves, and we raise a very effective defense system against those who see more clearly into ourselves than we do. It is very true that it is not advisable to lay open, bluntly and without discernment, the shortcoming of another.

Our shortcomings, our weak points, and our petty deceptions are most often compromises which help us to live and bear, as best we can, the burden we are to ourselves. To lay someone open and leave him defenseless is the height of folly. Not all truths are fit to say, for we cannot be sure that our way of saying them will not be more crushing than liberating.

Fraternal exchanges, however, in a sufficiently discreet and intelligent community can be of service. If they avoid getting into questionable or even salacious interpretations, which are a plague in our age when everyone has a smattering of three or four words

21 Ibid., 253.

of psychoanalytic jargon, these exchanges (a renewed version of "fraternal correction") can help each of us know ourselves better and thus avoid some mistakes, surprises, frustrations, or entanglements.

Rules for the Second Week

Having been forgiven and having heard the call of the Kingdom, the I wants to respond. Henceforth, for the I "the question is solely to choose between the greater and the lesser good. Ignatius is therefore no longer worried about the temptation in which freedom is captivated by the attraction of evil or hindered by the difficulty of the good. His sole concern is to describe the form that true freedom takes and to expose the illusion into which the I can fall in its quest for the greater good.

"These eight rules constitute an elaborate treatise on consolation. The first rule defines consolation in reference to its two possible sources, God and the good angels, and in opposition to the action of the evil spirit. The second rule characterizes the consolation that comes immediately from God and thereby assumes an unrivaled primacy. The consolations that do not come immediately from God, declares the third rule, can be the effects not only of the good angel but also of the evil spirit. This is then the case of false consolation which the fourth rule describes. A twofold criterion for discerning the nature of consolation is provided by the fifth rule and explicated by the two following rules. Finally, the eighth rule, without contradicting the privileges of the consolation that comes immediately from God, indicates how it can be subject to the criterion and process described in the previous rules."[22]

Rule 1: Consolation

Consolation is always the presence of the end, God, who frees me by making me share in his Freedom. And the gift of this presence is "true happiness and spiritual joy" [329]. The happiness is "the impulse of life that points upwards."[23] The joy expands the I, opening it up in all directions, permeating and filling all its faculties, forming a totality and plenitude like that of a full circle. "It is characteristic of the evil one to fight against such happiness" [329] by trying to counter the impulse that points upwards and discourage it by sadness. Into the soul unified by joy, the enemy

22 Ibid., 255.
23 Ibid., 256.

tries to insert divisive anxiety that wars with itself. We thus have four key terms: happiness and joy, and their opposites, sadness and anxiety. They signify an uplifting impulse and one that has collapsed, a sphere that is full and one that is rent, broken in two by anxiety.

Rule 2: Consolation without Cause

While analyzing the various "times" for making a correct and good Choice, we have already pointed out the analogy between the first time and this "consolation without previous cause." We are referring particularly to the Note (see page 132) on the immediate relation between God and the creature at the end of our chapter on the Choice.

The consolation without previous cause is the paradigm par excellence, the standard for all other consolations. "It belongs solely to the Creator to come into a soul, to leave it, to act upon it, to draw it wholly to the love of His Divine Majesty" [330].

This definition by Ignatius of the consolation without previous cause has been interpreted by Fessard in depth. "To come into" [*entrar*], "to leave" [*salir*]: "In the absence of a better interpretation, we are inclined to think that Ignatius thus wanted to indicate the come-and-go movement as it unfolds from 'the love that comes down from above,' attracts the I, and immediately returns to its source. Moreover, this instantaneous coming and going alone explains the discontinuity of this consolation without cause."[24]

The same word [*salir*] is found in paragraph [189] of the *Exercises*, in a passage where Ignatius universalizes the method for making the Choice and recommends the basic law of the entire spiritual life: "For every one must keep in mind that in all that concerns the spiritual life his progress will be in proportion to his surrender [*saliere*] of self-love and of his own will and interests."

How can we doubt that this "surrender of self-love and of his own will and interests" must be related to the "leaving" of the divine grace immediately after it has "come into" the soul? The "surrender of self-love," however, which conditions the "progress," the "coming into" God's love, is the appropriation by the soul of the movement which the Son accomplished first in the act of "emptying" himself at the Incarnation. Thus, the grace proper to the Creator, to the Father, "leaves" the soul

24 Ibid., 259-260.

into which it has "come" in order that the soul, in its turn, may "leave" self-love, as did the Son, and thereby "come in" and "progress" further into God's love. But the Contemplation to Attain the Love of God has shown that God's love is the very life of the Trinity, encompassing all his gifts, dwelling in all, laboring in all, in order that all may appear as an outpouring of his power and grace; in short, that God is "all in all."[25]

The consolation without cause makes us taste the first fruits of this life of God in everyone, which is the end point of our hope and the perfection of charity.

Now the question that remains is that of knowing precisely what "without previous cause" means. This is not a practical question of discernment, since this Instant of immediate encounter with God carries its own certitude. It is a question of definition. The discernment does not bear upon this consolation itself, but upon what takes place in "the period which follows it," as specified in the eighth rule [336]. And there one thing is decisive: By definition, God is freeing. Is the recipient of this sort of consolation obstinately attached to his own "awareness" (*évidence*)? And does he call upon that awareness despite every verification of what is *now* the case? If so, there is room to fear that he is being deceived. On the other hand, if he remains spiritually free to accept examination of what he holds as certain, there is reason to presume that he is not deluded.

As for the meaning of "without previous cause," we observe first of all that Ignatius explains himself: "I said without previous cause, that is, without any preceding perception [*sentimiento*] or knowledge of any subject by which a soul might be led to such a consolation through its own acts of intellect and will" [330].

The terms "perception" (*sentiment*) and "knowledge" suggest contents of consciousness. But "without previous cause" cannot mean the total absence of such contents in the period preceding the consolation. While we are awake, even if we are inattentive, we are never without some perception or knowledge. What Ignatius seems to have in view is rather a *disproportion* between these preceding contents of consciousness and the experience had in the Instant of consolation, and thus the absence of any cause-effect relationship. The Instant erupts by sundering the continuity of what preceded, breaking with the past. The Instant is novelty, irreducible to what went before, although it arises in a consciousness that is not disjoined from its past since there is a self-identical "I" that endures. The Instant introduces the dimension of the future into the present, which it provides with a very strong consistency (certainty, absence of doubt). Experienced certainty always concerns the future, but here the future suddenly becomes present with an extraordinary intensity. "A devout soul without hesitation, or the possibility of hesitation, follows what has been manifested to it," according to the definition of the first time for making a Choice [175]. The mysterious aspect of this consolation without cause is that the future —what God wills —irrupts into the present with such an intensity and certitude that it cannot be accounted for by appealing to the past.

My freedom thus experiences divine Freedom which, in relation to me, is always in front and comes towards me from the future. We will now look more closely at this encounter between my freedom and Freedom.

My freedom as such is unportrayable. I cannot represent it to myself except indirectly, by reflecting on the temporal body that my freedom provides itself: the moments of its becoming, before and after the instant of decision. But this body becomes part and parcel of my freedom. It is distinguishable from my freedom since it belongs to the objectivity that offers material for my reflection; but it is simultaneously related to my freedom. It constitutes the entirety of the conditions in whose midst freedom readies itself and precedes itself, from whose midst freedom springs and into which it returns after having posited an act that is inscribed in this body in the form of a change between Before and After. Reflection can always abstract from this act and spin a delicate continuity of determinate phenomena determining one another in time. All scientific explanations are formed in this very fashion. But a suitable training of our gaze succeeds in making us perceive, within this determinate continuity, a "residue" that is not "on a par" with it, an "unknown" coextensive with the known, an "irreducible reality" that reduplicates the entire determinate *continuum*, and which offers my freedom the means for recognizing itself in its works.

In the consolation without cause, it is as though freedom were suspended by the visitation of Freedom. The suppressed reflection is concentrated, as it were, in a point, a point where the "I" can no longer live out its own duration as duration nor stem it by thought. As a result, it is as though the body of conditions, the materiality of the Befores and Afters, were nonexistent. Hence the

225

expression "without cause" is used, even though the Instant does not happen apart from conditions (how could it?), but happens in such a way that the conditions are gathered into a whole without duration. For the reflection that *will follow*, it is an Instant which is between a past and a future only because it gathers up past and future more completely than the normal[26] present of the life of consciousness.

If such is the consolation without cause in consciousness, it does not seem that our present knowledge of the unconscious compels us to put the problem in totally new terms. It is sometimes said that, while the consolation without cause cannot be linked to a proportionate cause in the previous period of consciousness, it does come from the unconscious. Though it is without a conscious cause, it would not be without an unconscious one. And that would call in question the Ignatian theory about the spiritual authenticity of such an experience.

There seems to be a misunderstanding here. It is only insofar as one would have understood "without cause" to mean a non-intervention of consciousness that the unconscious, by the fact of its probable and even certain intervention, would call everything in question. The unconscious does intervene here, as does consciousness. First of all, this Instant of the consolation without cause is a present moment of consciousness, within the depth of consciousness. To admit that this depth goes down into the darkness of the unconscious presents no difficulty at all. Secondly, this instantaneous present is novelty in relation to the past only by virtue of the future irrupting more intensely than happens in the regular course of consciousness. Through the power of the future that looms up as present, the Instant is a unity of past and future, incommensurate with the dialectical unity of the ordinary present moment wherein I live out the intersecting of the time that flows by and of my reflection that stems it.

If such is the case, the consolation without cause in the Ignatian sense is left untouched, even though what happens there derives from paths that pass through the unconscious and are lost in the mists of time. There is no difficulty whatsoever admitting this intervention from the unconscious past. A difficulty would come

26 The word *normal* should not foster an imagination that would portray the Instant of the consolation without cause as some kind of psychic anomaly. The consolation without cause, especially in its most lofty forms, inserts itself into the duration of consciousness with a delicate continuity.

only from a theoretical viewpoint that would tend to reduce freedom to a product of the past, whereas it is a spurting at the intersection of past and future. If, by alluding here to the possible and even certain role of the unconscious, one would intend to curtail the role of the future completely, that is when the Ignatian theory of consolation without cause would lose all credibility.

But do analyses that explore the unconscious necessitate setting up a theory of man and freedom according to which each person would presently be solely the product of his past? It is possible that such a viewpoint prevails among some; then, however, we are no longer dealing with a strict analysis of the unconscious, but with the theoretical foundations of such an analysis. These foundations would be part of a conceptual framework that would certainly not be compatible with the doctrine of the consolation without cause. But it must be pointed out that this conceptual framework is not demanded by the analysis of the unconscious; on the contrary, the analysis would be based on it.

In short, is the consolation without cause nothing more than a "dream" in which the future present to the dreamer is, thanks to the dreamer's indestructible desire, modeled on the image of the past?[27] Or is the consolation without cause an Instant when the future does indeed become present and cause new creative energies to spurt forth from the midst of what was already there — a freedom that discloses itself instantaneously, with a certainty that nothing can destroy, not even the indestructible past?

It follows from what we have said that the consolation without cause cannot be treated as a simple product of the past.

Rule 3: Consolations Caused by the Spirits

After having defined consolation in the pure state as an immediate effect of the divine action vertically impinging on the horizontal duration of the I, Ignatius envisages consolation as it occurs more commonly, namely, given through the intervention of a preceding cause. In this case, it can have either the good angel or the evil spirit [331] as its sponsor. In order to discern true consolation from false, Ignatius quickly adds that it is enough to pay attention to their opposite goals. True consolation tends to make the I advance, causing it to grow in grace and rise from the good towards the better. False consolation, on the contrary, acts in the reverse direction, at

---

27 See S. Freud, *The Interpretation of Dreams* (New York: Basic Books, 1955).

first restraining the I in its ascent, then drawing it down, inclining it towards the perverse and wicked intentions of non-being.[28]

This criterion is identical with that already enunciated by the second rule of the First Week. There is one difference, however; here Ignatius stresses the intellectual aspect (considering the respective ends towards which true and false consolation tend). The second rule of the First Week emphasized more the affective dimension (sadness, anxiety, or on the other hand, encouragement, strength, and peace). But we will see shortly that, in Ignatius' eyes, the affective criterion has just as much importance in the Second Week.

Rule 4: False Consolation

In order to check the progress of the I which is rising from the good towards the better, the enemy disguises himself by assuming the appearance of what is light, strength (being). We saw in the First Week that an analogous move took place: To one who goes "from one mortal sin to another," the enemy proposes "apparent pleasures." Now that the I has been extricated from sin and is safe from these flagrant temptations that delight the senses, the enemy does not address himself to its affectivity, but to its understanding. Those who resolve on the better thing and go forward with determination are always tempted in their understanding. For their very disposition makes them receptive to every thought that seems to promise something better and to criticize the existing lesser good. Therefore, the enemy begins by entering into their plans and joining the direction of their progress. But this move is in order to come out, sooner or later, through "his own door," making them fall into his traps and perverse intentions: "He will suggest holy and pious thoughts that are wholly in conformity with the sanctity of the soul. Afterwards, he will endeavor little by little to end by drawing the soul into his hidden snares and evil designs" [332].

In the Gospel we see the enemy acting this way with Christ during the temptation in the desert: "Christ was victorious over this threefold assault by resorting each time to Sacred Scripture, that is, to the historical revelation wherein the Father announced the sending of the Son and the gift of the Spirit."[29]

---

28 *Dialectique*, I, 263.
29 Ibid., 265.

Rule 5: Discernment of False Consolation

In order to frustrate the enemy's deceits and snares, Ignatius recommended in the First Week (rule 13, [326]) opening oneself to a third party, a confessor or other spiritual person. Now he intends to initiate the I into the art of discerning these deceits and illusions by itself and thus make the I capable of helping others in turn.

The criterion for true and false consolation is the simple unfolding of what the third rule had mentioned: paying attention to their contrary goals. But we are going to see that it divides into an intellectual criterion (attention directed to the end towards which the movement of consolation is tending) and an affective criterion (the interior condition which the consolation creates or alters: peace, tranquillity, quiet, or a lessening of peace, then disquiet and anxiety). They complement each other. In order for both to be put into practice wittingly, they demand paying close attention to temporal determinations (before, after). The consideration of contrary ends is a practical and simple procedure when the problem for discernment is posed in a "crossroad" type of situation. This is the ordinary First Week situation where I have to convert myself from sin to God's will. Then I am at an intersection, and it does not take me long to notice whether I am moving towards the good or whether I am falling back into my old ruts.

In the Second Week, the situation is very different. Then I am striving to progress from the less good to the better, and the present moment wherein I have to reinforce this advance towards the better is more like a switching in a rail terminal. The point of divergence between the line of the better and that of the less good, which would end by leading me towards evil, is hard to distinguish here and now at the very spot of the switching. In Miami all the trains leave in the same direction, but some go to New York and others to Chicago. However, I need to discover the direction I have taken before I am in New York if I wanted to go to Chicago, or before I am in Chicago if I wanted to go to New York. In short, the problem of the fifth rule is to "discern those motions which, even if they are bound to be diametrically opposed before long, begin by coinciding and whose divergence at their source is as slight as possible."[30] This problem arises in every person's life as well as within the history of the Church and the

---

30 Ibid., 266.

world. How can we distinguish, at the outset, an authentic social reformer from a political opportunist? How differentiate between a true prophet of God who castigates abuses and a fomenter of discord who, while fighting real abuses, splinters the community?

Here the intellectual criterion is not enough because the "contrary goals" do not become clear until one has gone quite far in the good or bad direction. After a switching occurs, one needs to be able to make a decision about it, before the situation becomes too seriously compromised in the bad direction without one's noticing it. Such is the problem.

We can thus measure to what degree of precision the Ignatian dialectic pushes its analysis. The Exercises appear at first only to be interested in choices that decide a person's whole life. But Ignatius is not unaware that these major decisions, before acquiring their exceptional importance in the eyes of history, are fashioned and prefigured during the preceding period in the manifold orientations that the I has given to the winding train of its thoughts, day after day and even hour by hour, nay, minute by minute. These orientations are so infinitesimal that they are almost unconscious, and yet their summation has exerted a major influence on the will at the decisive moment.[31]

This is why, whatever the scope of the question for discussion may be, Ignatius first of all recommends that the I pay very close attention to the trend and tone of its thoughts: "We must carefully observe the whole course of our thoughts" [333]. And we ought to proceed in the same way, whether it is a question of evaluating an event in our own personal spiritual life, a thought that is unfolding, or an event in social and political life, national or international.

This appraisal will come about by examining the direction taken by the thought (or the event)—the intellectual criterion—and the affective state that it creates in the very moment when it takes shape: "If the beginning and middle and end of the course of thoughts are wholly good and directed to what is entirely right, it is a sign that they are from the good angel. But the course of thoughts suggested to us may terminate in something evil, or distracting, or less good than the soul had formerly proposed to do" [333].

31 Ibid.

We recognize here the intellectual criterion, considering the end. Next, the affective criterion is introduced in the same breath:[32] "Again, it may end in what weakens the soul, or disquiets it; or by destroying the peace, tranquillity, and quiet which it had before, it may cause disturbance to the soul. These things are a clear sign that the thoughts are proceeding from the evil spirit" [333].

And we will have noticed the temporal determinations: beginning and end; terminate in something less good than...formerly; the quiet which it had before.

Let us go back to the statements above that denote each of the two criteria. The first presents the intellectual criterion in a hypothesis where it is sufficient by itself: "If the beginning and middle and end of the course of thoughts are wholly good. ..." There are some cases where things verge on immediate transparency: the plan (the beginning), the intended means (the middle), and the end in view are entirely good, without the symptomatic gaps between initially "very pure" intentions, means "which are open to discussion," and an end which "looks nebulous." In this case there is no problem, provided, as Ignatius specifies, the beginning, middle, and end tend to what is *all good*. It is not enough for the sequence of "plan, means, and end" to be good and upright in the sense that it is wholly directed to the particular good one has in mind; it must, moreover, aim at *all good*, the supreme Good.

Here is a preciseness as important as it is apparently impractical. What we are saying, of course, is that the best of particular plans, carried out by honest means, with an eye to an intrinsically good end, can be held in suspicion if, while aspiring to work out one problem, it creates ten others. But is there a way, in practice, to include a really universal aim, or at least an attentiveness to the whole issue, within one plan? Ignatius does not pose the question here. But we will make a suggestion. We can assure ourselves that a project is sufficiently ordered to the good of all through communal deliberation. Several people striving after discernment can bring out the principal aspects of a problem or implications that were overlooked at first.[33]

The rest of the passage envisages the other eventuality: "But the course of thoughts suggested to us may terminate in something

32 [Translator's Note. Literally, "in the same movement of the sentence," because it is all one sentence in the original Spanish and in the French version. Puhl, however, begins a new sentence.]

33 See Claude Viard, "La délibération communautaire," *Vie chrétienne*, 130 (1970), 12-14: idem, "Délibération dans la vie quotidienne," ibid., 138 (1971), 12-15.

evil, or distracting, or less good...." We can see the gradation: (1) *less good*, scarcely discernible from the better because the less good is still good and can constitute a forward movement, though one which is slower and less decisive; (2) *distracting*, a movement with no other direction than the thread of time that runs by without anything happening, good or bad; (3) following the very inclination that goes from the less good to the distracting, *something evil*, which we will slip into imperceptibly and almost without noticing it.

But, supposing I have just crossed a switching point without knowing fully what happened, how can I really discern? How can I set up a comparison between (1) the After wherein the better was projected for me (in continuity with my previous movement from the good to the better) and (2) the After which is falling away from the better and giving way to the less good? In relation to the switch that I have just passed and which I recall, I am in one of these two Afters, but which one? I do not yet perceive the "end" clearly enough. As for the starting point, it is the switch itself where I see the two directions, good and bad, come together. Nothing is clear or fixed; everything is shifting and becoming confused.

Ignatius has enough experience of the spiritual life not to be unaware of the practical difficulty the I will run into when it tries to discern the "better" and the "less good" with the help of a criterion as purely intellectual as the consideration of the beginning and the end of its thoughts. This is why Ignatius hastens to point out another criterion, based on the affective dimension of advancing consciousness, which will allow it to eliminate this difficulty. Supposing, as a matter of fact, that consciousness does not manage, through its understanding alone, to see clearly the exact point where the "less good" diverges from the "better," it will profit consciousness nothing to pursue an examination in which it can only flounder in excessive precision. Consciousness should then stop scrutinizing the orientation of its thoughts in order to consider instead the inmost repercussion that their sequence produces. The enemy's action and the moment of its insertion into this sequence will disclose itself to the I under one of the following forms: a weakening of its momentum or of its interior concentration, disquiet, anxiety, or merely a loss of "the peace, tranquillity, and quiet which it had before."...That is enough to recognize that this entire course of thoughts is coming from the enemy not only of our spiritual progress, but of our salvation.[34]

If, at the switching, I have shifted unawares in the direction the enemy is suggesting, a change cannot help taking place in me (less of that peace, quiet, and tranquillity which are the fruit of the Spirit), since I have in fact started upon a way that will divert me from my true end if I stick to it. Sometimes a person who goes astray on a walk suddenly experiences an uneasiness, a strangeness, a discomfort, a vague feeling of no longer being on the right track, even when he is unable to get his present bearings. Ignatius is convinced that this is exactly what will happen here. On the basis of faith and hope, he knows that the Spirit does not abandon for a single instant those who want to walk in his presence: "...or if he asks for an egg, will give him a scorpion?...how much more will the heavenly Father give the Holy Spirit to those who ask him!" (Luke 11:12-13).

With this quite simple conjunction of a precise, but not always usable, intellectual criterion and an affective criterion which is always applicable with or without the other, but which presupposes the interior peace and harmony of a right intention, we are "at the heart of the Ignatian doctrine."[35]

We recognize the author of the rules for making a good and correct Choice who, while explaining the two ways of making a Choice in the third time, took us back to the second and even to the first time. For him, the work of reflection must be upheld and confirmed by a spiritual motion experienced in one's affectivity. Pure reason alone is never capable of making a categorical decision in a practical problem. For reason, by means of its universal and abstract concepts, cannot wholly coincide with the particular determinations of a concrete situation in order to effect progress through a precise deed decided in conformity with God. Reason is reason only when it is joined to a sensuous, corporeal organism that puts it in touch with what is and what ought to be. Just as affectivity is blind without the light of reason that sifts the feelings, so reason is impotent unless it is embodied in affectivity. It is the supple and steady connection of one with the other that allows the I to see clearly, to decide, and to act in conformity with God. Outside of that connection there is no decision, no discernment, and no spiritual life.

---

34 *Dialectique*, I, 270.

35 These are the words of Fessard, who analyzes this fifth rule ibid., 265-283. Our account does not replace those pages, which—let it be added—are easy reading.

Why this twofold criterion? We have just offered a very general answer. Now we must take a closer look at why every rational deliberation demands a practical test.

Let us say it immediately in order to clarify our argument: If Ignatius appeals to feeling in order to make a final judgment about the "better," he does so because, having begun with an utterly rigorous analysis of the power of the understanding, he also recognized its impotence when it claims to be the sole criterion of perfection. This is the dialectical reversal expressed by the proverb: The best is often the enemy of the good. For their part, spiritual writers agree in denouncing it [the understanding as the sole criterion] when they say that the pursuit of perfection for its own sake always runs the risk of turning into a subtle self-seeking. It is precisely in order to forestall such a perversion, a result of the enemy's strategem of passing himself off as the One who IS, that Ignatius then appeals to the affectivity, and by that very move transforms Satan's snares set before the soul into means which allow the soul to attain the highest perfection in total security.[36]

In the present problem there is no question of evaluating an objective content, appearing within fixed coordinates, under the aspects of good and evil. It is a question of my having to discern which of two relative goods is better for me now. In themselves one or the other could be better, depending on circumstances, person, and times. That is, there are no fixed coordinates by which I can appraise them. As a result, it is not a matter of asking a question like, "Must I pay my debts?" There is no doubt at all that I have to pay them. At the very most, depending on the circumstances, I could decide on an extension, a method of payment. Here, however, it is a question of a choice like: "Is it better for me to change my way of life by choosing, for example, the state of religious poverty, or is it better for me to retain control of my possessions, while renouncing 'the spirit of riches'?" One or the other could be the better choice, depending on what emerges from a great number of considerations viewed within the dynamics of a situation that includes many unknowns.

If I attend to the reasons which make the religious life of poverty appear better for me from now on, the possession of my own property will correspondingly appear a priori as a lesser good, which I ought to give up. But the opposite consideration is not thereby excluded. If I attend to other arguments, I can find it better to remain in material possession of my property, coupled with a spirit of detachment. Religious poverty will then appear to me as less good in relation to the life-style that was mine already and which, after being reformed, should continue to be preferred. How can I cut this Gordian knot in which my generosity and spiritual energy can dissolve into innumerable subtleties, which are precisely the wiles whereby the enemy is trying to trap me? The enemy's trick consists precisely in tempting the I through its generosity and having the I believe that, with the aid of its understanding alone, it can make a decision on a level with its spiritual fervor. He hopes to impel the I to an act of self-sufficiency, to an act of its own will. For the reasons in one direction or the other will be decisive only by virtue of a certain way of looking at the whole question. Now, who will decide this way of looking at the whole question? The enemy is trying to make sure that I decide by myself. Thus, under the guise of doing the will of God, which the reasons are presumed to point out to me, I will have secretly and fundamentally done my own will. This is the most subtle, but also the most common, danger that waylays those disciples most resolutely engaged in pursuing the greater good. And it is to ward off this danger that Ignatius suggests appealing to the affective criterion.

We will make all this more tangible through an example. We are going to propose a diagram for choosing according to the sole criterion of "reasons," when in fact our reasons are always more or less linked to the concrete by an affective appraisal of our situation. The example will therefore be artificial. But, as such, it will only highlight more clearly a lack which is ordinarily unnoticed and which we commonly rectify in an "unnoticed," that is, arbitrary, fashion.

Suppose the following deliberation: to embrace religious life by taking the vow of poverty, or to remain in possession of my property while practicing poverty of spirit. Below is the list of reasons:

Hypothesis 1: Vow of Poverty	Hypothesis 2: Remaining in Possession of My Property
—the vow establishes me in a state of dispossession;	—binds me to some permanent choices and thus to renewing my interior detachment, whereas
—it makes me depend on a community;	the vow establishes me in a routine not exempt from unsatisfied greed;
—thus I will be free to live according to the gospel.	—makes me live out the real condition of men forced to

earn their living and to become acquainted with the hazards of economic life.

On the other hand, retaining my property places me in danger of an attachment; it makes me live relying on my wealth rather than on God; it thus renders me less disposed for living the gospel.

Living in poverty of spirit and depending on Providence is a very practical way to learn the cost of things, whereas religious life would establish me in a kind of security.

Let us consider the respective arguments for each hypothesis; it is clear that they each depend on a presupposition and draw their strength from it. For the first set of arguments, the supposition is that poverty which is bound by vow is the means for living poverty of spirit. And for the second set of arguments, the supposition is that the spirit is worth more than the letter; poverty institutional-ized in a vow runs the risk of being the death of poverty of spirit. But what establishes the implicit presuppostion? My freedom does, short of the deliberation in which the arguments are stated and weighed. Now, to submit oneself to reasons within the framework of deliberation and tacitly to posit this or that principle in function of which one or another series of arguments will have value for me, is to do my own will under the pretext of following some reasons that supposedly point out the will of God to me. Conse-quently, I must submit to God on the level of the presuppositions themselves. The latter are principles which are part and parcel of what I am, in my consciousness and unconscious, body and soul, intellect and affectivity. From this depth of my being rise passions, anxiety, and disquiet, but also peace, light, and relish for the indwelling God.

Reason can and should prune the tangle of our lower affectivity; the whole pedagogy of the Exercises is directed towards this. But to sanction dark unconscious desires with fallacious reasonings would be to replace animality with the pride of pure spirit. Here reason, based on faith and hope, must submit to the best of affecti-vity, which is passivity to God. It is a time for distrusting one's instincts and even one's feelings. The time will come later on for giving in to what one feels is going in the direction of the peace that comes from God. The understanding, though, reserves the right, once it has been freed of all pride through an open acknow-ledgement of its carnal condition, to undertake an examination of the trail of spiritual affectivity (rules 6 and 7, [334-335]).

Below is a passage in which Fessard summarizes this whole body of doctrine:

Satan makes use of "fallacious reasonings and subtleties" in order to let the I believe that the determination of the better has been definitively left to its own sheer willing. Through many an example from his personal life, Ignatius recognized that divine Freedom, the sole ultimate source of such a determination, manifests itself to consciousness not only through the light of understanding, but also in the dark life-forces whence arises a good part of the course of our thoughts. In order to protect the I from self-seeking, he therefore prescribes that it look for the solution on the side of affectivity.

But, on the other hand, he is not unaware that the enemy, after having beguiled the soul into making itself the principle for determining the better, knows how to finish leading it astray through an opposite trick, namely, by inducing the person to interpret the promptings of feeling as directly divine inspirations. Knowing that our inmost dispositions are just as subject to the influence of Satan as to that of God, Ignatius will not give up enlightening them through the insights of the understanding. The latter is impotent when it claims to find the better through its own resources. Nevertheless, only the understanding is able to subordinate feeling to the control of reason and thus discern which element comes from above, from divine Freedom, and which rises from below, from carnal and sensual love.[37]

Thus we see Ignatius now offering us two new rules (6 and 7), the first to examine what has occurred along the course of thoughts described by the fifth rule and to recognize, if need be, how a deviation could have taken place. The second new rule is to teach us how each of the two spirits touches our affectivity, depending on our dispositions. We refer the reader to these rules and to Fessard's commentary on them.[38] We will simply summarize the second one as saying: "The Lord's grace does not have the harassing quality of the enemy's suggestions 'under the appearances of good'; it comes gently, in peace."

As for the eighth and final rule, we have already mentioned it in connection with the "consolation without previous cause." It advises us to "cautiously distinguish the actual time of the

37 Ibid., 278.
38 Ibid., 292-299.

consolation from the period which follows it....In this second period the soul frequently forms various resolutions and plans which are not granted directly by God our Lord. They may come from our own reasoning on the relations of our concepts and on the consequences of our judgments, or they may come from the good or evil spirit" [336]. Thus this "period which follows" corresponds to the situation envisaged by the fifth rule.[39]

By way of conclusion, we will quote the Ignatian maxim stemming from Gabriel Hevenesi:[40]

HAVE FAITH IN GOD

AS IF ALL SUCCESS DEPENDED ON YOU,

NOTHING ON GOD;

SET TO WORK, HOWEVER,

AS IF NOTHING WERE TO COME ABOUT THROUGH YOU,

AND EVERYTHING THROUGH GOD ALONE.

---

39 See above.

40 [Translator's Note. The quotation is from *Scintillae Ignatianae* (Vienna, 1705), p. 2. See the long discussion on the various forms of this maxim in Fessard, *Dialectique*, I, 305-363; and in Hugo Rahner, S.J., *Ignatius the Theologian*, trans. Michael Barry (New York: Herder and Herder, 1968), pp. 25-31, with further references given there; also, J. de Guibert, S.J., *The Jesuits: Their Spiritual Doctrine and Practice* (St. Louis: The Institute of Jesuit Sources, 1972), p. 148; and J. W. Padberg, S.J., *Studies in the Spirituality of Jesuits*, X, no. 5 (Nov. 1978), p. 320.]

The Institute of Jesuit Sources
Fusz Memorial, St. Louis University
3700 West Pine Blvd.
St. Louis, Missouri, 63108, U.S.A.

This Institute consists of a group of Jesuits in St. Louis, Missouri, assisted by collaborators in many English-speaking provinces of the Society. The chief aim of the Institute is to make the sources of Jesuit thought more readily available to the scholarly world in English-speaking countries, especially by publishing English translations of important books written in other languages by or about Jesuits. The titles of the books published so far follow.

Pedro Arrupe, S.J. *Challenge to Religious Life Today. Selected Letters and Addresses—I.* Edited by Jerome Aixala, S.J. 1979, 290 pages.
Pedro Arrupe, S.J., *Justice with Faith Today. Selected Letters and Addresses—II.* Edited by Jerome Aixala, S.J. 1980, 336 pages.

Series I. Jesuit Primary Sources, in English Translations

No. 1. Saint Ignatius of Loyola. *The Constitutions of the Society of Jesus. Translated, with an Introduction and a Commentary,* by George E. Ganss, S.J. 1970, 432 pages.

No. 2. *Documents of the 31st and 32nd General Congregations of the Society of Jesus.* A translation of the official Latin texts, prepared by the Jesuit Conference, Washington, D.C., and edited by John W. Padberg, S.J. 1977, 608 pages.

No. 3. *Jesuit Religious Life Today. The Principal Features of Its Spirit, in Excerpts from Papal Documents, St. Ignatius' Constitutions, the 31st and 32nd General Congregations, and Letters of Father General Pedro Arrupe.* Edited by George E. Ganss, S.J. 1977, 190 pages.

Series II. Modern Scholarly Studies about the Jesuits, in English Translations

No. 1. Joseph de Guibert, S.J. *The Jesuits: Their Spiritual Doctrine and Practice. A Historical Study.* Trans. by W. J. Young, S.J. 1964, 717 pages.

No. 2. *Ignatius of Loyola: His Personality and Spiritual Heritage, 1556-1956. Studies on the 400th Anniversary of His Death,* by F. Wulf, S.J. (Ed.), Hugo Rahner, S.J., Karl Rahner, S.J., and others. 1977, 318 pages.

No. 3. Josef Franz Schütte, S.J. *Valignano's Mission Principles for Japan. Part I: The Problem (1573-1580).* Trans. by John Coyne, S.J. 1980, 452 pages.

Note: *Part II: The Solution (1580-1582)* is planned to be published in 1981.

No. 4. Edouard Pousset, S.J. *Life in Faith and Freedom. An Essay Presenting Gaston Fessard's Analysis of the Dialectic of the Spiritual Exercises of St. Ignatius.* 1980, 268 pages.

Series III. Original Studies, Composed in English

No. 1. David M. Stanley, S.J. *A Modern Scriptural Approach to the Spiritual Exercises*, 1967, 374 pages.

No. 2. John Carroll Futrell. S.J. *Making an Apostolic Community of Love. The Role of the Superior according to St. Ignatius.* 1970, 239 pages.

No. 3. William V. Bangert, S.J. *A History of the Society of Jesus.* 1972, 570 pages.

Series IV. Study Aids on Jesuit Topics

No. 1. Ignacio Iparraguirre, S.J. *Contemporary Trends in Studies on the Constitutions of the Society of Jesus: Annotated Bibliographical Orientations.* Translated by Daniel F. X. Meenan, S.J. 1974, 94 pages.

No. 2. David L. Fleming, S.J. *A Contemporary Reading of the Spiritual Exercises: A Companion to St. Ignatius' Text.* 1976, 112 pages; revised, 1980, 112 pages.

No. 3. Thomas H. Clancy, S.J. *An Introduction to Jesuit Life: The Constitutions and History through 435 Years.* 1976, 423 pages.

No. 4. Jean-Yves Calvez, Ignacio Iglesias, Edward F. Sheridan, Carlo M. Martini, Vincent T. O'Keefe, John Correia-Afonso, Cecil McGarry, Francisco Ivern (all S.J.) *Conferences on the Chief Decrees of Jesuit General Congregation XXXII: A Symposium by Some of Its Members.* 1976, 173 pages.

No. 5. Harvey D. Egan, S.J. *The Spiritual Exercises and the Ignatian Mystical Horizon.* With a Foreword by Karl Rahner S.J. 1976, 198 pages.

No. 6. William V. Bangert, S.J. *A Bibliographical Essay on the Society of Jesus.* 1976, 92 pages.

No. 7. David L. Fleming, S.J. *The Spiritual Exercises of St. Ignatius: A Literal Translation and a Contemporary Reading.* 1978, 272 pages.

No. 8. Thomas H. Clancy, S.J. *The Conversational Word of God: A Commentary on the Doctrine of St. Ignatius concerning Spiritual Conversation, with Four Early Jesuit Texts.* 1978, 84 pages.

No. 9. Anthony de Mello, S.J., *Sadhana: A Way to God. Christian Exercises in Eastern Form.* 1979, 146 pages.